ARISTOPHANES' *Frogs*

OXFORD APPROACHES TO
Classical Literature

SERIES EDITORS
Kathleen Coleman and Richard Rutherford

Ovid's *Metamorphoses*
ELAINE FANTHAM

Plato's *Symposium*
RICHARD HUNTER

Caesar's *Civil War*
WILLIAM W. BATSTONE
CYNTHIA DAMON

Polybius' *Histories*
BRIAN C. McGING

Tacitus' *Annals*
RONALD MELLOR

Xenophon's *Anabasis*, or *The Expedition of Cyrus*
MICHAEL A. FLOWER

Aristophanes' *Frogs*
MARK GRIFFITH

ARISTOPHANES'
Frogs

Mark Griffith

OXFORD
UNIVERSITY PRESS

Oxford University Press publishes works that further
Oxford University's objective of excellence in research,
scholarship, and education.

Oxford New York
Auckland Cape Town Dar es Salaam Hong Kong Karachi
Kuala Lumpur Madrid Melbourne Mexico City Nairobi
New Delhi Shanghai Taipei Toronto

With offices in
Argentina Austria Brazil Chile Czech Republic France Greece
Guatemala Hungary Italy Japan Poland Portugal Singapore
South Korea Switzerland Thailand Turkey Ukraine Vietnam

Copyright © 2013 by Oxford University Press

Published by Oxford University Press
198 Madison Avenue, New York, New York 10016

www.oup.com

Oxford is a registered trademark of Oxford University Press

All rights reserved. No part of this publication may be reproduced,
stored in a retrieval system, or transmitted, in any form or by any means,
electronic, mechanical, photocopying, recording, or otherwise,
without the prior permission of Oxford University Press.

Library of Congress Cataloging-in-Publication Data
Griffith, Mark, PhD
Aristophanes' Frogs / Mark Griffith.
pages. cm.—(Oxford approaches to classical literature)
ISBN 978-0-19-532773-1—ISBN 978-0-19-532772-4 1. Aristophanes. Frogs. I. Title. II. Series:
Oxford approaches to classical literature.
PA3875.R3G75 2012
882'.01—dc23   2012008786

1 3 5 7 9 8 6 4 2
Printed in the United States of America
on acid-free paper

Editors' Foreword

The late twentieth and early twenty-first centuries have seen a massive expansion in courses dealing with ancient civilization and, in particular, the culture and literature of the Greek and Roman world. Never has there been such a flood of good translations available: Oxford's own World Classics, the Penguin Classics, the Hackett Library, and other series offer the English-speaking reader access to the masterpieces of classical literature from Homer to Augustine. The reader may, however, need more guidance in the interpretation and understanding of these works than can usually be provided in the relatively short introduction that prefaces a work in translation. There is a need for studies of individual works that will provide a clear, lively, and reliable account based on the most up-to-date scholarship without dwelling on the minutiae that are likely to distract or confuse the reader.

It is to meet this need that the present series has been devised. The title *Oxford Approaches to Classical Literature* deliberately puts the emphasis on the literary works themselves. The volumes in this series will each be concerned with a single work (with the exception of cases where a "book" or larger collection of poems is treated as one work). These are neither biographies nor accounts of literary movements or schools. Nor are they books devoted to the total oeuvre of one author: our first volumes consider Ovid's *Metamorphoses* and Plato's *Symposium*, not the works of Ovid or Plato as a whole. This is, however, a question of emphasis, and not a straitjacket: biographical issues, literary and cultural background, and related works by the same author are discussed where they are obviously relevant. Series authors have also been encouraged to consider the influence and legacy of the works in question. As the editors of this series, we intend these volumes to be accessible to the reader who is encountering the relevant work for the first time; but we also intend that each volume should do more than simply provide the basic facts, dates, and summaries that handbooks generally supply. We would like these books to be essays in criticism and interpretation that will do justice to the subtlety and complexity of the works under discussion. With this in mind, we have invited leading scholars to offer personal assessments and appreciations of their chosen works, anchored within the mainstream of classical scholarship. We have thought it particularly important that our authors be allowed to set their own agendas and to speak in their own voices rather than repeating the *idées reçues* of conventional wisdom in neutral tones.

The title *Oxford Approaches to Classical Literature* has been chosen simply because the series is published by Oxford University Press, USA; it in no way implies a party line, either Oxonian or any other. We believe that different approaches are suited to different texts, and we expect each volume to have its own distinctive character. Advanced critical theory is neither compulsory nor excluded; what matters is whether it can be made to illuminate the text in question. The authors have been encouraged to avoid obscurity and jargon, bearing in mind the needs of the general reader; but, when important critical or narratological issues arise, they are presented to the reader as lucidly as possible.

This series was originally conceived by Professor Charles Segal, an inspiring scholar and teacher whose intellectual energy and range of interests were matched by a humility and generosity of spirit. Although he was involved in the commissioning of a number of volumes, he did not—alas—live to see any of them published. The series is intended to convey something of the excitement and pleasure to be derived from reading the extraordinarily rich and varied literature of Greco-Roman antiquity. We hope that these volumes will form a worthy monument to a dedicated classical scholar who was committed to enabling the ancient texts to speak to the widest possible audience in the contemporary world.

Kathleen Coleman, Harvard University
Richard Rutherford, Christ Church, Oxford

Preface

Almost every aspect of the classical Greek experience of life comes into play in Aristophanes' incomparable comedy, *The Frogs*: war, politics, labor, mythology, aesthetics, the arts, religion, death and salvation, freedom and slavery, sex and gender . . . and—of course—humor of all kinds. It is impossible for one person to do full justice to this fantastic play in one short book, though it has been a hugely enjoyable challenge to make the attempt.

My debt to the scholarship and ideas of others is very extensive, much too great to describe here; and I regret that the constraints of this series forbid detailed references and critical discussion. The "Suggestions for Further Reading" provided after each chapter, and the consolidated "Bibliography" at the end, represent just the tips of several large icebergs. I hope that the many Aristophanic—and other—scholars whose work is not mentioned in the bibliography but who have nonetheless helped me get closer to an understanding of *The Frogs* will recognize the places where they have been helpful and will forgive me for not citing them explicitly; and I hope that those with whose positions I have disagreed will forgive me too for not engaging in more direct dialogue with their views. It goes against the grain for me to write briefly and dogmatically; but in this case it was sometimes necessary.

In particular, I should like to thank the following individuals for advice, corrections, and help of various kinds: Zachary Biles, the late Crawford Greenewalt Jr., Foivos Karachalios, Sarah Pirovitz, Laurialan Reitzammer, Daniel Walin, and all the Berkeley students who took my class on *The Frogs* in spring 2008. I am especially grateful to Naomi Weiss and Daniel Esses for their valuable comments and editorial assistance, and to Elizabeth Wahle for her wonderful drawings of the Weighing Scene, the Brygos Painter's singing Dionysus, and Charon's ferryboat of souls. Above all, I thank the series editors, Kathleen Coleman and Richard Rutherford, for inviting me to write this book in the first place, for their encouragement and firm discipline in helping me reduce it to the proper scale, and for useful criticisms in its penultimate stages.

I hope this book will be found entertaining as well as helpful, and will encourage readers of all ages and backgrounds to go (back) and read Aristophanes' play for themselves—preferably, in more than one translation. There is so much to enjoy.

Contents

Editors' Foreword   *v*

Preface   *ix*

List of Illustrations   *xiii*

1
Comedy at Athens   *3*

2
Aristophanes and His Athenian Audience   *22*

3
What Happens in *Frogs*? (The Plot)   *55*

4
Agôn Sophias: Judging the Arts in Classical Greece   *80*

5

Old and New Styles in Tragedy: Aeschylus, Euripides, and the Rest *115*

6

Underworld and Afterlife: Dionysus and Greek Fantasies of Salvation *150*

7

Dionysus' Verdict and the Ending/Message of the Play *200*

8

Reading and Performing *Frogs* After Aristophanes—Reception *220*

Glossary of Personal and Geographical Names *259*

Bibliography *279*

General Index *285*

List of Illustrations

1-1. Two sketches of the Theater of Dionysus as it might have looked for the first production of *Frogs* in 405 BCE: **11**
(a) Circular configuration. Drawing by H. Wirsing, from H. Bulle and H. Wirsing *Szenenbilder zum griechischen Theater des 5. Jahrhunderts vor Chr.* (Berlin 1950).
(b) Trapezoidal configuration. Drawing by Elizabeth Wahle.

3-1. Fourth century vase painting apparently illustrating a scene from near the beginning of *Frogs*. Apulian (South Italian) bell-krater ca. 375–350 BCE (so-called "Berlin Heracles"). Formerly Berlin, Staatliche Museen F3046 (destroyed or plundered during World War II). **61**
Photo from M. Bieber *Die Denkmäler zum Theaterwesen im Altertum* (Berlin 1920) Tafel 80.

3-2. Terracotta figurines of comic actors, Athenian ca. 400–350 BCE. **64**
(a) New York Metropolitan Museum of Art 13.225.13; photo courtesy of The Metropolitan Museum of Art/Art Resource.

(b) London, The British Museum 1852,0728.752 (T741); photo courtesy of the Trustees of the British Museum.

5–1. Two examples of Dionysian music, as represented in Athenian vase-painting of the fifth century: **144**
(a) Dionysus plays a *barbitos* (lyre) while two satyrs dance and play *krotala* (castanets). Interior of Red-figure kylix-cup by the Brygos Painter, ca. 480 BCE (ARV^2 371,14: Cab. Méd. Inv. 575). Drawing by Elizabeth Wahle.
(b) A young man plays the *auloi* (double-pipes), presumably at a symposium, while a woman dances with *krotala* (castanets). Red-figure Athenian kylix-cup by Epictetus, ca. 500 BCE (ARV^2 72,16: London E38, 1843,1103.9). Photo courtesy of the Trustees of the British Museum.

6–1. Charon, ferryman of souls, with Hermes and a dead woman. Attic white-ground lekythos, fifth century BCE (ARV^2 846,193). National Museum, Athens ANM 1926. Drawing by Elizabeth Wahle. **161**

6–2. An Athenian trireme (warship): **167**
(a) Replica of a trireme, *Olympias*, proceeding under oar-power with sails furled (approaching Tolo, Greece, August 1990); photo courtesy of The Trireme Trust.
(b) Interior of the trireme, showing cramped arrangement of the three banks of rowers (whence the term "trireme"); photo courtesy of Rosie Randolph and The Trireme Trust.
  This full-scale trireme replica was researched and designed by John Coates and John Morrison, and was commissioned into the Greek navy in 1987. The crew in these photos were members of the Greek navy, together with British and American students.

8–1. The page of the parchment manuscript R (Ravennas 429: 10th century CE) that contains the opening lines of *Frogs*. **233**
  The original MS is in the Biblioteca Classense, Ravenna. This photo is from the facsimile edition, *Aristophanis comoediae undecim cum scholiis: Codex ravennas 137, 4, A*, ed. J. van Leeuwen (Leiden 1904).

8–2. Program cover for the 1892 production of *Frogs* by the Oxford University Dramatic Society at the New Theatre, Oxford. Program designed by Charles Wellington Furse. *248* (John Johnson Collection, OUDS Box 2. Bodleian Library, Oxford). Photo courtesy of the Bodleian Libraries, The University of Oxford.

Aristophanes' *Frogs*

· 1 ·

Comedy at Athens

"Shall I say one of the usual things, Master—the things that the audience always laugh at?" (*Frogs* 1–2). So begins our play. The opening lines immediately remind the audience that they have seen many, many plays of this type before, while implying that "the usual things <jokes>" may be both expected and yet to some degree dubious and inadequate. The audience expects that each new play adhere to a traditional format and a familiar set of social and verbal norms ("the usual things"), even as it demands something new, adventurous, different.

What were "the usual things" that an Athenian audience would "always laugh at" in the Theater of Dionysus? What did theatergoers expect from their *kômôidoi* when the festival competitions got under way each year? Without a good grasp of the conventions and traditions of Athenian Old Comedy, we will miss much of Aristophanes' humor and, worse still, fail to understand many of the moral, aesthetic, and political issues with which his play is engaging. *Frogs* was written and performed in 405 BCE, winning first prize in that year's Lenaea festival competition. The play was re-performed soon thereafter (perhaps with minor revisions), a rare occurrence for comedies in those days, and it has ever since been admired and quoted by readers and critics. It thus has proven itself to possess a timeless and almost universal appeal. Yet there are many elements of the play that are extremely specific to Athens and to a particular historical moment, and which need some explanation if modern audiences and readers are to get the point. This chapter is intended to supply some of the requisite comic context.

Comedy and *kômôidia*

The English words "comedy" and "comic" come from the Greek *kômôidia, kômikos* (via Latin *comoedia, comicus*). In ancient Greek contexts, a *kômos* was a group of revelers, a semi-riotous party, often fueled by wine and music, that would roam through the streets, singing, shouting, making jokes among themselves or accosting others with mockery and insults. A *kômos* might be a celebration of a recent happy event, or the final stage of a symposium or feast; but it might also be an opportunity for one group of aggressive young men to assert their collective social clout and challenge others to offer any resistance—something akin to the semi-ritualized behavior of a modern neighborhood gang or college fraternity. A century or two before Aristophanes, the early *kômôidoi* (lit. "revel-singers") were apparently formal or informal choral groups that sang and danced in ritualized celebration and/or abuse of others, usually in the name of the god Dionysus. It is from these "comedians" that Attic Old Comedy must have evolved, though similar "comic" groups apparently flourished in many other parts of Greece as well.

Visual representations, especially vase paintings, provide our best evidence for these kômastic predecessors. Corinthian, Attic Black-Figure, Boeotian, and other sixth-century pots depict choruses of more or less grotesquely padded "fat-men" dancing in groups and/or sexually engaged with women. Some show men in animal costumes. Often such groups include someone playing the double-pipes (*auloi*—the instrument most consistently associated with Dionysus; see further chapter 5), and sometimes also ithyphallic paraphernalia of one kind or another (i.e., erect phalluses, whether natural or as artificial costumes). Usually these groups are drinking, sometimes around a mixing-bowl—so presumably these are Dionysiac ritual-songs of some kind. But we cannot tell whether the activities represented on these vases constitute a specifically human/sexual celebration, or are basically symposiastic, or are directed towards fertility and seasonal productivity more generally. Nor can we tell whether any kind of story is being enacted in such scenes, that is, whether these are proto-dramas or simply dances and skits. (The dancers do not generally appear to be wearing masks, as they always do in later Athenian dramatic performances.)

These visual remains are confirmed by Aristotle's brief remarks in the *Poetics* (ch. 4. 1449a–b), where he states that comedy evolved "out of those leading off the phallic things <dances, choruses>," adding that these were originally improvised, not based on written scripts (4. 1449a9), and that the first Athenian comic poet to introduce coherent stories and plots rather than random lampoons, jokes "of the iambic type," etc., was Crates (active ca. 450 BCE). Aristotle also remarks that comedy began earlier in Sicily than in Athens.

From this angle, then, we may say that the essence or origin of Greek "comic drama" was ritual choral dance and group celebration of Dionysus, presumably designed to promote some kind of group solidarity and fertility/potency. (The procession and song to Phales at Aristophanes *Acharnians* 237–79 may be a quasi-authentic representation of such a traditional kind of phallic song-procession, complete with a strong element of male sexual aggression.) But a wrinkle is introduced to such explanations by the fact that in Athens, in particular, aristocratic symposiasts sometimes liked to adopt animal or exotic (foreign) costumes (though not, as far as we can tell, masks) to enhance their *kômos* activities. So we cannot necessarily draw a clear distinction between rustic fertility rituals and sophisticated elite masquerades. All of these influences seem to have contributed to the "origins" of Attic theater comedy, leading up to its institutionalization at the City Dionysia in 486 BCE.

On the other hand, by any definition (including Aristotle's), comedy and the comic also have a lot to do with laughter and humor, and these need not always have a sexual, ritual, or riotous focus. This might seem to bring us twenty-first-century moderns to a more universal, less "primitive" point of contact with the Greeks: Aristophanes' plays were—and are—appreciated because they are funny, witty, and clever. That is to say, regardless of its probable ritual origins, by the late fifth century Attic comedy had evolved into a highly sophisticated art form whose chief goals seem broadly similar to those of innumerable modern plays, TV shows, and movies: getting an audience to laugh and to appreciate typical—or extreme—quirks of human character, situations, and fantasies.

Notions of what is laughable, humorous, or worthy of ludicrous representation before an audience vary greatly from one society to another, and this is not the place to discuss such issues in any detail. Laughter (or smiling), to be sure, is a physical, observable act, manifested by almost all human beings in very similar ways. But that does not mean that everyone laughs or smiles at the same things. Verbal jokes, visual and audible incongruities, unexpected outcomes or combinations of events—all may arouse laughter in certain contexts, though the laughter may be more or less friendly (joking, banter, self-depreciation) or hostile (taunting, mockery, satire, ridicule). By and large, however, it seems that all of these sources of laughter can qualify as "comic," and almost any art form that employs any of these triggers for laughter can be regarded as a "comedy."

Ancient Greek humor and notions of the "comic" tended very often to involve heavy doses of mockery, disapproval, and the ridiculing of others. In fact the Greeks tended to associate both the origins and the essence of Old Comedy quite closely with practices of ritual abuse and invective. Thus *psogos* ("censure, invective") and the poetic forms known as *iambos*, as exemplified by Archilochus of Paros (seventh century), Hipponax of Ephesus (sixth century), and others, were seen as the direct ancestors of Aristophanes. These poets had employed down-to-earth—often downright foul—language and simple meters to insult their personal enemies, mock socially unacceptable behavior, and present exaggerated and often grotesque accounts of their own or their acquaintances' sexual, scatological, or otherwise nefarious behavior. Tradition had it that such invective poetry was sometimes so potent in its social impact that these two poets' chief targets (Lycambes and Bupalus respectively—both of them men of wealth and prominence in their communities) were shamed to the point of committing suicide. Whether or not this is historically true, the notion that poetic ridicule could expose vicious behavior and social deviance, and thereby bring down the punishment of the gods and/or the disapproval of the rest of the community, was certainly widely held. It was sometimes a matter of strong disagreement whether such invective was socially beneficial (in exposing and eradicating vicious behavior and socially undesirable individuals) or whether it tended to be more harmful (in promoting bitter personal hostilities and indecorous conduct within the community). Aristophanes' own practice altered somewhat during the course of his career, and *Frogs* contains significantly less ad hominem abuse and foul language than several of his earlier plays. Nonetheless the expectation remains integral to all Aristophanic drama that a "comic" performance, like that of an invective poet, may include insults and mockery directed at particular prominent individuals, as well as scenes of low-life characters behaving in ways normally forbidden, unmentionable, or regarded as disgraceful.

Ritual obscenity and joking/mockery were widespread in Greece, as in many other parts of the world. Sometimes there was no discernibly malicious or critical intent behind it, as, for example, in the "Homeric" *Hymn to Demeter*—a thoroughly "serious" and respectable hexameter poem—and certain moments of the annual Thesmophoria festival, and even the Eleusinian Mysteries, all of these honoring Demeter and her Daughter, Kore/Persephone; indeed we hear allusions to these from the Chorus of Initiates in *Frogs* (416–30, esp. 417 "Let's mock Archedemus . . . etc!").

At the heart of many of these sources of laughter there usually lies some kind of inversion of the normal order of things, an overturning of expectations and/or social structures through incongruous juxtapositions, exaggerations, and reversals. These are usually effected (in the fictional, comedic realm) in a way that suggests unexpected possibilities—humiliation of the mighty and self-important, empowerment of the underdog, relaxation of oppressive rules and restrictions—while simultaneously reassuring those laughing (the audience) that (in reality) a good and proper social order will be restored, even strengthened, by the eventual outcome. In the Classical Greek context, this notion of inversion was especially strong because both *iambos* and Old Comedy regularly presented language and characters that were decidedly "low," in marked contrast to the kings, heroes, and elevated diction of epic, choral lyric, and tragedy. Thus the successful escapades of low-life characters and the public flaunting of vulgar language and behavior in themselves, along with outright parodies and burlesques of heroic/tragic expressions and situations, represented a reversal of entrenched cultural rules and a temporary validation of an alternate reality.

But in addition to these various types of "ridiculous" action and behavior, another type of "comic" activity and a quite different origin for Attic comedy needs to be acknowledged. Fictional narratives such as the *Odyssey*, involving romantic encounters and "happy endings," present an obvious contrast to the grim stories of death, loss, and suffering encountered in the *Iliad* and the majority of our surviving Greek "tragedies." By the standards of modern criticism, and also those of certain ancient Greek theorists, the *Odyssey* should be counted as comic (like Dante's *Divine Comedy*, or, e.g., Jane Austen's novels), even though in Aristotle's terms the language, characters, and action of the *Odyssey* adhere quite properly to the rules of "serious, high" epic. Indeed, certain aspects of *Frogs*, as of several other Old Comedies, may remind us quite vividly of epic-style adventure stories or sacred hymns: a visit to the Underworld, a poetic contest, encounters with Heracles, Plouton, and others; and the quest to "save the city" is in itself a serious venture, however fantastic and even farcical much of the language and stage action may be.

In any case, whatever psychological, social, ritual, and poetic origins we may identify for "Old Comedy," by the time Aristophanes began to compose plays in the last third of the fifth century Athenian *kômôidia* had evolved into a distinctive art form of its own. Tragedy doubtless contributed to this evolution too. Certainly the form of drama that emerged by the 450s or so, in the hands of the early masters of Attic Old Comedy, Magnes, Crates, and others, had quite a bit in common with *tragôidia*: a story acted out by two or three speaking actors (plus some nonspeaking extras) along with a singing and dancing chorus—all of these wearing masks; the whole drama about 1200 to 1500 lines long (70 to 90 minutes in performance time), with alternations between episodes of spoken dialogue, mainly from the speaking actors, and more or less elaborate chants and songs, mainly, but not exclusively, from the chorus; the sung portions were all accompanied by a pipe-player (*aulêtês*). Probably the early Athenian comic poets were influenced also by the already well-established tradition of comic drama in Syracuse (Sicily), where Epicharmus had achieved much success and more than local fame with comedies based mainly on mythological themes. But, unfortunately, too little survives from Epicharmus' plays to give us much of an idea of the scale or flavor of their overall plots, and we cannot even tell what kind of a role (if any) the chorus played.

No texts survive from the earliest period of Attic comedy (480s–40s BCE), apart from scraps. The earliest Athenian comic playwright of whose work we possess substantial—though still fragmentary—amounts is Cratinus (fl. ca. 440–20). But we do have enough titles and fragments from the predecessors and rivals of Aristophanes overall to see that the range of subjects and techniques of comic presentation were already quite wide-ranging, i.e., by no means confined to, or dominated by, invective and personal criticism, as some ancient critics imply. Some of the comedies were based on traditional myth, others (perhaps the majority) involved contemporary and topical subjects, drawing on the old traditions of *iambos*. Some combined both, mixing heroic characters into contemporary situations, or vice versa. Prominent politicians and other public figures would often be ridiculed (a feature especially of Cratinus' comedies, it seems), and at one point in the play the chorus was expected to "step forward" (*parabainein*, as at *Acharnians* 629; hence the term *parabasis*) to offer directly the playwright's own statement to the audience about matters of social and political interest, and often some competitive self-advertisement about his own poetic talent and worth.

The primary venue for this newly developed dramatic form was (at least by the mid-fifth century) the Theater of Dionysus, situated on the south slope of the Acropolis, where performances of comedies took place at two major festivals each year, the Lenaea (January) and the City Dionysia (late March–early April); see further chapter 6. The Theater itself underwent many alterations and transformations over the centuries, such that it is almost impossible to determine its precise configuration during those early years. Figures

1–1a and b present two different configurations, one of them based on the surviving stone theaters of later periods, the other following the recent tendency of archaeologists and theater historians to reinterpret the early evidence from the Theater of Dionysus in the light of the somewhat better-preserved remains of the old regional theaters that have been excavated from the rural demes (parishes) of Attica. So in Fig. 1–1a we have a circular plan and massive stone structures for the stage-building (*skênê*), and raised stage and seats, which is the way Greek theaters were imagined by Victorian and early twentieth-century scholars, and certainly the way theaters came to look by the late fourth century (as, e.g., at Epidaurus and Syracuse). On the other hand, Fig. 1–1b presents a much smaller, wooden *skênê* (rebuilt each year for the festival), no raised stage, and a rectangular or trapezoidal dance floor and auditorium. This latter configuration probably comes much closer to recapturing the contours and flavor of the Theater of Dionysus in Aristophanes' day.

Plays might also be restaged in the (smaller) deme theaters (Thoricus, Icarion, Rhamnous, Eleusis, etc.), at the so-called "rural Dionysia" (*ta kat' agrous Dionusia*: cf. *Acharnians* 250). The Lenaea and the City Dionysia were governed by somewhat different arrangements and rules concerning the dramatic competitions: the latter was a five-day event, drawing visitors from all over the Greek world in addition to the local residents of Attica, and featuring parades, dithyrambic competitions for choruses of men and boys, and contests in tragic drama as well as comedy, whereas the Lenaea occupied just three days, was restricted to Athenians and metics (resident aliens), and involved competitions just in comedy. Five comic playwrights generally competed each year at the City Dionysia, three at the Lenaea (though it seems that the arrangements were occasionally modified during tight economic times, especially during the Peloponnesian War).

In both festivals prizes were awarded to the victorious poet, producer, lead actor, and pipe-player. *Frogs* won first prize at the Lenaea of 405, and we are told that the Athenians appreciated the play (especially its *parabasis*) so much that the poet was awarded a special crown and was (most unusually) granted a chorus to restage

Figure 1–1. Two sketches of the Theater of Dionysus as it might have looked for the first production of *Frogs* in 405 BCE.
(a) Circular configuration.
Drawing by H. Wirsing, from H. Bulle and H. Wirsing *Szenenbilder zum griechischen Theater des 5. Jahrhunderts vor Chr.* (Berlin 1950).
(b) Trapezoidal configuration.
Drawing by Elizabeth Wahle.

the play; but we do not know when or where this second production may have taken place (see below, chapter 8).

The sacred context of performance—a festival of Dionysus, a *theatron* located within the precinct of his temple—obviously needs to be borne in mind in assessing the social function and meaning of Aristophanes' plays (as too of the tragedies performed in the same context). But it is notoriously hard to determine exactly what this sacred significance amounted to. Athletic competitions were religious events too (honoring Zeus at the Olympic Games, Athena in the Panathenaic Games, etc.); yet one does not usually think of the charioteers or boxers in the heat of a contest as performing a sacred ritual so much as exerting their physical and technical abilities to the maximum in order to outdo one another and earn honor and acclaim from their watching peers, and a prize. A relatively small proportion of the surviving plays and known play titles from classical Athens, whether tragedies or comedies, have plots that involve anything that has much to do with Dionysus: most of them are about other gods and heroes, or (in the case of comedy) about practically anything imaginable under the sun.

Frogs, like Euripides' *Bacchae* (from almost exactly the same date), is thus unusual and especially intriguing since the whole drama focuses not only on the city of Athens and its cultural life—tragedy and comedy, above all—but also on the figure of Dionysus himself. It also presents scenes involving Eleusinian mystery cult and some kind of life after death, topics that we would certainly regard today as quintessentially "religious." We shall return in chapter 6 to these issues of comic (and Dionysian) religion.

Conventions and Characteristics of Attic Comedies

While Athenian "Old Comedy" includes several ritual and performance features that can be found in numerous other societies, ancient and modern, in certain respects it was a very specific, indeed unique, cultural phenomenon that evolved as it did in response to its particular place, time, and context. Aristophanes' plays were very much a product of—and were designed to address—Athens' socioeconomic structures, its democratic system, the cults and geographical-ecological features of Attica, the specific opportunities, controversies, and life challenges presented by the growth of imperial power and the vicissitudes of the Peloponnesian War, and a multitude of other social and intellectual issues that were continually flooding into Greece's largest urban center and cultural hub during this period. Aristophanic comedy reflects these processes—and anxieties about them—at every turn, since the plots of these plays could allow the most extravagant and fantastic mixtures of topical and traditional, personal and political, sexual and religious features to coexist, with cheerful disregard for realistic standards of plausibility or verisimilitude. Thus they brought on stage not only figures from the Greeks' collective mythological and religious traditions (Heracles, Dionysus, Paris and Helen, Prometheus, Hermes, etc.), but also contemporary Athenians, both real and fictional (and often a few Spartans, Megarians, Scythians, Persians, etc. as well), men and women such as one might meet any day in the agora, or sit next to as one rowed in a trireme (warship: see Figs. 6–2a and 6–2b), or see arguing public policy in the Assembly.

The amazing variety and imaginative range of Old Comedy can be seen even from the surviving eleven plays of Aristophanes (leaving aside the hundreds of lost comedies by him and his rivals, of which we have many titles but usually not much more). So, for example:

Acharnians (425 BCE): an enterprising Athenian citizen declares a private peace of his own with Sparta.

Clouds (423 BCE): an old man has run into debt because of his son's expensive habits. He decides to go to study with Socrates (!) so that he can learn fancy rhetorical strategies for outwitting juries and creditors ("making the worse argument stronger").

Birds (414 BCE): two Athenian men, disgusted with the interfering, litigious, frantic lifestyle of Athens, decide to travel to find a more tranquil spot to live. They end up joining the birds and construct their own *polis* in the sky ("Cloudcuckooland").

Lysistrata (411 BCE): wives from all the Greek cities stage a collective sex strike and occupy the Athenian Acropolis, to force their husbands to end the Peloponnesian War.

And so on.

The plots of these plays are elaborate and sophisticated (if not always entirely self-consistent and tidy—nothing like the clockwork precision of Menander, Terence, or Oscar Wilde). Furthermore, the structural elements out of which each play is built, with multiple meters, alternating lyric and recited forms, and spoken dialogue, are complex and their deployment somewhat regular and stylized. The plays are thus, despite their wild and crazy flavor, very carefully planned and executed. Where did this structural "plan" come from?

While most modern scholars agree with Aristotle in surmising that Attic Old Comedy grew out of improvised iambic/phallic performances, there is much less agreement concerning the stages through which such "improvisations" must have passed before they became institutionalized as scripted dramas and introduced into the annual festival competitions. Nor is it at all clear how typical, or distinctively different, the eleven surviving plays of Aristophanes are in their structure and plot elements when compared with the comedies of his main predecessors and rivals. The surviving remains of Cratinus, Eupolis, Pherecrates, and the others, along with ancient testimony about their careers and respective comic styles, amount to a fairly substantial body of evidence; yet we have no complete plays from any of them, and most of the fragments exist in isolation from one another, making it impossible to reconstruct even single scenes in any detail. So our account of the "history" of Attic comedy is necessarily rather speculative.

The most widely held view of this history divides it into three fairly distinct phases: "Old" (fifth century), "Middle" (ca. 400–350), and "New" (fourth century), while also tracing an evolution within Old Comedy itself from a cruder to a more sophisticated set of formal and thematic possibilities. Old Comedy is supposed to have been heavily weighted at first towards political satire and topical themes; then, by the late fifth century, as political comedy became less acceptable, Middle Comedy gravitated to mythological and allegorical themes; and eventually the character- and situation-based New Comedy emerged as the dominant form. This is certainly how later (post-Hellenistic) scholars liked to explain the differences between Aristophanes (along with his rivals Cratinus and Eupolis, in particular) on the one hand ("Old"), and Menander on the other ("New"). But the fragmentary remains of the various other comic playwrights do not well support this account; nor do we find earlier scholars (such as Aristotle) endorsing it. Instead, we see that many of the titles and themes of mid-fifth-century comedies were taken from mythology, or were allegorical or literary parodies—that is to say, they fit the definition of Middle rather than Old Comedy; conversely, some of Menander's contemporaries wrote plays that seem somewhat akin to Middle Comedy. So it may be more appropriate to think of fifth-century Attic comedy, like the Sicilian comedies of Epicharmus, as ranging quite broadly in topics and plot-types.

There is likewise much uncertainty as to the structure and dramatic technique of pre-Aristophanic comedy. Working back from the structural elements that are found most consistently in Aristophanes' earlier plays (those of the 420s) but less frequently or obviously in his later ones, modern scholars have reconstructed a hypothetical framework for early Attic comedy, a framework that some have suggested might be connected to pre-existing ritual forms. In this framework, each play begins with the entrance of one or two characters, whose opening dialogue (*PROLOGOS*) sets the scene and launches the main plot-idea; then the chorus arrives (*PARODOS*) with an elaborate song and dance; some kind of confrontation or contest then takes place (*EPIRRHEMATIC AGÓN*) between the hero and one or more opponents; after this is resolved, the chorus "step forward" and speak directly to the audience in alternating song and chant, more or less speaking as (in the person of) the playwright himself (*PARABASIS*), and usually offering advice or criticism to the city at large. In the later stages of the play, a sequence of "arrivals" and brief dialogues takes place (*EPISODES*), as different characters attempt to join or oppose the hero in his/her venture; and finally a celebration takes place (*EXODOS/KÓMOS*), with eating, singing, and perhaps a sexual triumph or marriage for the hero.

Whether or not any such regular structure did exist in the very early days of Attic comedy, even the few plays of Aristophanes that we possess display quite a lot of structural variation among them; and as his career progressed he seems to have taken greater liberties. Most of these structural elements are found—though not quite in this same order, and with some duplication—in *Frogs* (see chapter 3). But the fact that comedies were performed in the same theater as tragedies guaranteed that audiences were generally familiar also with the distinctly different formal structure of this other kind of drama, one in which scenes of spoken dialogue from the actors generally alternated with strophic songs from the chorus and with occasional actors' monodies inserted at moments of emotional climax. Greek comedy often imitates or parodies tragedy; and comedy occasionally drew from satyr-drama as well, so theater audiences in the middle and late fifth century perhaps had a pretty open mind as to what to expect, and in what order.

Aristophanes and the Other Fifth-Century Athenian Comic Playwrights

Of all the hundreds of comedies written and performed in Athens during the fifth and early fourth century, only eleven—all by Aristophanes—survive in complete manuscript form. However, hundreds of fragments exist from the other great playwrights of that era, mostly in the form of quotations, titles, and comments by later writers, along with a few (sometimes quite extensive and fascinating) papyrus pieces excavated from Egypt. Valuable and informative though these fragments are, it is very hard—usually impossible—to form any reliable idea of what any of those plays were really like, scene by scene and in their entirety, though we can often get quite a good sense of their exuberant and varied language.

It is by no means certain that Aristophanes was the most popular or the most successful of them all in his own day. It is a curious fact, for example, that whereas ancient sources tell us the number of victories won by Eupolis (seven victories, in fourteen or fifteen productions) and Cratinus (nine victories), no such figure is recorded anywhere for Aristophanes. We have to piece this information together from various different and incomplete sources. We do know that several of his plays did not in fact win first prize (*Wasps, Peace, Birds,* and the first version of *Clouds*); victories are only certain in the case of *Acharnians* (425), *Knights* (424), and *Frogs* (405)— all at the Lenaea—though probably he won also at the City Dionysia with *Babylonians* (426) and perhaps with *Banqueters* too (427). (We do not know the placing of *Thesmophoriazusae*, *Lysistrata*, *Assembly-women*, or *Wealth* in their respective competitions.) References within his plays to their author's brilliance and sophistication may not be entirely trustworthy as indices of audience favor, and it is quite possible that, like Euripides, Aristophanes was widely known, loved by some, but not universally admired during his own career, only emerging in later generations as the most popular and widely read of all the Old Comedians.

It has been suggested that Aristophanes' frequent encounters with Socrates as described by Plato (he is mentioned in several works, appearing unforgettably in the *Symposium*) may have contributed to this posthumous success; or else that his plays may in fact have come to be regarded simply as better (aesthetically? stylistically? morally?) than those of any of his rivals, especially for school reading. But in any case, a word or two about (especially) the plays of Crates, Pherecrates, Cratinus, Eupolis, and Phrynichus, is called for here, since two of these were frequently mentioned by Aristophanes himself. Knowing something about their dramas can help us to understand better what Old Comedy had already accomplished before *Frogs* was written, and what Aristophanes' audience would have regarded as "the usual things" for a comedy.

CRATES and PHERECRATES were apparently active in the generations before Aristophanes, though Pherecrates' career overlapped with his (Crates 450s–430s; Pherecrates 440s–400 or so). Both of them were best known for comedies with mythological plots and relatively little political invective and personal abuse. One of Pherecrates' plays, *Crapataloi* (*Sprats*), is of particular interest in relation to *Frogs* since its action was apparently set in the Underworld and involved Aeschylus as one of the characters. Little else is known about the play, however. Pherecrates' amusing musical parody in *Cheiron* will also come into our discussion later (chapter 5).

The biggest name in Athenian comedy before Aristophanes was undoubtedly CRATINUS, who is mentioned prominently in *Frogs* and elsewhere in Aristophanes. Cratinus is credited by ancient sources above all with developing topical and political invective on a sustained scale, but it appears that he was also a sophisticated critic and competitor with a strong self-image as poet and public performer. His best-known plays included *Dionysalexandros*, in which Pericles was ridiculed and criticized for bringing unnecessary wars on Athens (presumably, like Paris/Alexandros with regard to Troy); the *Ploutoi* (*Wealth-gods*), based on the release of the Titans from the Underworld; *Odysseus and Friends*, based on the Cyclops episode of the *Odyssey*; and *Pytinê*, in which old Cratinus made himself the central character, at first engaged in a love affair with a woman named Methê ("Drunkenness") until he is persuaded to give her up and return to his true mistress/wife, Kômôidia ("Comedy"). This last play seems to have been a huge hit and to have played cleverly off Aristophanes' own criticisms and jokes about Cratinus as a drunken, aging, lecherous has-been. Overall, it is clear even from the limited remains that Cratinus' plays were varied and creative: mythological burlesque, allegory, political satire, literary criticism, self-parody are all well represented.

Although Cratinus is often ridiculed in Aristophanes' early plays (*Acharnians* 848–53, 1173; *Knights* 400, 526–36), he is mentioned with some nostalgia shortly after his death (*Peace* 700–04), and by the time of *Frogs* we find him invoked by the Chorus in their *parabasis* as the virtual culture-hero of Comedy itself:

> You must mind what you say (*euphêmein*) and speak only
>   holy words:
> There is no place in our celebrations for those who are
>   inexperienced
> In this kind of language, or those who are impure of mind,
> Or those who have not seen or danced the noble celebrations
>   of the Muses,
> And have not been initiated into the Bacchic rites of the
>   tongue of bull-eating Cratinus! (*Frogs* 354–57)

In several respects, indeed, the contest between Aeschylus and Euripides in *Frogs* seems to mirror the longtime comic contest between Cratinus and Aristophanes himself (especially during the 420s), with the same contrasting images of (old-style) wine-drinking, potency, inflation, and inspiration versus (modern) neatness, cleverness, slimness, and art. Indeed one ancient source remarks that Cratinus modeled his style on that of Aeschylus (*eis ton Aischulou charactêra*), while a fragment of one of Cratinus' plays (we do not know which: *PCG* fr. 342) includes a reference to someone as "a Euripides–Aristophanizing kind of guy" (*euripidaristophanizôn*), which suggests some affinity (in the minds of the old guard) between those two modernists. (See further chapter 7.).

EUPOLIS was an exact contemporary of Aristophanes, though he apparently died much younger, drowned in a shipwreck in 411. It was said (e.g., by the Byzantine encyclopedia known as the Suda) that Eupolis and Aristophanes sometimes collaborated amicably; but mutual accusations of plagiarism flew back and forth, with Eupolis claiming to have been himself the chief author of Aristophanes' *Knights* (Eupolis fr. 89), whereas Aristophanes insisted (*Clouds* 553–54) that the borrowing went the other way—Eupolis had stolen most of the ideas and even some of the language for his comedy *Maricas* (421 BCE) from *Knights*. Certainly Eupolis was a kindred comic spirit in many respects. Two of his most successful plays in fact anticipated some of the central ideas of *Frogs*: in *Taxiarchoi* (*Officers*) he had Dionysus join the navy (cf. *Frogs* 197–270), while in *Dêmoi* (*Demes*), his most celebrated play, four politicians from Athens' glorious past (Solon, Miltiades, Aristides, and Pericles) are brought back from Hades to advise the city (rather as Aeschylus is chosen by Dionysus in *Frogs* "to provide advice," 1420–21).

PHRYNICHUS was another of Aristophanes' contemporaries. Little of his work survives, even in fragments; but we do know that he was the author of one of the comedies that competed against *Frogs*, and that this play, oddly enough, also involved a trip to the Underworld and an encounter with the Muses.

To conclude this preliminary survey of Athenian comedy in its various phases and styles, we may return to where we began: the opening lines of *Frogs*. Of course Aristophanes wants to employ as many of the "usual things" as possible. So he will make sure to give us luggage-carrying slave routines (1–10, 88 "my shoulder's killing me"), scatological jokes (e.g., 10 "I'm going to burst!," 479 "I've shat myself!," 484 "Is that where you keep your 'heart'?"), slaves being beaten, ridicule directed at well-known Athenian politicians (Cleophon, Theramenes, Alcibiades, etc.) and at socially marginal or deviant types of people, along with plenty of bizarre costumes and incongruous visual and musical effects. At the same time, Aristophanes takes care to remind us just how old and corny several of these elements are—and he thus gets extra mileage out of them as he contrasts his own sophistication with the more pedestrian and unoriginal efforts of his rivals (e.g., 13–14 criticizing Phrynichus, Lycis, and Ameipsias). Whether in fact Aristophanes was any more refined than they in eschewing slapstick, routine, and visual humor in favor of more subtle literary allusion and thoughtful moralizing, as he himself claims, we are not in a good position to judge.

Several of the main characters and plot elements that Aristophanes employs in *Frogs* had certainly been attempted before in comedy: Heracles' adventures in the Underworld, Dionysus attempting to perform an unaccustomed new role, a judgment of the dead, the salvation or resurrection of a soul through Dionysus and initiation ritual, perhaps others too. We even hear of other plays with frogs in them (by Magnes *PCG* V. 628, and by Callias *PCG* IV. 42). Criticism and parody of the bad poetry and playwriting of others, or of tragedy in general, were likewise not in themselves a new idea, as we have seen; nor was the combination of traditional mythological characters and themes with contemporary Athenian politics and social problems. These were all part and parcel of "the usual things that audiences always laugh at." So we might say that *Frogs* presents itself at every turn as a typical and exemplary *kômôidia*, and expects to be judged as such. The play is nonetheless enormously and captivatingly original. As the author had earlier remarked (in the *parabasis* to *Clouds*, 547–48), "I am a clever and sophisticated enough artist (*sophizomai*) that I can keep bringing on fresh ideas (*ideas kainas*), not all the same, but all super-smart (*dexias*)!"

Suggestions for Further Reading

Fuller information about Aristophanes' career and about the history and nature of Old Comedy can be found in the standard books and editions of Aristophanes: see especially Dover (1972),

Henderson (2002), MacDowell (1971), Olson (2004), Sommerstein (1996), and Revermann (2013). On the origins of Greek comedy, the traditions of *iambos*, and Dionysian ritual and phallic dance, see especially Bierl (2001/2009), Csapo and Miller (2007), Rosen (1988), Rothwell (2007), and (for the organization of the Athenian comic festival performances) Rusten 2011. For good discussions of humor, both ancient Greek and modern, and theories of comedy, see Apte (1985), Frye (1957), Halliwell (2008); also Silk (2000).

On the archaeological evidence for assessing the shape, size, organization, and configuration of the Theater of Dionysus at Athens, see Wilson (2007), and especially the "Archaeological Appendix" (pp. 116–23) by H. R. Goette to E. Csapo's article, "The men who built the Theatres."

On the other poets of Old Comedy, their relationship to Aristophanes, and the nature and evolution of Attic comedy in general through the fifth and fourth centuries, see Bakola (2010), Biles (2011), Csapo (2000a), Harvey and Wilkins (2000), Rosen (2000), and Storey (2003).

· 2 ·

Aristophanes and His Athenian Audience

Growing up in Late Fifth-Century Athens

We know very little about Aristophanes' life and family. Most of the information we do have is derived from the plays themselves and much of that may be untrustworthy. (Comic poets are not obligated to tell the exact truth all the time.) He was apparently born in the early or mid-440s, making him almost fifty years younger than Sophocles, and some twenty years younger than Euripides and Socrates. Alcibiades was a close contemporary of his, Plato and Xenophon both about fifteen years younger. He thus grew up during a period when Athens had already risen to a position of dominance within the Greek world both culturally and, in many respects, militarily and politically as well. Memories of the Athenians' glorious repulse of the Persians in the infantry battle at Marathon (490) and the sea-battle of Salamis (480) were still vividly present in the memory and imagination of the older generation of Athenians, and these events had become much-publicized symbols of Athens' political heritage and of the city's claim to leadership of the rest of Greece. Aristophanes was a teenager when the Peloponnesian War broke out between Sparta and Athens (431); he presumably became eligible for military service a year or two after he heard Pericles deliver the Funeral Oration recorded for us by Thucydides (2. 34–46); and he lived as an adult to witness the defeat of Athens by Sparta (404), the destruction of Athens' fortifications (the Long Walls) and imposition of an oligarchic junta, the "Thirty" (404–403), the restoration of the democracy (403), and the steady recovery of Athens to a state of stability and prosperity—though no longer of such enormous expansionist and imperialist ambitions—during the 390s and 380s. He seems to have died before 380.

The *Life of Aristophanes* contained in the Suda, like the rest of the entries in that multifarious work, is a curious jumble of valuable facts and implausible fictions. Sometimes it is not possible to tell the two apart, and all too often "information" about a playwright's life, character, and career has apparently been gleaned or merely inferred from the texts of the plays themselves rather than from any independent testimony. This *Life* is clearly written from an intensely pro-Aristophanic point of view, crediting him with inventing or maintaining all that was good in Old Comedy while dissociating him from its defects and blaming these on other playwrights (whose works are all lost to us, as they were to the Byzantines as well). Nonetheless, this is much the fullest continuous account available to us, and we have to begin from it even while exercising all due caution.

> Aristophanes the comic poet was the son of Philippus; he was an Athenian; his deme was Cydathenaeus, his tribe Pandionis. He seems to have been the first to transform Comedy, which was still wandering erratically in its early stages of development, into something more morally serious and worthwhile, while Cratinus and Eupolis were writing a scurrilous type of comedy (*blasphêmountôn*) that was fiercer and more undignified than was proper. He was also the first to display the style of New Comedy, in his *Cocalus* [a lost play], from which Menander and Philemon got their start in composing plays.
>
> He was very careful to begin with, and well-brought-up, so he presented his plays at first under the name of Callistratus and of Philonides . . . but later he competed in his own name. He was especially hostile to Cleon the demagogue, and wrote

the *Knights* against him, criticizing his thievery and tyrannical ways; and when none of the costume-makers dared to make a mask of him because of their extreme fear . . . nor would any of the actors dare to play that role, Aristophanes acted the role himself, smearing his own face with red dye . . . etc.

There seems no reason to doubt that Aristophanes' family was prosperous, if not aristocratic. The Suda's additional statement that they owned property on the nearby island of Aegina is plausible, though it may be no more than an inference from Aristophanes' own remarks in the *parabasis* of *Acharnians* (652–55). Their home deme (Cydathenaeus) where Aristophanes, like his father Philippus, was registered lay right in the city-center of Athens itself. Like all of his age-mates, he will have trained to fight as an infantry soldier and also probably to row in a trireme (see Fig. 6–2). Fighting as a hoplite or cavalryman was generally regarded as a mark of citizen valor, appropriate to an aristocrat or a man of solid social standing; honorific inscriptions confirm this. Rowing in the fleet, which was generally the job of poorer citizens and hired mercenaries, was less glamorous, and usually anonymous (Fig. 6–2b); yet it was at least equally dangerous, since loss of life in sea-battles tended to be heavier than in land-battles (if your ship sank, it was hard to both escape the enemy and avoid drowning). Athenian foreign policy, grain supplies, and military success depended heavily on naval power, and the *Frogs* reminds its audience constantly of the importance of the navy and good seamanship. Indeed, in Aristophanes' world a man who does not know how to pull properly on an oar is a dunce, or a softy, or both. In the sea-battle that occurred at Arginusae shortly before the production of *Frogs*, hoplites (i.e., middle-class infantry soldiers) had been required to row, an emergency measure; hence surely arises some of the humorous point of Dionysus' unexpectedly having to learn to use an oar at *Frogs* 190–270. Earlier (48–50) he had described himself serving on an Athenian warship in a previous campaign as a "marine" (*epibatês*), i.e., a gentleman-hoplite, not a rower.

More likely than not, Aristophanes' father and/or other close relatives were expert in music and poetry: for playwriting, like other occupations, tended to be a family affair (and Aristophanes' own sons, Ararus and Philippus, in due course both became successful comic poets). In any case, in addition to (presumably) attending the Theater of Dionysus every year, he will have grown up with epic narratives, hymns and encomia, wisdom poetry, and invectives (*iamboi*) all around him, since not only were these part and parcel of every well-brought-up boy's education (see *Clouds* 961–1023 on the "old, traditional education," esp. 964–72), but such poems were also performed at public festivals and recited piecemeal at upper-class dinners and drinking parties (*symposia*; cf. Philocleon in *Wasps* 1122–64).

Some of the songs performed at festivals were delivered by expert solo singers (cf. *Frogs* 1281–1300), but many were sung and danced by a chorus. The annual City Dionysia in particular involved several hundred choral singers, both boys and men, in the competitions of dithyramb, tragedy, and comedy. So a musically inclined young man had many opportunities to develop his skills as a performer as well as his understanding of choral composition—opportunities also to make friends and connections with others who might collaborate with him in the future. There was no need for play-writing classes or music conservatories: one learned to be a poet-musician by practicing and performing from childhood on.

"Music" (*mousikê technê* = "the art belonging/pertaining to the Muses") was a much less peripheral or optional component of a citizen's life in classical Athens than it is for citizens of most Western societies today—a closer modern analogy might be West Africa or Brazil, even rural Greece, at least until very recently, i.e., societies where a vital component of male or female elegance, even social power, may consist of singing, dancing, story-telling, and various kinds of musical performance. As it is stated in Plato's *Laws* (2. 654a), written some thirty years after Aristophanes' death but in a traditionalist frame of mind, "anyone who is not chorally trained (*achoreutos*) is uneducated (*apaideutos*)." So Aristophanes could count on many of his audience members bringing with them a lifetime spent in musical performance, recitation, and appreciation. Furthermore, they shared a general sense that a person's whole character could be "read" from his (or her) way of moving, dancing, talking, and singing. "Music" was not merely a form of entertainment or aesthetic refinement, it was a social and ethical matter as well, and musical taste often went beyond personal preference to involve group identity and affiliation, gender, and class position.

But Aristophanes was also part of a generation—perhaps the first generation in Western history—that grew up with books and could study the wisdom and artistic techniques of past authors in written form as well as experiencing them live. In the late fifth century, both oral and literate education were going strong in Athens, side by side, and a cultural shift was in fact taking place between the traditional system of athletics, choruses, and musical-poetical performance and the newer program that was rhetorically oriented and would eventually become the standard for future centuries.

At school, then, not only were Homer's epics and Hesiod's wisdom poetry recited and memorized, along with passages from the hymns and healing-spells attributed to Musaeus and Orpheus (see *Frogs* 1031–33), but so too were the verse and prose fables of Archilochus and Aesop, the lyrics of Simonides, Sappho, and Anacreon, and probably excerpts from the great tragedians as well. Written texts of all these works, and of the histories, ethnographies, and genealogies of various kinds (including natural-scientific and Orphic) that were being produced by various progressive thinkers and teachers, were beginning to become more widely available, though by no means mainstream: likewise, technical writings on medicine, astronomy, mathematics, even "philosophy," such as the little book of Anaxagoras that Socrates says he read as a young man (*Phaedo* 97b–98d; cf. *Apology* 28d–e).

It is likely that the young Aristophanes was exceptionally interested in collecting literary texts. Even though, like most Athenians, he would have been far better at oral memorization than most Westerners today, the detailed parodies and allusions that we find in his plays seem too numerous and often too subtle not to have required some textual study. And to put the matter beyond dispute, his plays themselves make frequent reference to "reading" and to "books" (*biblia*, esp. *Frogs* 52–53, 943, 1114, 1409). But he probably did not expect very many members of his audience to have read much, if at all. Nor did he expect most of his audience to be sympathetic to the new rhetorical methods of schooling. In his *Clouds* (first composed in 423), Aristophanes presents an unforgettable (if unfair and far-fetched) portrait of Socrates as a shameless exponent of rhetorical ingenuity, cheating, and intellectualist hair-splitting; and he includes an extended debate-scene (*agôn*) between the "old-style" and "new" systems of education (*Clouds* 889–1112; see too Plato *Apology* 19c). Such a view of Socrates recurs elsewhere in Aristophanes' plays (as at *Frogs* 1491–93); and, in general, the playwright's traditionalist/populist comic vision is quick to mock newfangled ideas—about the gods, about science, and about the various fashions in clothing and behavior—that were winning a following among the Athenian elite. This suspicion of hyper-intellectualism and pretentious novelty is also a central factor in Aristophanes' presentation of Euripides, in *Frogs* and elsewhere (see chapter 5).

By the late fifth century, not only was the technology of writing beginning to transform the processes of cultural production and consumption, but there was also something of a revolution taking place in the world of musical composition and performance—a revolution that, as far as we can tell, had little to do with books or literacy. We will discuss these developments in the "New Music" in more detail in chapter 5, since many of them involve Euripides. The comic playwrights were necessarily quite minutely attuned to the latest sounds and fashions of tragedy, and Aristophanes' own metrical and musical style clearly owed much to these developing trends and possibilities—though the degree of his resistance or acceptance of them is sometimes hard to determine since references within his plays are ambivalent. Whether or not Aristophanes himself was an actor or singer (or accompanist) of any particular talent—and we have no reliable evidence about this—he certainly had grown up in the midst of both the old and the new kinds of music, and he must have been intimately familiar with their respective techniques and with the arguments adduced by both sides as to their merits and flaws.

It would be interesting to know more about Aristophanes' personal habits, friends, family, social status, etc.; speculations in particular about his relationship to Socrates (and Plato) have been rife since antiquity, given the frequency of cross-references in both directions (Plato's *Apology* and *Symposium*; Aristophanes' *Clouds* and *Frogs*). But these can be no more than speculations. Likewise the nature and degree of his collaboration with other comic playwrights, and with his own playwright sons, can only be guessed at. (See chapter 1 for discussion of Eupolis, and below for Philonides in particular.)

Becoming a Dramatist: *kômôidos–chorêgos–didaskalos*

The career path of a comic dramatist (or tragedian, for that matter) at Athens was distinctly different from that in most subsequent European societies. Nobody in Athens really made a living financially out of playwriting (as did, for example, Plautus, or Shakespeare and Jonson, Racine and Molière). An Athenian playwright's ambitions were instead focused mainly on, first, gaining the approval of the eponymous archon (the senior city official responsible for organizing the festivals) so that he would be selected as one of those playwrights to be "given a chorus" to compete in one of the major annual competitions, and then winning first prize in that competition by impressing the judges in a single performance in the Theater of Dionysus. The reward for the victors was not cash (though this was surely a big factor for the pipe-player and actors) but prestige, of which there was plenty in the form of fellow citizens' recognition and approval, including a permanent victory monument inscribed with the names of the *chorêgos* and poet (*kômôidos*). This monument was usually erected in a conspicuous spot on (what is now) the Street of Tripods or somewhere else close to the Theater itself. (The *chorêgos*, literally "chorus-master," that is, producer, was a wealthy citizen assigned this duty for a year as a kind of super-tax. Other such civic duties ("liturgies") involved paying for a trireme or for repairs to the city's walls.) The *choregos* and the playwright presumably shared responsibilities for "teaching" (*didaskein*) all the performers their parts, unless a third person was employed as "chorus-teacher" (*chorodidaskalos*)—a term that also meshed nicely with the poet's implicit function as "teacher" of his fellow-citizens (see chapter 4) The expenses for a theater production (drama or dithyramb) were quite considerable and were mostly borne by the *chorêgos*. The city may have paid the salaries of the actors directly, but the task of selecting and looking after the chorus belonged to the *chorêgos*. The dramatist himself was not paid, so he too had to be wealthy enough to be able to devote months on end to the processes of composition, design, auditioning, casting, rehearsing, rewriting—and all of this while aware that there might only ever be one production of his play.

Several of Aristophanes' plays were presented, not under his own name, but under that of a collaborator, though it seems to have been no secret who the true author was. So the first three known comedies of Aristophanes, performed when he was still hardly more than an adolescent, were officially presented by Callistratus (*Banqueters* in 427, not preserved; *Babylonians* in 426, also not preserved; and *Acharnians* in 425). In the *parabasis* of *Wasps* (422), Aristophanes makes quite an issue out of all this (1018–22); and he goes on to point out proudly that the first play produced under his own name, *Knights* (424), involved an uncompromising attack on Cleon, Athens' most fearsome politician.

But it was not only at the very beginning of his career that Aristophanes chose to produce plays in someone else's name. This was apparently a common practice among comic poets in general (as we noted in chapter 1, concerning Eupolis and Aristophanes, though there the relationship may not always have been amicable). Likewise, Euripides apparently worked with a musician-collaborator, Cephisophon, in composing several of his tragedies (see *Frogs* 944, 1408, 1452–53; also 1046?). In the case of *Frogs*, Philonides receives credit as producer of the play, which he had been earlier at least twice (in 422, perhaps *Wasps*; and in 414, *Amphiaraus*, now lost). Philonides was himself a comic poet of some distinction, as was his son Nicochares. So it is likely that he and other "producers" contributed ideas and direction, as well as rehearsal time, to these productions. Late in Aristophanes' career, he apparently preferred that his plays be presented under the name(s) of his sons. So whereas our extant *Wealth* (388) was announced as his own, *Aeolosicon* and *Cocalus* were apparently presented by Ararus. As for Iophon and his father Sophocles (*Frogs* 72–82), see chapter 5. All of these references may be taken as confirming our general impression that writing and presenting plays, whether tragedies or comedies (satyr-dramas too), was often a family affair and always a team effort. Unlike a lyric poem or epic, one person cannot create a play. Theatrical talent always involves some collaborative genius.

In any case, once Aristophanes, with or without a co-producer, had requested and been granted permission by the archon in a given year to "teach/train a chorus" (= produce a play) on the topic he had announced in the preliminary application process, he and the *chorêgos* together would enter upon a process that must have taken several months, pooling the poetic talents of the one and the financial-logistical capacities of the other, as they worked to complete a script, design masks and costumes, compose music and choreography, select and rehearse a chorus of twenty-four skilled dancers, meet with their team of four actors, hire and rehearse a pipe-player (*aulêtês*), and prepare to mount a production that would be as spectacular, sophisticated, and appealing as possible.

Many attempts have been made by critics to determine Aristophanes' political preferences and aversions on the basis of the surviving plays and additional scraps of evidence and hearsay about his career. For the most part, the results have been inconclusive or contradictory, and we need not explore here all the ins and outs of these previous discussions. *Frogs* does not happen to engage with some of the topics on which these debates have focused most fiercely (most notably, gender and the status of women); and in any case we should surely let the play speak for itself rather than beginning with preformed expectations as to what its author is likely to have intended. A few basic facts about Aristophanes' political position and views do seem to be well established, however, and are worth bearing in mind. (1) He and his family were prosperous landowners. (2) Several of his plays (*Acharnians*, *Peace*, *Lysistrata*) advocate finding a way to make peace with Sparta—an attitude generally characteristic of the landed Athenian aristocracy but much less common among the poor and among the populist leaders who most vigorously promoted Athenian expansionism and imperialism. (3) The one politician whom Aristophanes most consistently and virulently attacks in several plays is Cleon, a nonaristocrat and also the most conspicuous proponent of those populist and expansionist policies (continuing from Pericles). (4) Whereas Aristophanes' plays are full of scornful and scurrilous criticisms of individual politicians, he rarely includes among his targets any member of the traditional Athenian aristocracy: only demagogues, parvenus, foreigners, etc. The conclusion, not in itself particularly surprising, seems inescapable: however in tune with and sympathetic to the manners and predicaments of regular working peasants and laborers Aristophanes may have been, he was himself more comfortable with the economic and political positions—and maybe the company (as Plato's *Symposium* might suggest)—of the traditional Athenian aristocracy. At the same time (5) there is no evidence at all to suggest that Aristophanes was a radical reactionary, a Spartan sympathizer (Laconizer), a secret oligarch, or anything other than a staunch supporter of the democracy. But democracy of course could be practiced—and imagined—in several different ways among the Athenians, and Aristophanes' own opinions may well have shifted from time to time during the turbulent years of the Peloponnesian War, especially its later stages.

The Audience

Athenian theater audiences were large and not very homogeneous (by classical Greek standards) in their character and tastes. The seating capacity within the Theater itself in the late fifth century was probably 6,000 to 8,000, perhaps even greater, and some additional seating (or standing room only?) seems to have been available above the Theater precinct, in the area "beyond the poplar tree." We do not know whether women could attend the theater, nor whether wealthier citizens were disproportionately represented. Scholars argue vigorously on both sides of these questions. But even if (as the evidence seems mostly to suggest) admission to the Theater was officially restricted to men and to have cost two obols (not a negligible sum) per day, in practice a good number of women, slaves, and poorer citizens may well have watched the dramas from one or another location. In any case, Aristophanes' plays themselves make clear that their audience contained not only members of the intellectual and political elite of the city but also a large number of ordinary, unsophisticated peasants, laborers, and artisans. So when his characters or (especially) the chorus refer to "the city" or to "us" or "you," they must have quite a broad range of mentalities and experience in mind.

But what did it mean to be a (typical, good, ideal) "Athenian"? What was the audience of *Frogs* like (or how did it imagine itself to be)? The shared experience of being a fully qualified Athenian would entail the following: passing a physical, legal, and ethical examination (*dokimasia*) at the age of eighteen within one's deme, so as to be registered as a full citizen; serving as either an infantry soldier or as a rower in the navy, or both; voting in elections of annual administrative officers, and perhaps at one time or another running for office oneself within one's deme (e.g., the local council, or a priesthood) or within the Athenian polis at large, and/or serving for a year as a member of the Council (*Boulê*); attending the Assembly meetings once a month, listening to debate there and voting; probably serving too on juries at some point in one's life (after the age of 30) and thus gaining the experience of judging rival speeches and bodies of evidence, and committing oneself to a relatively quick, yet responsible, verdict (criminal trials lasted only for half a day). In these terms, most of the audience members could probably regard themselves both as true Athenians and as veteran "judges" of what was best for the city. And even if one was not a citizen but a registered metic (*metoikos*), that is, a non-Athenian—but usually Greek—immigrant residing permanently in Attica, one would still probably have served in the Athenian military, and might perhaps have performed in musical events too, though without the opportunity to vote, serve on juries, or run for office.

What about slaves? As far as we can tell, a high proportion of Athenian households owned slaves, and slaves were ubiquitous both within the home as domestic servants and throughout the city as laborers, craftsmen, clerks, accountants, tutors, musicians, and sex workers. In some areas (most notably, the silver mines of Laureium) slaves worked in grim and miserable conditions doing work that no free Athenian would wish to undertake. But in several professions slaves worked side by side with free men and women (citizen and metic) doing similar work. During the late fifth century slaves increasingly had performed military service as well, rowing in the fleet and participating as light-armed troops in land-battles. Some of these slave enlistees had been rewarded with the gift of freedom, even citizenship. So even while the legal and ideological gulf between free and slave, Greek and non-Greek ("barbarian"), remained in some respects unbridgeable, every Athenian citizen had to be well aware of the mutual familiarity and numerous—quite intimate—experiences that they shared with some of their "non-Athenian" and socially inferior co-residents.

Most of the slaves owned by Athenians were of non-Greek origin (Thracian, Scythian, Syrian, Anatolian, Egyptian, etc.), though many must have been second- or third-generation (i.e., born to slave parents who were already residents of Attica) and thus entirely fluent in Attic Greek dialect and speech patterns and thoroughly familiar with Athenian culture in general. Some would have been detectably non-Greek looking: the name Xanthias, for example, means "Redhead, Sandy," probably indicating Thracian or Scythian appearance; others were more or less indistinguishable from Athenians and other Greeks. (We read complaints from conservative-minded Athenians that distinctions are not being clearly enough drawn, in terms of dress, behavior, etc.; for example, sometimes you may find yourself stepping aside in the street for someone you later realize is a slave. Other cities, it is implied, are less egalitarian.)

Theater was one of the media through which free–slave relationships and anxieties could be imaginatively but harmlessly explored. Even in tragedy, we find some eloquent and perceptive slave characters (labeled simply Nurse, Watchman, Tutor, etc.) whose interventions and observations throw significant light on the behavior of their elite masters and who sometimes elicit audience sympathy in their own right. In Aristophanic comedy—and especially in *Frogs*—the dynamics of master-slave trust and mistrust, privilege and deprivation, interdependence, violence, sexual competition, and resentment are explored more pointedly, and while we never encounter in Old Comedy a "cunning slave" or plotting mastermind of the fully developed kind that we meet later in Menander and Plautus (the so-called *servus callidus*), Xanthias in *Frogs* already exhibits several of these characteristics—to a greater degree, in fact, than any previous comic slave. Thus, not only do we find sharp verbal exchanges and put-downs between slave and master (1–35, 107–117, 189–196, and an amusing short scene in which Xanthias and one of Plouton's servants compare notes on the small joys of surreptitiously getting back at one's master (738–55), but the whole central part of the play during which Dionysus and Xanthias enter the Underworld together involves a hilarious switching back and forth of roles between them (272–673), culminating in an absurd (and, to us at least, rather disturbing) scene in which each is flogged by the Underworld authorities in a concerted attempt to establish which is the "true" slave (605–73). (We shall have more to say about Xanthias's role and significance in chapters 6 and 7.)

Athens provided its citizens with numerous opportunities to develop some familiarity with different kinds of musical and dramatic performance. Overall, quite a high proportion of those sitting and watching *Frogs* (several hundred at least) must themselves have participated at some point in their lives as chorus members in dithyrambic or dramatic competitions and thus possessed more firsthand knowledge about poetic/musical/choreographic technique than most modern theater- or concert-goers. Among the rest, the level of musical experience and literary-poetic "competence," as well as of education and literacy, must have varied greatly, from high-brow to groundling, as in the theater of Shakespeare or the cinema of the Marx Brothers. Aristophanes knew well how to appeal to both ends of this spectrum and also—perhaps most importantly—to make them all ("all of you, us") feel included and respected within the terms of his comic drama. His language mixes crude slang, puns, and everyday conversational idioms with subtle poetic allusions and moments of high-flown lyric, and his humor manages to draw from all kinds of physical, verbal, topical, and fantastic sources.

Even if Aristophanes' audience was generally more homogeneous than an average modern theater or cinema audience, this Athenian polis included many different kinds of people and points of view. Attica was a large and populous region, containing 139 separate demes, some rural (*chôra*), some urban (*astu*); in each, there were rich and poor, free and slave, citizen and noncitizen, old and young, male and female. Each of these constituencies doubtless held different assumptions, desires, opinions—and, presumably, would tend to have different responses to any particular piece of literature or drama. Can we nonetheless make any general statements about the expectations of this heterogeneous—yet implicitly, and ideally, united—audience when it assembled in the theater?

Certainly it was often claimed in classical Greece that drama, like other forms of literature, should enlighten, educate, and edify its audience ("poets teach and give advice . . . make the citizens better . . ., etc.," *Frogs* 1009–10, 1030–35). So somewhat paradoxically, it seems, Aristophanes and his rivals were supposed to be providing educational examples and salutary advice to their fellow citizens, even while a large part of the appeal of comedy plainly lay in its sheer outrageousness in flouting social and moral norms and in the coarseness and shamelessness of its characters: comedy is indeed *meant* to be ugly and gross. (As Aristotle phrases it, "comedy represents people worse than we are . . ."; it is "a representation of base, ugly and laughable action . . .," [*Poet.* 2. 1448a, 4. 1454a].) This is a potentially confusing and contradictory task for the comic playwright—how to be shameless, gross, and offensive, but only in the right ways and to the proper degree. We shall examine some of these issues (especially those concerning notions of propriety/decorum and moral instruction) further in chapter 4.

Comic License?

One closely related issue that modern scholars have discussed extensively, and one on which a lot depends with regard to Aristophanes' intentions and procedures in writing a play like *Frogs*, is the freedom (or otherwise) of poets in Athens to write what they wished. What constraints, legal or social, explicit or implicit, existed to limit the dramatists' play of fantasy and their willingness to offer particular or general critiques of the Athenian community, its leaders, and its policies? It is hard to know how much to trust the evidence of the ancient commentators on Aristophanes' plays (the scholia) and other sources that refer to "decrees," lawsuits, and fines involving Aristophanes and other Athenian playwrights and the contents of their plays. But on the whole it appears that few formal restrictions existed.

Comic poets were indeed expected to refer to topical events and issues, and also to mock prominent individuals—this had always been a tradition within *iambos* and comic drama. And whereas reference is occasionally made in our sources to actual censorship, in the form of special laws being introduced forbidding certain topics or types of performance—particularly the "ridiculing by name" (*onomasti kômôidein*) of individual citizens—and whereas the text of Aristophanes' plays also contains references to citizens (mainly Cleon) reacting vigorously and publicly to being lampooned by him on stage and thus making a great deal of trouble for the playwright, the evidence overall is spotty and inconclusive. Indeed, the rules may well have changed at different times.

Here (briefly) is what we can reconstruct with a fair degree of certainty. In his earliest plays, especially *Babylonians* (426), Aristophanes had virulently attacked Cleon. He mentions this in *Acharnians* (425), stating that Cleon had retaliated: "Because of last year's comedy, he dragged me before the Council and slandered me (*dieballe*) and made up a bunch of lies . . ." (*Ach.* 378–80). In the following year his *Knights* (424) was a full-blast attack on Cleon from start to finish. But two years later, in *Wasps* (422), he states (1284–91) that Cleon had "bitten" him quite severely and "caused [him] a lot of trouble," so that he (Aristophanes) had recently made some kind of concession or compromise with him (1290)—mainly because he had not found anyone else to stand up on his behalf (1286–89). Not long after this, Cleon was killed in battle, and Aristophanes does not appear to have engaged so fiercely with any particular politician again. There is no record of any legal or other interactions with aggrieved individuals outside the theater, as there had been for Cleon. In *Frogs*, a brief reference is made to Cleon and Hyperbolus, who are now apparently the ace lawsuit-bringers in the Underworld (569–70), and plenty of living individuals are named in passing with brief mockery and abuse: Cleisthenes (48, 57, 422), Callias (428), Cleigenes (709), Clitophon (967), etc. All of this appears to be standard comic procedure. But not even against the slippery Theramenes (540, 967–70) or the populist anti-Spartan leader Cleophon (678, 1504, 1532) is any serious or sustained criticism mounted.

Outside the text of the plays themselves, we are told (again, by the Suda) that at some point a charge was brought against Aristophanes by someone (implicitly Cleon) that he was a "foreigner," that is, a noncitizen, apparently because of his family's connection with Aegina. This prosecution seems not to have been successful, and other "accusations" too apparently failed. Altogether, close examination of all of this evidence, together with a number of other— mostly quite unbelievable—remarks in scholia and elsewhere about particular laws and decrees being passed at various points during the fifth century banning mockery by name completely, leads to the conclusion that Cleon's attacks on Aristophanes were probably not based on any particular law about comedy or festival invective, but were simply attempts by an infuriated victim to find some recourse on the basis of general social norms of decency. Aristophanes generally had a very free hand to criticize whom he wished.

Athenian Politics, the War—and *Frogs*

The Athenian political system was a direct democracy—the first in history, involving the whole citizen body of 30,000 to 40,000 men. Then as now, not all members of the *dêmos* ("people") always saw eye to eye with one another about policy, about their leaders, about the interpretation of what "democracy" itself should really entail, even about whether or not it made sense at all as a political system. Athenian politics were volatile and often violent.

Between 508 (when the Cleisthenic democracy had first been introduced) and the performance of *Frogs* just over a hundred years later, the Athenians had experienced several extremes of success and failure, optimism and despair, about their city and its constitution.

Athenians looked back with pride and nostalgia to the days of Marathon (490) and Salamis (480), to their brief period of co-leadership of the Greek world with Sparta (in the early 460s), and to their subsequent decades of increasing domination over the large confederation of their "allies" (originally the "Delian League"), i.e., the many islands and cities of the Aegean which came under their control during the 460s to 440s—decades during which the magnificent new temples on the Acropolis were being built and visitors flocked to Athens to watch the plays and admire the monuments.

Athenian self-image and self-confidence were thus based both on the Athenians' past military successes—along with the freedom and independence that these guaranteed—and on their continuing cultural preeminence. Since the Persian Wars, Athens had become unquestionably the intellectual and artistic hub of the Greek world (as Pericles claimed, the "school (*paideusis*) for all of Greece," Thuc. 2.41). By the time of *Frogs*, however, much had changed—mostly for the worse, in terms of material comforts, collective self-confidence, and military outlook—and opinions differed radically about current policies, prospects, and leadership. Much of the empire (or the "allies") had been lost, forever. Athens was hated by a high proportion of the other Greek city-states. The Persians—always likely to be a major player in Greek politics given their much greater financial resources and centralized and better organized foreign policies—were now paying close attention to the task of helping the Peloponnesians build an effective navy, a task which, if successful, inevitably spelled defeat for Athens. Several of the most talented, or most reasonable and sensible, of the Athenian politicians had died, or were in exile. Consensus on anything was hard to achieve.

In early spring of 405, the Athenians were in the twenty-sixth year of an agonizing and seemingly never-ending war. Their empire was in tatters, with only the large island of Samos still a loyal and significant ally in the war effort. Yet the need for a powerful naval presence throughout the Aegean and especially around the Hellespont continued to be as strong as ever, since this was the means of securing access to much of Athens' grain and other crucial supplies. The ships and men lost in the disastrous expedition to Sicily eight years previously were still a vivid memory; and month by month, day by day, every Athenian lived with the reality that a Spartan-occupied fortress sat in Decelea on the northern edge of Attica, sending out raiding parties to ravage the fields and orchards, and severely curtailing both agriculture and travel throughout the region. Thousands of Athenians whose homes—house, fields, workshops, shrines—lay in one of the rural demes of Attica had been living most of the last twenty-five years cooped up in the city center of Athens itself or in the port of Piraeus, or else in the temporary housing constructed in the narrow corridor of land between the two parallel defensive walls (the "Long Walls") that ran between them. Overcrowding, deprivation, and fear had long been endemic to Athenian life.

Just the previous summer (406), an Athenian force of over 100 ships had won a critical sea-battle over a Spartan navy (largely built from Persian funding) off the islands of Arginusae near Lesbos (Xen. *Hell.* 1.6.24–38). Inspirational though this victory was in several respects, since a defeat would probably have spelt the immediate end of the war, the means by which it was achieved, and its political aftermath, were controversial and in some ways demoralizing for the Athenian population at large, as is made very clear by the text of *Frogs*. Before the battle, the Athenians had passed a decree offering not only citizenship to metics and foreigners but even freedom and citizenship to any slaves who would volunteer for service. Slaves were not normally part of the official Athenian war effort (in contrast, for instance, to Roman practice, where the galleys were routinely manned by slaves and convicts); so this decree was an extraordinary departure from usual practice, and not every Athenian felt that such a sweeping extension of their jealously guarded rights of citizenship was justified. Nor had the battle of Arginusae itself been an unmitigated success. Twenty-five Athenian ships had been lost (the Spartans had lost seventy-five), and thousands of crewmen had drowned in stormy seas—probably the biggest loss of life in any single Athenian campaign of the Peloponnesian War, apart from the Sicilian expedition. In the aftermath, some said that the generals commanding the fleet were to blame for failing to rescue those in the water, and all eight generals were hastily (and illegally) prosecuted and convicted by the Assembly (cf. Plato *Apology* 32b). Six were executed; the other two survived only because they had prudently decided not to return to Athens at all. (They were tried and convicted in absentia.) Among the instigators of popular rage and recrimination against these generals were two ship-captains who had themselves become leading politicians, Thrasybulus and Theramenes (*Frogs* 540–41, 967–70). Personal opportunism and animosity, as usual, played a big role in the city's decision-making.

One of the convicted generals was Erasinides, a moderate democrat and apparently a decent human being, mentioned at *Frogs* 1196 as an example of someone whose life was as undeservedly unfortunate as Oedipus'. Feelings about the victory, the dreadful loss of life, the incompetence or ill-luck of the generals and/or the irresponsibility of the prosecutors—and of the Assembly itself—in rushing to judgment, continued to trouble the Athenians in the months that followed. These feelings clearly fuel several references in *Frogs* to sailing, to sea-battles, to Erasinides, and above all to the freeing of the slaves. Thus not only is Xanthias found early in the play making the rather feeble excuse "No, I didn't fight in the battle—I had an eye-infection" (190–92), but the Chorus Leader devotes the two major segments of the *parabasis* (686–87, 718–37) to a discussion of Athenian citizenship, its privileges and entitlements, and the purity of the citizen body.

Some six years earlier (411), Aristophanes' heroine Lysistrata had presented an elaborate simile of the city as a "fleece" (*Lys.* 574–86), an abundant tangle of wool that needs to have the dirt washed out of it and the knots teased out before the weaving of any patterned garment can begin. The allegory in that famous passage (designed explicitly in terms appropriate to the traditional female activity of textile production, in accordance with the social politics of that play) conveys a similar message to what we find in *Frogs*: the Athenian democracy ("the people") needs to be selective, yet inclusive and well-integrated. In *Frogs*, rather than wool-working, we find the city's coinage being used as Aristophanes' symbol of civic integrity and collective worth (*Frogs* 717–37), and we will look closely at that passage in a moment.

The familiar political game of inclusion and exclusion ("us" and "them") within a broad but limited franchise—as pervasive in democratic Athens as in the modern West—involved careful maneuvering ("spin") on the part of every politician and popular leader. Comic playwrights often contributed to that spin, much as talk-show hosts or cartoonists may do nowadays. And for both politicians and comic poets, the chief goal was to create a sense of solidarity among a large body of supporters (ideally, among the whole community) in one of two ways: either through appeals to the whole city ("we, the people," "men of Athens") reinforcing its collective sense of pride in achievements past and future ("remember Marathon and Salamis . . .," or "The Star-spangled Banner," "The Dunkirk Spirit," etc.); or else, less inclusively, through a populist discrimination between a valorized "us" and a demonized "them." Such ways of thinking of course need not be cynical or consciously manipulative: any sincere and committed social activist or artist may easily begin to feel him/herself thus engaged with the community and with the world at large, and the degree of polarization that ensues will vary from one individual and context to another. But, on the whole, for an Athenian comic dramatist an attitude of inclusiveness and nonpolarization seems to have been preferred.

Thus, on the one hand, you wanted everyone in your audience to feel included (at least potentially) and to share some fellow feeling with one another, and with you, as a group of implicit "equals" with common interests and tastes (as at *Frogs* 688: "First and foremost, we must make all the citizens equal!"). But, on the other hand, you needed to establish yourself individually as being wiser and more experienced (i.e., better) than they and than others of your rivals, so that they (the audience) should feel inclined to pay attention and vote for you. If you appear too much better—or to be making such a claim—your audience/voters may resent this and reject you. But if you are merely one of the crowd, just like the rest of them, you surely do not deserve to be singled out for special praise and trust. Aristophanes shows himself to be a master at walking this thin line, as he works engagingly to create a sense of solidarity ("us") among the audience, even while acknowledging that actual consensus of opinions and political positions may not be achievable or entirely desirable. Indeed, as we noted, modern scholars generally cannot agree as to whether his plays push consistently for any particular political position or platform, and whether or not they favor any particular group, class, or individuals. And this very fact may be said to reflect Aristophanes' skill at appealing simultaneously to disparate groups and subject-positions within his audience, in a way that ultimately enables almost all of them to feel included—as the ones whose opinions and favor matter, the ones who best represent the city of Athens, the ones who belong in this Theater as worthiest recipients and judges of Aristophanes' own comic wisdom.

That is not to say that there are not moments—plenty of them—at which an Aristophanic character may criticize the audience sharply for its stupidity or past mistakes. But every one of Aristophanes' comedies evolves in such a way that by the halfway point most of the audience is on the hero's side and rooting for the same goals that s/he is about to achieve, however absurd and fantastic these may be (a private peace with Sparta, a city in the sky, women running the Assembly, etc.). Thus they can feel that their own deepest problems are being confronted and taken seriously, even as they themselves are perhaps being intermittently ridiculed and their problems curiously distorted. At some level these problems are thus being ameliorated, or at least temporarily transcended, through this very comic performance, even if no particular policy decision is advocated or likely to result.

In *Frogs*, this process of inclusion and creation of solidarity is most strikingly evident in the choral *parabasis*, especially in the two passages of formal "advice" (686–87, 718–37) that are technically known as *epirrhêma* and *antepirrhêma* (which may be loosely translated as "back-and-forth," or alternating lyric and spoken discourse). We also find here specific reference to past political mistakes and recommendations for future remedies. The lines are chanted and sung by the Chorus of Initiates, but they are clearly to be understood as expressing the views of the poet himself, as is common in a *parabasis*. Here, the chorus begins by singing a short prayer, inviting the Muse to join them:

> Set foot among the sacred choruses . . .
> And come to see the great mass of people here,
> Whose many-thousand-fold wisdom
> Sits here waiting. . . .
>
> (673–78)

By crediting the mass audience in the Theater with multiple forms of "wisdom" (*sophia*, a word that suggests also "good taste, artistic skill") and suggesting that they will be joined by the Muse herself as fellow spectator of what is to follow, Aristophanes invites the Athenians to think of themselves as both enormously versatile (677–78 *muriai* = "ten-thousand-fold") and unerring in their discrimination, an opinion that is reinforced by the accompanying insults directed against the foreign-sounding and inept "twitterings" of Cleophon (678–82).

So far, this is all very democratic and inclusive, apart from the exclusion of Cleophon—who actually, with his strident repudiations of Spartan offers of peace, had been the most successful Athenian politician of recent months. In what follows, however, the Chorus begins to make some crucial distinctions, both about their own identity and relationship to the audience, and about their opinions concerning the Athenians' recent political decisions and their consequences. Disapproval is mixed here inextricably with encouragement: things have gone badly wrong (for which the democracy is to blame, with its recent foolish decisions) and yet the people may still redeem themselves and "set everything to rights" (735) if they can just manage to recover their true, time-tested identity and align themselves properly with their own best and brightest members.

The *parabasis* is framed by references to the Chorus' intentions of providing "advice and teaching." They assert that "it is just . . . to give useful advice to the city" (686–87: language that recalls that of many an Athenian orator in the Assembly), and they echo repeatedly the formulaic language of state decrees: "It seemed <good> to the Athenians" or "to the people," i.e., "It has been decided by popular vote. . . ." Thus they begin the first passage of advice, "It seems good to us . . ." (688), and the second one, "It seemed good to us . . ." (718), while both passages conclude with further occurrences of this same verb (*dokeô*, "seem, appear, decide"), though now in a personal rather than impersonal construction: 705 "we won't seem to be thinking sensibly," 737 "to the wise you will seem. . . ." Thus the Chorus/poet seems to identify himself and his audience closely with the language and operations of the *dêmos* as it conducts its business in the Assembly, and also with their past and future history of policy-making, with himself (in the guise of the "sacred chorus," [674, 686]) now invested with the authority and trust of an ideal democratic leader. Yet at the same time the repeated use in both passages (687, 717) of the word "us," as distinct from "the city" (686, 718), requires that both the speaker and the audience locate themselves somewhere in relation to these two alternative positions. Is the poet "one of us," or is he a sacred and privileged "adviser and teacher"? Are "we" (the audience) the same people as the "city" and "the citizens" (686, 688, 704; 718, 719, 727, 732) who have made the various mistakes that the Chorus are now pointing out? Or, with our "ten-thousand-fold wisdom," are we now capable of "thinking better" and making better decisions than they did then? The terms "we" and "you," "city" and "citizens," keep shifting subtly.

Whether or not the audience consciously notices these shifts, the implicit distinction between good and bad citizens, and between what the city ("you") decided to do (wrong) in the recent past, and what it ("we") needs now to decide to do in order to set things right, turns out to be crucial to the whole message of the *parabasis*—and of the play. For, in the final words of the second advice-speech (718–37), the formula is used with a crucial modification: "You will seem to *the wise*. . . ." These imaginary "wise men" (*sophoi*) who will be passing judgment on the policies and conduct of the Athenians are presented here as a group distinct from, and much more select than, the polis as a whole (the verdict of posterity?), even though the same decree-formula is employed (737, cf. 718). Thus the Athenian audience is surreptitiously, but perhaps reassuringly, offered several different categories of decision-makers and sufferers, citizens good and bad, and present or future assessors with whom they may align their own subject position: "us," "you," "the city," "the <best> citizens," and "the wise."

Two recent sequences of events of very different kinds—both of them causing considerable dismay and disagreement among the Athenians—lie behind the advice offered in this *parabasis*. The first is the awarding of citizenship to the slaves who fought at Arginusae, together with the continuing exile and disenfranchisement of others—mostly wealthy citizens of respectable families—who had participated in the oligarchic revolution of 411. The second is the issuing of a new coinage in 407–406. Let us consider the latter of these first, as it is presented by the Chorus:

> All too often it's seemed to us that the city has gone
>   through the same process
> With regard to its best and finest citizens
> As it has with its old coinage and the new gold.
> Those [old coins] weren't counterfeit, but recognized as
>   finest of all currencies,
> The only ones properly struck, tested to ring true as a bell,
> Accepted everywhere, all over Greece and the rest of the
>   world.
> But we're not using them at all. Instead we've got these
>   sleazy coppers
> That were struck just yesterday or the day before, the basest
>   coinage ever.
> Likewise with our citizens: those we know to be nobly-born
>   and well-behaved,
> Honest, fine gentlemen, raised in the wrestling-schools,
>   choruses, and the arts,

> We reject them; and we keep on making use instead of the
>   base-metal types—
> Foreigners, red-heads, low-life types from low backgrounds,
> The most recent arrivals off the boat, people that the city
>   previously
> Would never have made use of even for random scapegoat
>   rituals!
> So, come on now, you idiots, it's not too late: change your
>   ways,
> And make use of the good and useful ones again!
> If you are successful, and you get everything straightened
>   out,
> It will have been a praiseworthy move; and if instead things
>   come unstuck
> And something really bad happens, at least the opinion of
>   wise observers
> Will be that you are "being hung from a worthy tree."
>   (718–37)

The "ancient coinage" that is mentioned here (720) refers to the famous silver "owls of Athena," which had circulated for many decades as Athens' main currency and had been a key symbol of the city's prosperity and international standing. Minted from silver ore that was mined from the huge deposits of Laureium in southern Attica, these were the best known and most widely used coins in the Greek world throughout the fifth century; for, while many different cities issued their own coins, only Athens' silver was trusted universally for purity of metal and consistency of weight. The Spartan occupation of Decelea severely affected production at these mines, and several thousands of the slaves who worked there escaped to freedom by that route. The supply of "owls" in Athens therefore began to dwindle, and in 407–06 the Athenians replaced the owls with a currency made of bronze that was merely faced with a thin layer of silver—a technique previously used only by counterfeiters and by cities less scrupulous than Athens about the purity of their currency. This new coinage (here scornfully described as "worthless bronze," [725]) was not acceptable for payment to nonlocals (e.g., merchants and many of the rowers in the navy); so at this same date the city decided also to strip the gold from the splendid statues of Victory (Nikê) in the Parthenon, melt this down, and produce from it an issue of small gold coins. This was the "new gold" (720), a currency fine and reliable indeed—nobody could complain about pure gold—but probably reserved mainly for payment to foreigners since gold coins, however small, would carry too high a face value for daily use in the market, workshop, or fields. The switch from the reliable old silver "owls" to the new and adulterated (silver-plated) bronze for all domestic use was a constant source of shame, a reminder that Athens was no longer able to live up to its traditional ideals or maintain its "old standards" (720, 722 *nomisma*).

The whole of this passage—which ancient sources tell us made a deeply favorable impression on the original Athenian audience—owes much of its rhetorical and moral force to Aristophanes' use of the long-standing association in Greek culture between the "stamp" of a coin and the "character" of a person. Thus *typos* is originally in Greek the "stamp, imprint" of a design on a coin (or sculpture mould) and hence comes to mean a person's character "type," i.e., personality; *charactêr* means "engraved pattern" and hence a person's "character." Both of these usages entail the expectation that the coinage of a particular community will bear a guaranteed mark of consistent quality and value, and that a person's character should be reliable, true through-and-through, and recognizable from the outside. The Greek word for "currency, standard," *nomisma*, was indeed derived from the same root as *nomos* ("law, custom, belief, tradition"), in both cases denoting "assigned value," "something that can be believed in." In English, the words "metal" and "mettle" were likewise originally the same.

The best, truest coins will be made entirely of pure metal/mettle (gold or silver), not adulterated with "base" metals (bronze or lead) nor merely plated-over with a thin layer of that precious metal. How can one tell the difference? By careful testing. The language—and the practice—of "testing" coins for their purity and value was extensive, and it too was employed to refer to the assessing of human character: the noun *basanos* = "touchstone" (i.e., a hard stone that can be rubbed against a piece of silver or gold to see if dark (baser) metal shows up under the surface). The verb *basanizô* became standard Greek for "examine, test" or even "torture" as the means to extract proof and determine truth (as at *Frogs* 616, 618, 625, 629, 642; and so also 802, 826; 1121, 1123; 1367 for the "purity," "weight" and worth of poetic language!). Other terms too for "weighing" and "counting" are likewise common in both kinds of contexts. A coin that is "fake, counterfeit, adulterated" (as at *Frogs* 721) will be exposed; one that is of pure metal will "ring true," as "clear as a bell" (as at *Frogs* 723).

In the first segment of "advice" (686–705), it is the integrity of the citizen body itself (the people, rather than their coinage) that occupies the Chorus' attention. Over the previous six years or so, several political upheavals, as well as the extraordinary measures surrounding the recent sea-battle, had brought about major shifts and uncertainties about who was (or should be) a bona fide participant in the Athenian *politeia*. During the thirty years or so of Athenian successes preceding the Peloponnesian War, the constitution had remained fairly stable and the leadership had been entrusted almost uninterruptedly to Pericles (himself a blue-blooded aristocrat of the Alcmeonid clan, but staunchly democratic in his policies), despite fierce competition at times from rival aristocratic leaders. And, from at least the 460s, all male citizens had full voting rights on all issues, and state pay was provided for jurymen and officeholders: no qualifications of wealth, birth, or education were required. At the same time, Pericles had enacted a law (in 451) stipulating that henceforth only the children of two citizen parents could be legitimate citizens, which meant that scrutiny of legitimate parentage became more meticulous and accusations of foreign birth not uncommon, especially as a tactic to discredit political rivals or disinherit the wealthy (hence the "Thracian swallow" slur directed against Cleophon at 681).

There had always been a segment of the Athenian population— especially the wealthier citizens, some of whom, but by no means all, came from aristocratic families and so could be described as "well-born" (*eugeneis*), "worthy, honest" (*chrêstoi*, as at *Frogs* 735; cf.

783, 1011, 1035, 1455) or "the fine and good" (*kaloi kai agathoi*, as at *Frogs* 719)—who disapproved of this radically egalitarian and inclusive constitution and preferred the idea of either a limited democracy within which only those possessing some wealth would hold the franchise, or outright oligarchy. Up until the time of the Sicilian expedition (415–413 BCE), such voices of conservatism and disapproval of demagogic leadership had certainly been audible in Athens, not least in Comedy. But they had not been orchestrated into any serious counter-democratic action. Aristophanes' own fierce and hilarious attacks on Cleon in *Babylonians*, *Knights*, and *Wasps* were merciless (and quite controversial), while in previous decades both Cratinus and Eupolis had been equally vociferous (and funny) in their criticisms of Pericles. In many Greek cities, on and off throughout the fifth century and especially since the 430s, bitter civil conflicts had occurred, including assassinations, massacres, expulsions, and wholesale coups d' états. In Athens itself, by contrast, no concerted political opposition to the democratic status quo seems to have been organized until the later years of the Peloponnesian War. It was only when things began to go increasingly badly in the war, and Athens' economic as well as military prospects became desperate, that the idea of abolishing the democracy and establishing some kind of oligarchic replacement (perhaps involving also a peace with Sparta) began seriously to catch on.

In 411, a group of energetic anti-democrats called a special Assembly meeting in Colonus (a couple of miles away from the Pnyx, the usual meeting-place) and orchestrated a vote by which the democratic constitution was replaced by a Council of Four Hundred. The ringleaders of this oligarchic coup were Phrynichus, Pisander, Theramenes, and Antiphon; their motives seem to have varied (Phrynichus, for example, seems to have been driven above all by rivalry and fear of Alcibiades, who was himself exiled from Athens throughout this sequence of events), but all of them apparently favored the opening of peace negotiations with Sparta and resisting any move to bring Alcibiades back to Athens. As for Alcibiades, he possessed, despite his checkered political career—which in addition to exile from Athens in 415 included a prolonged stint as military adviser to the Spartans—and despite his flamboyantly aristocratic and narcissistic behavior, indisputable military talent and an almost irresistible appeal for the people at large. So he was seen by many as the obvious—and only possible—successor to his adoptive father, Pericles, as leader of Athens' war effort. Consequently, the Athenians' interest in, and attachment to, Alcibiades was almost obsessive, and in *Frogs* Aristophanes appropriately makes him the final and deciding topic on which the choice between Aeschylus and Euripides will depend (see chapter 7).

Within a year of the establishment of the Four Hundred, however, Phrynichus had been assassinated, Theramenes had changed his tune and was collaborating with those who wanted the democracy back, and the swing back to the regular democratic constitution was under way. The Four Hundred were quickly overthrown and democracy was restored. In the months that followed, despite a naval defeat by the Spartans off Euboea, things returned more or less to normal; yet anxieties—and divisions—persisted. Pisander and other ringleaders of the 411 coup had fled to Decelea and remained in exile; several additional supporters of the Four Hundred were also subsequently prosecuted and exiled. Those responsible for the assassination of Phrynichus were recognized with an honorific decree (*IG* I^3 102), and at least one non-Athenian from among them (Thrasybulus of Calydon) was awarded Athenian citizenship as a mark of gratitude.

All of this had occurred during the five years leading up to the production of *Frogs*. Now (winter-spring 406–405), in the immediate aftermath of Arginusae, the Athenians had even expanded ("debased"?) their citizen body through the addition of hundreds of new citizens. Democracy indeed! Confidence in the progress of the war was now somewhat elevated by the victory, and the democratic leader Cleophon had won majority votes in the Assembly on several occasions to reject what some moderates thought were quite attractive proposals from the Spartans for peace terms. Yet the prospect of total defeat was still very real.

Of course, nobody could know exactly what was in store: that within eighteen months of the performance of *Frogs*, Cleophon would be prosecuted (on feeble, trumped-up charges), convicted, and executed; Alcibiades would be murdered while visiting Anatolia; the Athenian fleet would be annihilated at Aegospotami; Lysander would lead the Spartan navy into the Piraeus; and a junta of extreme oligarchs ("the Thirty Tyrants") led by Plato's uncle, Critias, would be installed to rule the city with the help of a Spartan garrison and a new constitution. The city walls would be torn down, to the glee of all those cities that had felt the burden of Athenian imperialism and military hostility over the previous decades. Massacres of democrats, banishments, legal and illegal confiscations of property would ensue on a horrendous scale; but the reign of the Thirty would in turn soon be ended by a democratic counter-revolution (403), bringing on a wave of lawsuits and recriminations that included the prosecution and execution of Socrates (a friend of Critias and of Alcibiades) in 399. To the surprise and relief of many, Lysander and the Spartans in 404 would in fact resist the call by the Thebans and Corinthians for wholesale execution of Athenian men and enslavement and deportation of women and children—a policy that the Athenians themselves had carried out against others on more than one occasion during the War. But Athens' ascendancy was shattered, and the "salvation of the city," so earnestly invoked in *Frogs*, was not in fact to be achieved—at least, not in the terms meant by Dionysus, Plouton, Aeschylus, and the others.

Aristophanes himself and his family, as far as we know, were not directly affected by these radical shifts of military and political fortune. He continued to write and produce comedies throughout the 390s and early 380s, though it is noticeable that the two that survive from that period (*Women at the Assembly*, *Wealth*) contain less ad hominem invective and less contemporary political humor than his previous plays. Whether this was because of a change in the moral-political climate of fourth century Athens, or was simply the result of an evolution in the tastes of audiences and playwrights—or both—is debated by modern scholars. But most of them agree that *Frogs* represents (even if Aristophanes and his audience were not fully aware of this at the time) his last full-blooded engagement with the traditional forms of Old Comedy—including personal abuse, direct address to the audience in a *parabasis*, and extensive choral song and dance. Thus we might think of this play as being almost as much about the past, future, and ideal form of comedy, as it is about old and new tragedy. We will return to this topic in chapter 7.

In *Frogs*, as we have already seen, the audience is asked again and again, both implicitly and explicitly: Who are (we) the true Athenians now, and who should best represent them (us), in the Assembly and in the Theater? By "the city" and "the Athenian people" (or "us") do we mean—to put the issues in exaggeratedly class-conscious and polarized terms, as the play's agonistic framework encourages us to do—the Arginusae ex-slaves, along with those Euripides-loving low-life democrats led by Cleophon, Nicomachus (1506), and the rest, hell-bent on continuing the war and on victimizing all those who had shown the slightest sympathy for the Four Hundred ("anyone who made a mistake after being tripped up by Phrynichus' slippery moves . . .," [689])? Or should we value instead as our "best citizens" the "useful/worthy" ones (733 *chrêstoi*), equivalent in their nobility to pure "gold" (or to the trusty "old standard" of the familiar silver owls), those pure-bred elites who, after long years of trusty service to the city, found themselves so doubtful about the war-policies and demagogic habits of Athens' leadership that they joined the Four Hundred for a few confusing months, and are now consequently in exile, disenfranchised, their property confiscated and their names besmirched?

Aristophanes' inclusive appeal is powerful. Concerning the award of citizenship to those battle-veteran slaves, his Chorus, in its most authorial mode, insists explicitly, "I approve" (695–96); and at the same time it suggests that this might also be the right time to grant amnesty for those other "mistakes" so as to rally together all elements among the citizens, old and new, noble and former slave, in Athens' hour of crisis (687–705). As for Alcibiades, one-time promoter of democratic causes, brilliant general, heir-apparent in so many respects to his adoptive father, Pericles—yet also exiled for his suspected role in the sacrilegious mutilation of the Herms in 415 and since then an intermittent but all-too-effective collaborator and adviser to both the Spartans and Persians: what is now the city's best policy in dealing with him? (See further chapter 6.)

All in all, this is a very disparate list of potential members—and leaders—of "our" Athenian community and theater audience, to be sure; and this sense of radical disparateness and oppositionality is exploited by Aristophanes again and again, in Charon's rejection of a slave passenger (Xanthias), in the arguments and role-reversals of Xanthias and Dionysus, in the confrontations and costuming of Dionysus and Heracles, and above all in the contest between Euripides and Aeschylus. Concern for the health and well-being of the city is characteristic of Old Comedy, and most of Aristophanes' plays from one angle or another confront quite squarely the questions, what does it take to be a (good) Athenian and what do we need to do in order to restore the city's integrity and strength. But perhaps in no play more than *Frogs* does the sense of urgency, of near-desperation, emerge so forcefully: the city of Athens is in deadly peril, and it is terribly divided against itself.

Aristophanes' comedy promises to restore integrity, to "teach" the city how to think sensibly and recover its former values, to recognize the virtues of its "best citizens," to regain a sense of purity, of integrity, of salvation. This will involve bringing together the best of the past and the present—while perhaps eliminating the worst of the present too—in such a way as to recover that long-lost (perhaps illusory) sense of community as it might have existed in the good old days. It takes a heroic trip to the Underworld to bring back our dearly departed loved-one, a Dionysian process of initiation and rebirth for our souls, the recovery of a former generation's musical and poetic spirit. All of these processes are required if we are to "save the city" (1419, 1436, 1450, 1458, 1501–02). As we, the audience of rich and poor, democrats and (would-be) oligarchs, (former) slaves and masters, "sit together in thousand-fold wisdom" (677) in the precinct of Dionysus, we look to the "sacred chorus" and attendant Muse (674–76, 686) as allies in the project of reinvigorating the art of poetry and bringing back—if only for an hour or two—the days of Marathon, of unity, of victory. A fantastic notion, to be sure: Aristophanic in the extreme.

Suggestions for Further Reading

The evidence concerning Aristophanes' life and career is clearly laid out and well discussed in MacDowell (1995). For the procedures, locations, and rules concerning the dramatic competitions at Athens, see Csapo and Slater (1995), Wilson (2000); also Rusten (2011), Wilson (2007).

On the composition and character of theater audiences in Athens, see Ehrenberg (1962), Roselli (2011); and for the range of their political positions and opinions, McGlew (2002). On their (and Aristophanes') reading habits and degree of literary sophistication, see Woodbury (1976), Lowe (1993), Silk (2000); and on audiences' expertise in judging choral and dramatic performances, Revermann (2006) and chapter 4 below. In general, on the classical Greek educational system, still useful is Marrou (1956).

On issues of censorship and comic license, I find persuasive the discussion of Halliwell (1991). See too Rosen and Sluiter (2004).

On Aristophanes' political biases, see De Ste. Croix (1972) Appendix 29. See too Henderson (1990) and Cartledge (1990).

· 3 ·

What Happens in *Frogs*? (The Plot)

Aristophanes' plays are not like Menander's or Molière's—situation comedies in which the whole plot is driven by character, coincidence, misunderstandings, and (usually) love affairs, with the audience's delight, scene-by-scene, depending greatly on the fact that they know things that the characters (as yet) don't and on their comfortable awareness that the spirit of Aphrodite/Eros and of Good Fortune is guiding events toward their desired outcome. Even though Aristophanes was credited by the Suda (above, chapter 2) with anticipating late in his career the New Comic techniques of romance, rapes, pregnancies, character-types, mistaken identities and recognitions, etc., his surviving plays all present bigger and wilder scenarios, often involving the whole city of Athens (or Cloudcuckooland) and confronting large issues of politics, morality, sexual identity, and the gods. This is certainly true of *Frogs*.

The plots of New Comedy (and of the European tradition that derives from it, via Plautus and Terence, Shakespeare, Molière, Sheridan, Wilde, etc.) are more tightly constructed and intricate: every detail counts, every overheard conversation and long-misplaced recognition-token contributes to the resolution of the plot, and that is part of these plays' appeal. In Old Comedy, by contrast, plots tend to be quite loosely connected, even at times a little incoherent. Individual scenes, or tropes, can take on a life of their own that may occupy a large chunk of stage time—and provide enormous comic entertainment to the audience—without really advancing the main plot at all; and some of Aristophanes' plays, including *Frogs*, have been accused of changing direction rather radically as they proceed, so as to end up with a quite different denouement and eventual pay-off (message?) from what was apparently announced at the beginning. To state the issue baldly: Dionysus at the beginning of our play seems to be entirely focused on bringing back Euripides, on whose poetry he himself dotes completely; yet by halfway through, the focus of the action has shifted, first, to the extended contest between Aeschylus and Euripides, and then to "saving the city of Athens," culminating in the god's final decision to bring back Aeschylus. This outcome is obviously very different from what is outlined at the beginning. Did Aristophanes change his plan as he went along? Is it a mistake to look for much "unity" in the plot of his plays? Or is there in fact a stronger connecting thread, a more cohesive and unified dramatic movement, one that we should recognize as underlying and informing the play as a whole?

(One) Great Idea?

Many of the plays of Old Comedy are built around a Great Idea, an expansive, wild-and-crazy scheme that is adopted by the hero and brought to unexpected fruition through a fantastic series of events: Let's Make a Private Peace with Sparta (*Acharnians*)! Let's Stop This War (*Peace; Lysistrata*)! Let's Get Rid of Cleon (*Knights*)! Let's Emigrate and Found a New and Better City in the Sky (*Birds*)! Let's Stop This New-fangled Education (*Clouds*)! Let's Grab Political Power for the Women (*Assemblywomen*)! Some critics have even zeroed in on this tendency and identified it as the single key to Aristophanic comedy, with a concomitant notion of a larger-than-life (yet in some ways socially disadvantaged) Comic Hero who is whole-heartedly committed to an eccentric, extraordinary vision of a better world or alternate reality, and who—miraculously, comically—succeeds in achieving it. This model works well for many plays but much less well for a few others (e.g., *Clouds, Thesmophoriazusae*) in which the "hero" seems rather small-minded and is not in the end entirely successful.

It is interesting to look at *Frogs* through this lens. On the one hand, we can see at once that Dionysus is seriously deficient as a "hero" of this type in so far as he is generally indecisive, ineffectual, cowardly, and dependent on others. Unlike such admirably assertive heroes and heroines as Dicaeopolis (*Acharnians*), Trygaeus (*Peace*), Pisetaerus (*Birds*), or Lysistrata (*Lys*.), he is constantly out-argued and out-maneuvered by others (including his slave, Xanthias), loses his nerve, changes his mind at crucial moments, and vacillates up to the last moment as to how to save Athens. But, on the other hand, Dionysus does have a Great Idea—to bring the best tragedian back to life in order to save Athens—and he does show himself to be an extraordinarily appropriate and effective "everyman" figure, as he manages at one point or another (in combination with his slave) to embody quite engagingly and convincingly the ideal theater-spectator, our hope for an afterlife, and even the whole city of Athens.

Aristophanic heroes are normally Athenians, and the action of Aristophanes' plays is usually centered on Athens and its concerns (which is not to say that these concerns might not involve also the well-being of all of Greece, as in *Peace, Lysistrata*, and *Wealth*). In *Frogs*, it is striking once one stops to think about it (but perhaps taken for granted, without question, by an actual theater audience) that Dionysus behaves in such an Athenocentric fashion throughout. He seems actually to be a resident of Athens, with a domestic (human) slave who is entirely Athens-focused, refers to his own recent service as a marine on an Athenian warship, mentions his passion for the Athenian dramatist Euripides, and is clearly aware of all kinds of details of the city's recent political and cultural history. Yet his status as an Olympian divinity is also vital to the logic of the play and to his success in visiting the Underworld, as is his expertise as patron of the theater. At one and the same time, this Dionysus-character thus presents himself both as a regular Athenian guy (if a somewhat eccentric one—bumbling, cowardly, physically incompetent, and mentally quirky) in his life experience and interests, and as a god who is supposed to be exempt from normal human limitations (such as pain or fear of death). And of course he is also not only the presiding genius of the very Theater the audience is sitting in, but also a chief (yet oddly unrecognized) object of devotion from both the play's choruses: frogs in the Marshes and Eleusinian initiates in the Underworld.

Yet, as we shall see, it is a curious comic twist or "disconnect" that neither of these choruses directly acknowledges the god in their midst: the frog-chorus does not seem to realize that the individual they are tormenting is the "same" divinity as they are honoring in their song, while the Chorus of Initiates in their opening hymn of celebration never appear to notice Dionysus at all, as he sits to the side of the orchestra (316ff), and he likewise in his comments never makes any direct reference to his involvement in their cult. But he does at one point (297) run across the orchestra to beg protection from the Priest of Dionysus, whose throne was in the center of the first row; and the Chorus' repeated address to "Iacchus" (316, 324, 340, 398, etc.) must be noticed by the audience, even if the god himself does not respond. See further chapter 6.

This ambiguous identity is vital to Dionysus' role throughout the play. At the end, his verdict as to who is the best poet, and which dead soul he is going to bring back to life in Athens, however arbitrary and whimsical it may appear, is at some level accepted as an authoritative, blessed, and salutary outcome for all (i.e., for all of us Athenians). Nobody else could have pulled this off; and nobody else but a god intently focused on the well-being of Athens in particular would have taken so much trouble. And, in the final scene, as Plouton and Persephone invite Dionysus and his friends to "come inside and enjoy a dinner" with them before they "sail away" (1479–80), the camaraderie and sense of community is strong. The Chorus sums it up:

> Blessed (*makarios*) is the man who has exact intelligence (*xunesin*);
> One can learn this by many examples:
> And this man here, who, it was decreed, has thoroughly good sense,
> Will return home again

> For the benefit of the citizens
> And for the benefit of his own relatives
> And nearest and dearest—
> Because he is so intelligent (*sunetos*).
>
> (1482–90)

After the dinner (which is imagined as having taken place indoors during the choral song at 1482–99), Plouton leads out the celebrants and continues in the same vein:

> Off you go, Aeschylus, with gratitude and rejoicing,
> And save our city with your good notions (*gnômais agathais*) . . .
>
> (1500–02)

So Plouton, god of the whole Underworld, speaks of Athens as "our city," and treats both Aeschylus and Dionysus as his guests (perhaps even Xanthias too? see chapter 7). The references to the "man" (1484 *anêr*) who will save them/us through his good sense seems to suggest a transference of the audience's focus from the god to the mortal, from Dionysus onto Aeschylus. The inept yet well-meaning comic hero who began the play "yearning for . . . a man . . ." (55–58) has indeed found a different, better man, and has brought him back to save us. Dionysus and Aeschylus are now almost (as) one, and the play's plot has turned out to be a unity after all.

The Formal Structure

The formal structure of the play, as analyzed in the terms used by ancient scholars of comedy and by many modern commentators too (especially in relation to the questions of origins that we briefly considered in chapter 1), is the following:

1–208: *PROLOGOS* ("prologue" or opening scene); spoken dialogue in iambic trimeters.
209–268: (First) *PARODOS* ("arrival" of the chorus); sung lyrics, with brief sung responses from Dionysus.

268–322 Resumption of *Prologos* (or else an *Episode*)

323–459 (True) *PARODOS* ("arrival" of main chorus); sung lyrics, with brief interjections from Dionysus.

460–673 *EPISODES* (short dialogue scenes), with brief choral interjections.

674–737 *PARABASIS* ("stepping-forward" of chorus) ode & antode sung in lyrics (674–85, 706–16), *epirrhêma* & *antepirrhêma* chanted in trochaics (686–705, 718–37).

738–1499 *EPISODES* ("scenes," including *AGÔN*); mostly iambic trimeter dialogue, but with sung segments too.

1500–end *EXODOS* ("departure-scene"); victory songs, *kômos* (feasting-celebration) and final procession.

The shifting and contrasting registers and performance techniques of these different meters and structures (including several scenes of alternating song and recitation, as the summary above shows) are vital to the dynamics and dramatic effect of Old Comedy. In English translation it is not always easy (or even possible) to follow or capture the effects of such shifts and contrasts: some translators are more scrupulous than others in indicating them with stage directions and/or with different metrical schemes or typefaces. But very often the contrast in tone and mood between one agitated character who is singing and another who is speaking more calmly, or the rapid back-and-forth exchanges between two interlocutors who are alternating or even splitting lines between them, contribute crucially to the building of anticipation, the setting up of jokes, or the sheer incongruity of cross-purposes and radical disagreements out of which so much Aristophanic comedy is built. (The formal structures of some of these standardized "type-scenes" also perhaps in their own way contribute to the audience's aesthetic enjoyment of the whole play, in the same way that a four-movement symphony or an operatic alternation of aria and recitative each satisfies its respective audience's expectations.) But, for the purposes of this chapter, it will be more helpful for the most part to follow the plot as it develops without paying too much attention to these formal and metrical distinctions.

What Happens, Scene by Scene?

Two figures enter from the side: one wears a bizarre combination of saffron robe and lion-skin, and carries a club; the other is dressed simply as a laborer or servant (we learn immediately from line 1 that he is the other one's slave), and is sitting on a donkey—either a real one, or a stage prop. The slave is carrying a pole from which is hanging a heavy bundle of luggage (see Fig. 3–1). From their dialogue it quickly emerges that these are the god Dionysus and his personal slave, Xanthias (literally, "Red-haired one," "Sandy"). In conventional hymnic and mythological contexts, Dionysus obviously would not have a human slave (though he himself might well be riding a donkey—this is common in Athenian vase paintings, though less so in literature); his attendants would normally be

Figure 3–1. Fourth century vase painting apparently illustrating a scene from near the beginning of *Frogs*.
Apulian (South Italian) bell-krater ca. 375–350 BCE (so-called "Berlin Heracles"). Formerly Berlin, Staatliche Museen F3046 (destroyed or plundered during World War II). Photo from M. Bieber *Die Denkmäler zum Theaterwesen im Altertum* (Berlin 1920) Tafel 80.

satyrs. But in the world of Athenian comedy, as we noted above, Dionysus can become, in effect, an Athenian citizen (so at line 22 he introduces himself formally as "Dionysus, son of Wine-jar [*Stamnion*]" even as he remains, illogically, an immortal god and the patron of drama). It is not uncommon in Greek myth (and drama) for Dionysus to adopt a disguise or to transform himself; but in this play his disguise is only intermittently effective, and for much of the time he is indeed being himself. In any case, of course, the mask helps—he (the actor playing him) can "be" whoever he wants, from one moment to the next.

The two of them seem to be traveling through the streets of Athens, arguing about this and that, as masters and slaves do. Or perhaps we are to think that they have already traveled several miles outside the city: the setting is indeterminate. But they certainly cannot have reached Thebes (some sixty miles from Athens and over the last several decades continuously at war with the Athenians) or Argos (seventy-five miles away), the two cities conventionally most closely associated with Heracles' birth and career. Nonetheless, by comic logic, after a couple of minutes they are able to knock at the door of a house (35–37 ". . . here I am now right by the door that's supposed to be my first stopping-place"), which we immediately learn is Heracles' residence. One of the ancient "prefaces" to the play even states (*hypothesis* I(b) Dover), "It is not specified where the play is set, but it's most logical to think that it's in Thebes, since Dionysus is from there and he arrives at the house of Heracles, who is (also) a Theban." Alternatively, the Athenian audience may have understood Dionysus to be arriving at Heracles' shrine near the Diomeian Gate, on the outskirts of Athens, here imagined as a house. Wherever they are imagined as being—and perhaps we should concede that this is "nowhere in particular"—the fact that Heracles himself answers the door constitutes another comic departure from realism: a mighty aristocrat such as he would normally have servants to answer the door for him, as Dionysus expects (37 "Boy! Hey there! Hello? Boy?"). So both Dionysus and Heracles, for all their divine/heroic status and their track records of past achievement, appear to be living and behaving like lower-middle-class Athenians.

Heracles is huge, burly, pot-bellied, as often in comedy (see Fig. 3–2b). He is highly amused to see the foppish, slender Dionysus trying to impersonate him. (Of course they know each other well already, being both, in mythological terms, sons of Zeus, and thus half-brothers: cf. 60 *adelphidion*, "little bro".) Now at last the conversation turns to the topic that the audience has been awaiting: *why* is Dionysus dressed like this (47), and "where on earth" is he traveling to (48)? (The title of the play, THE FROGS, which will have been announced some days earlier at the public "Preview" (*Proagôn*) advertising the festival, will not have provided much of a clue as to its subject—merely leading us to expect that a chorus dressed as amphibians will show up at some point.) Dionysus reveals that he is in love and in mourning for someone dearly departed: Euripides. He wants to bring him back from Hades (49–70)—and that is a task at which Heracles uniquely excels, since he had been required in one of his Labors to capture Cerberus, watchdog of the Underworld, and bring him back up to earth. On another occasion, too, Heracles went down and wrestled Thanatos (Death) to claim from him the recently deceased Alcestis to be reunited with her husband Admetus (an episode included in Euripides' *Alcestis*); and yet again he went down to rescue his own comrade Theseus (or to help him release his beloved friend Pirithous: versions vary) who had been detained against his will in Hades by Persephone and Plouton. Thus if the most heroic of all heroes' quests is a journey to the Underworld and back—a return from the dead—then Heracles is indeed a hero several times over.

So this, the audience now realizes, is the reason why Dionysus is wearing all this Heraclean paraphernalia, and why he has stopped off now for advice from the veteran traveler to the Underworld. A couple of additional Underworld voyages are left out of consideration here, though they will begin to come into partial focus later in the play: Orpheus' attempt to recover Eurydice through the power of music and song, and Dionysus' own journey to recover his mother Semele (or Persephone; see chapter 6). In *Frogs* it is made abundantly clear that Dionysus has never set foot in the Underworld before and has no idea how to set about it or even how to get to the entrance.

Figure 3–2. Terracotta figurines of comic actors, Athenian ca. 400–350 BCE. (a) Actor costumed as a slave character.

New York Metropolitan Museum of Art 13.225.13; photo courtesy of The Metropolitan Museum of Art/Art Resource.

Figure 3-2. (b) Actor costumed as Heracles.
London, The British Museum 1852,0728.752 (T741); photo courtesy of the Trustees of the British Museum.

So the Great Idea is revealed. As Heracles asks him why he is so passionately eager for Euripides in particular (67–91), Dionysus replies that, now that Euripides and Sophocles have both recently died, there are no decent tragedians left in Athens: "However hard you might look, you couldn't find nowadays a really 'potent poet,' one who can utter a phrase that is nobly conceived" (96–97). Mission impossible—hence perfect for Comedy.

In what follows (107–64), with both Heracles and Xanthias constantly interjecting absurd and disruptive jokes (Heracles' about quick ways of reaching Hades through suicide, Xanthias' about the weight of the luggage that he is still carrying), Heracles does explain to Dionysus the geography of the Underworld: one large area of darkness and mud designated for the torment of the wicked (145–53), and another of light, meadows, and trees reserved for the blessedly good, including those initiated into the Mysteries (154–63). These initiates, he says, will be able to guide Dionysus the rest of the way. <*Exit Heracles, back into his house.*>

So Dionysus and Xanthias set off, and after a brief and unproductive encounter with a funeral cortège (167–78) they reach the edge of the Lake where Charon, ferryman of the dead, operates his boat. (Charon was a familiar figure to Athenians, as he is often represented on vases wearing his short tunic and pointed hat, punting the weightless, winged souls across the Lake in his little boat; see Fig. 6-1.) Charon quibbles at first and refuses to take a slave on board (191–95); so Xanthias is ordered to run all the way round the Lake <*Exit Xanthias*>—comic logic can ignore the fact that there should be no footpath conveying the living to the Underworld; and perhaps the actor extracted further humorous mileage by threading his way among the rows of seats in the auditorium in his detour to Hades (see chapter 8). Meanwhile Dionysus climbs on board the boat. But, in a neat twist that reflects both Athenian citizen culture in general and recent military events in particular, Charon is not going to punt them across with his pole but requires instead that Dionysus himself sit at the oar(s) and row.

The result, of course, is a fiasco: Dionysus is hopelessly unskilled and feeble, and doesn't know even which way to face. As Charon calls out the time like the boatswain of a trireme, "Ô-op-op, Ô-op-op"

(208), and Dionysus tries to get into the rhythm of rowing, suddenly a chorus of exuberantly singing voices bursts out—in a quite different, and very lively, rhythm (209–20): "*Brekekekex koax koax!*" The singers may be invisible to all (beneath the water, as it were; or in the reeds at the sides of the "lake"), or more likely the audience can see that these are the "frog-swans" that Charon had mentioned at 207, while Dionysus is facing the wrong way to see them. (See center stage of Fig. 1–1a.)

The chorus sing a hymn of praise to Dionysus (unaware, obviously, that the figure clad in a lion-skin in the boat is that very same divinity): "the hymn which once we sang for Dionysus in the Marshes, for the Festival of the Pots (*Chutroi*) . . ." (208–19). So we realize that these are the ghosts of frogs who once lived in Athens and who used to celebrate the Anthesteria festival there (see chapter 6). Their song goes on to praise the Muses, Pan, and Apollo, whose lyre makes use of the reed-canes that are their own home (228–34), and they refer to their own perennial habit of performing pastoral songs all day long, rain or shine (242–48). Every stanza is capped with the same refrain of *brekekekex koax koax*. Meanwhile Dionysus sings short stanzas of exasperation back at them, complaining about how much his backside hurts from rowing. At first, the frogs' rhythms are too fast and complicated for him; but soon he begins to catch on, and from line 250 on he is able to match their refrain: "There, look! I'm taking it over from you!" He has now learned how to row—like the slaves drafted into the Athenian fleet at Arginusae—as he yells out, "I will defeat you all with my *koax*!" (262–63). Maybe Dionysus is not quite so clueless, or as useless to Athens, as he at first appeared to be.

So Dionysus reaches the other side of the orchestra (i.e., of the Lake), and disembarks from the boat (270): he is now in the Underworld. Almost simultaneously, Xanthias comes running (back) in from the side to rejoin him, having traveled (he says) through the criminals and perjurers in the mud. The two of them start making their way forwards, anxiously imagining that they see all kinds of hideous apparitions and monsters around them, with Dionysus each time trying to hide behind Xanthias, or even (299) scampering across the orchestra to seek the protection of the Priest of Dionysus in the front row of the auditorium. In the midst of all this, Dionysus is found to have shat himself (309—as he does again at 478–85). Then (313–15), just as Heracles had predicted, they hear the sound of pipes and singing, and the Chorus of *Mystai* ("Initiates in the Mysteries") enters: a group of twenty-four, comprising both men and women (unusually for a dramatic chorus), singing and dancing in praise of the god Iacchus (another name for Bacchus/Dionysus).

The content and dramatic function of this long and complex choral song (316–459: the so-called *parodos* or "Arrival-Song") will be discussed in chapter 6, in relation to the religious elements of the play. For now, we may observe just the action. At first, Dionysus and Xanthias are hiding and watching from the side (321 "It's best to keep quiet . . .," 339 "Keep still!"). But when the Initiates start singing about the fun of dancing with a pretty girl (409–12), Dionysus cannot restrain himself any longer. He and Xanthias eagerly emerge: [Dion.] "I've always been an eager follower of the dance, and I want to dance and play with her as well!" [Xa.] "Me too!" (413–15). Then they talk with the Chorus-leader, asking for directions to Plouton's house (431–32), and it turns out that they are right there already.

So Dionysus, still dressed as Heracles, approaches the door. Xanthias encourages him: "Don't waste time—get cracking on that door, in the style and spirit of Heracles!" (462). He knocks with the club, very loudly. Over the next few minutes, the action moves rapidly back and forth (464–673), as first a bulky and bad-tempered Doorman and then a much more friendly Maidservant come into view and address the visitors. (Some ancient and modern commentators have identified this Doorman as "Aeacus," who is better known as one of the three Judges of the Dead, but there is nothing in Aristophanes' text to support this idea.) Both of them, clearly, remember Heracles' previous visit very vividly and think that he has now returned: but their reactions are diametrically opposite. The Doorman is furious and belligerent, threatening to tear Heracles to pieces with the help of various Underworld creatures (464–78), while the Maidservant invites him inside for a dinner tête-à-tête with Persephone, dancing, and sex (503–18). In response to the Doorman's threats, Dionysus quickly makes Xanthias put on the Heracles costume in his place, which means that, when the Maidservant enters instead, it is "Heracleo-Xanthias" (499) who actually gets invited in for the intimate dinner. Then, after Dionysus (predictably) insists on taking over again as Heracles in order to enjoy these enticements himself (522–48), two different servants suddenly come out, recognize "Heracles" as the man who stole and ate vast amounts of their food not so long ago, and summon help from within to catch and punish him. So of course Dionysus quickly prevails upon Xanthias again (582 "please, Xanthi-poo . . .!") to put on the Heracles costume so that he will be the one to get punished (579–604).

The pace accelerates and the slapstick humor escalates as the Doorman returns with some guards, who grab Xanthias-Heracles and are about to punish him, painfully—when he cleverly comes up with a notion based on actual judicial practice (612–28): he swears an oath of innocence, that he has never been down here ever before in his life (613), and offers to the court that they may torture his slave for his confirmatory testimony (the standard procedure in the Athenian courts). After many back-and-forth claims and counterclaims, as to which of them is the slave and which the master, Dionysus blurts out his true identity (Dionysus, not Heracles) and insists that, as a god, he must be immune from such legal procedure (628–32). An absurd (and to modern tastes, cruel and rather disturbing) test is put into effect: both of them will be flogged, to see which one of them feels pain and is therefore actually a slave, not a god. Each turns out to be as sensitive as the other: they both shriek out in pain, but each tries to disguise his own shrieks as some other kind of exclamation (a prayer, a casual remark, a poetic quotation, etc.). Eventually, with the issue still unresolved, it is decided that they should both go inside—since Plouton and Persephone should actually be able to recognize their fellow divinity Dionysus by reason of their superior discernment and previous acquaintance with him (670–73). So the first half of the play ends, with all the characters trooping inside. <*Exeunt omnes.*>

The Chorus is left alone in the orchestra, and we await the *parabasis* (674–737), i.e., the moment when the chorus traditionally "steps forward" to address the audience directly, breaking the dramatic illusion and singing/speaking more or less as the mouthpiece of the poet himself (see chapter 1). We have looked at this *parabasis* already, tracing Aristophanes' use of the Chorus of Initiates to present an intensely inclusive appeal to Athenian solidarity, with the goal of restoring the "gold standard" of earlier days (see chapter 2). Here we may note that this theme of moral restoration and recovery of past glories, once voiced, never really fades from the rest of the play. Even though the formal *parabasis* ends, and the action of the play resumes, the audience's experience of the Chorus' invitation is not forgotten. Indeed, the play may be said to evolve in a new direction from this moment on.

For in the next scene (737–812) the action takes a somewhat unexpected turn, though this is managed so neatly and quickly that the audience may hardly notice the change of direction and purpose. Whereas in the opening scenes Dionysus had been dead-set on finding Euripides and bringing him back up to Athens at all costs, now he has been suddenly appointed to a rather different task: judging an Underworld poetry contest. The new twist is introduced in the course of a short and seemingly trivial conversation between two slaves, Xanthias and one of Plouton's servants. They begin by joking about the ways in which slaves like to score off their masters in retaliation for the beatings and inconveniences they constantly suffer. As the two of them embrace in cordial appreciation of their shared values and experience (753–55), they—and the audience—hear a loud argument taking place inside. Plouton's slave explains what is going on:

> There is an established custom (*nomos*) here,
> For the crafts that are the greatest and most skilled,
> That the man who is best among all his fellow-professionals
> Receives free meals in the Prytaneum, and a seat next to
>   Pluto . . .
> . . . Until someone more expert at the craft arrives:
> And then he has to give up his seat to him . . .
> . . . Aeschylus had the throne for tragedy,
> As being the best at that craft. . . .
> . . . Well, when Euripides came down here, he started
>   showing off his abilities

> . . . To the masses in Hades. And when they heard his
>   counter-arguments
> And twistings and weavings of words, they went totally
>   crazy
> And considered him the most expert;
> So then he got all puffed-up and laid claim to the throne
> Where Aeschylus was sitting. . . .
>
> (761–78)

So a "trial" or "test" *(krisis)* has been arranged, to determine who is the "most expert" and best of all the tragic poets in Hades. (It is explained that Sophocles, who has also recently arrived down there, is perfectly content to grant the seat of honor to Aeschylus [786–94]—it is only the upstart, loud-mouthed Euripides who would be so bold and impolite as to challenge him.)

Dionysus, as the divinity perennially responsible for drama in Athens (and music everywhere else too), has been invited to be the "judge" (805 *krinei*) of this contest. There was apparently "a shortage of expert humans" (806) who might qualify for this highly responsible task: Aeschylus has refused to let the Athenians in Hades be the judges—they are too low-class and unrefined; but everyone else is "too stupid and ignorant about the true nature of poets and poetry" (809–10). So the god's mission to Hades has now taken on a new purpose; instead of being just an eccentric and monomaniacal Euripides-lover, he is now trusted—even by Aeschylus—as the all-time expert in tragedy, ancient and modern alike.

So it will not be a surprise that, when we next see Dionysus (entering at 830), he is no longer wearing the Heracles-costume. He is now the god of Athenian tragedy—still comic (padded, phallic, grotesque), but no longer on a mission to raid Hades and violate the guardians of the Underworld. Instead he wants to help everyone there find the best tragedian who ever lived. And his conversational companion now is not Xanthias, his Athenian slave, but Plouton, king of the Underworld. For most of the second half of the play, the two of them are probably sitting next to one another (perhaps with Persephone as well; see Fig. 1–1b); and when Dionysus is not engaging directly with Aeschylus and/or Euripides, he will be chatting to Plouton.

The contestants enter from indoors (perhaps wheeled out onstage? see chapter 8), together with Plouton, Dionysus, and various attendants. As previously reported by the Servant of Plouton, Aeschylus and Euripides are already furious at one another: but their anger manifests itself in different ways, as Euripides is grabbing at Aeschylus' throne and talking vociferously, while Aeschylus sits in grim and disdainful silence. We can already see that Dionysus' role is as much that of umpire and peacemaker as of judge. After some preliminary sparring and fussing around (830–906), Dionysus gets the two of them to join him in a prayer (875–904) accompanied by a brazier and incense, whose smell would quickly pervade the whole Theater. Aeschylus invokes Demeter and the Mysteries as he sprinkles incense on the flames (886–87), but Euripides says "No, thank you" to the incense (888) and addresses his own new-fangled divinities of "Sky . . . Understanding . . . and Keen-scented Nostrils" (892–94).

So the two great tragedians begin their competition (*agôn*). This contest will occupy almost all the rest of the play so that in terms of the stage action things are mostly quite straightforward, with relatively few entrances and exits or new characters. But even if the action is simple, the verbal, musical, and choreographical texture keeps changing in brilliantly unexpected ways, and Aristophanes has come up with numerous visual gimmicks to point up the stylistic and ethical contrasts between the two dramatists. As a backdrop to the whole contest—most of which presumably is conducted downstage, in the orchestra and close to the front rows of the audience—stand the weighing machinery (giant scales, large enough for a man or two to climb onto each of the pans), various measuring devices (set squares, plumb-lines), and perhaps other tools for carpentry, coin-testing, and stone-cutting as well. And the judges, Plouton, maybe Persephone, and Dionysus himself, sit on thrones at the back, supervising the whole procedure (see Fig. 1–1b). At the beginning of the scene, Aeschylus is apparently sitting on a throne too (830), next to Plouton; but he vacates it as he enters into the contest.

Everything about the two competitors is a visual—and audible—contrast: costumes, body type, gait, pitch of voice, vocabulary, with Aeschylus dressed in fine robes, moving sedately and speaking sonorously, while Euripides is quicker on his feet, wears simpler clothing, and uses more everyday language. But of course each of them spends quite a bit of the contest criticizing and parodying the other one's mannerisms, with the result that much of the humor comes from seeing and hearing these exaggerated distortions of more or less recognizable tragic passages and familiar styles coming from such incongruous sources. Euripides characterizes his old rival's Muse or "Art" (*technê*) as fat and overweight (939–40); he himself had to "get her in shape" and slim her down by using shorter words and clearer forms of expression—language that was available for all to use, even the lower classes (948–49). This "fat lady" is obviously a metaphor for the "grandness" and "inflation" of Aeschylean style, and much Aristophanic humor depends on thus concretizing, and making visible, notions that are usually purely conceptual (elsewhere, bad-tempered jurymen as wasps, a "Cloud-cuckoo" city in the sky, etc.). Having Aeschylus and Euripides on-stage as the embodiments of old and new styles of tragedy allows for particularly vivid and grotesque contrasts.

The topics of disagreement between the two of them come quickly into focus: elevated vs. normal language; concentration on upper-class heroes vs. inclusion of lower-class characters too, and their appropriate costuming; focus on warlike themes vs. female characters and erotic relationships; and so on. Euripides suggests that drama should be democratic (954 "I taught these people here [meaning the audience] how to talk!"), while Aeschylus insists instead (1009–42) that all undignified and morally questionable actions should be suppressed, and the poet should be a moralist, providing only useful and beneficial advice and instruction: (1054) "children have their schoolteachers, grown-ups have the poets." So playwrights should select only good examples for their audiences to learn from and should aim to keep on producing brave soldiers like Lamachus, the noble old Athenian general from the 420s (whom Aristophanes had mercilessly ridiculed in *Acharnians*).

It is a crucial moment in the play—but one that passes quickly and without debate or demur—when Euripides cheerfully agrees with Aeschylus that the criteria of a poet's worth are not only "skillfulness and thoughtful advice" (1009) but also "that we make people better members of their communities" (1010) and "teach worthwhile things" (1057). This means that both of them will be equally ready to debate, on the one hand, practical issues of "skill" and dramatic technique, and, on the other, moral and political issues, as to what is best for Athens and how to make the best possible citizens.

The contest proceeds. Technical issues come first: how to begin a play (1119–1248 prologues and opening lines); lyric meters and musical phrasings for choral or solo songs (1249–1364). In rapid succession, the tragedians each quote liberally from each other's work, or else from their own, with occasional interjections and jokes from Dionysus; the passages are taken to pieces, phrase by phrase and word by word; contradictions, absurdities, ambiguities, redundancies are seized upon and ridiculed; old-fashioned or new-fangled musical phrasings are exaggerated and mocked. After a while, Dionysus calls a halt to this (1364), and Aeschylus immediately calls for "the scales" (1365): "The weight of our words will provide the true test of our mettle/metal!" (1367; see chapter 2, pp. 45–48). The impressive paraphernalia of scales, balances, and weights are prepared, and the ludicrous process of loading each poet's chosen words into the pans on each side begins (1378–1410), with Aeschylus' phrases (about a river, Death, and chariots) invariably proving to be "heavier" than Euripides' (about a sailboat, Persuasion, and a spear). All three times, the pan sinks immediately down on Aeschylus' side. The victory appears to be his, as he scornfully challenges his frustrated opponent:

> I don't need any more of that line-by-line weighing now—
> He can climb on the scales himself, and his children,
> And his wife, and Cephisophon, along with all their books too!
> I'll just recite two verses of my poetry <and that'll be enough>!
>
> (1407–10)

But the contest is not to be decided so cleanly and quickly.
Once again Dionysus speaks up to modify the terms and conditions
on which the verdict is to be based (1411):

> "These men [Aeschylus and Euripides] are my friends;
> And I'm not going to judge between them and thereby
> Make myself an enemy of one of them.
> I think that one of them is a great skilled poet (*sophon*); and
>   the other one,
> I really enjoy . . . (*hêdomai*)."
>
> (1411–13)

This supreme act of evasion (and of ambiguity, since it is far from
clear which of the two poets Dionysus is privileging as "expert,
skilled" (*sophos*), and he is no longer, it seems, quite the obsessive
Euripides-lover that he was at the start of the play) brings them, as
Plouton pointedly observes, to an impasse:

> [Plouton] "So you'll be accomplishing nothing of what you
> came here for!" (1414)

But this hesitation is only momentary, and the impasse is quickly
resolved through a maneuver that finally reveals the true and most
far-reaching goal of this play's Great Idea—a goal of which neither
the audience nor Dionysus himself, it seems, has hitherto been fully
aware, though at some unconscious level we (and he) may have
sensed it since very early in the play:

> [Dion.] And if I do pass judgment?
> [Plouton] Then you can leave, taking one of them with you,
> Whichever one you choose. Then you won't have come
>   for nothing.
> [Dion.] Thanks indeed, and bless you!
> Come on, you two; listen to what I have to say:
> I came down here to fetch a poet. Why?
> So that the city may be saved and may keep on celebrating
>   choruses.
>
> (1414–17)

A mission that began as a desperate raid to capture Euripides at all costs (Heracles-style), for Dionysus' personal satisfaction, and that then evolved into a contest to see which poet in the Underworld deserves to sit on the throne of tragedy, now turns out, in its third and most satisfying formulation, to involve the salvation of the whole city of Athens. Through the resurrection of the finest poet—whoever that is deemed to be—the spirit of the Theater can be redeemed and the citizens can be reborn. Apparently, Dionysus' experiences in the Underworld have taught him something. Like the audience themselves, he has witnessed the Initiate Chorus, the gracious reception of the visitors by Plouton and Persephone, and the high poetic claims of Aeschylus and Euripides; and these various perspectives on death and oblivion, on Athens' political and military glories, past and present, and on the power of music, poetry, and dance (*choroi*) to transform and enrich human life have (perhaps) qualified him at last to arrive at a responsible and salutary decision: which poet to bring back?

The final choice cannot be simple, nor even entirely reasonable. So many criteria have already been invoked and explored; how will Dionysus decide which one to make final and decisive? His procedure, picking up on the two poets' agreement from early on (1009–10) that they should be expected to "give advice, and make people better members of their community," is now to ask each of them to provide "a bit of good advice" about the city's present problems.

So he asks them both first what their view is of Alcibiades (1422) and then (after their answers about him seem equally ambivalent) the more general question:

> Each of you, state just one opinion about the best way
> You can offer for the city to find salvation and security
> (*sôtêrian*).

(1435–36)

The Greek text of this whole next passage (1437–1466) is in a very confused state, and modern scholars disagree as to how to restore it to exactly what Aristophanes wrote for the first performance of the play. It seems that at least two different versions of this episode were written and subsequently jumbled together in our manuscript tradition. Disentangling which version is which, and even determining in several places which character says which lines, has proven to be quite controversial. I shall here follow the reading and interpretation of Alan Sommerstein, but without complete confidence. Fortunately, not too much is at stake in terms of the particular responses that Euripides and Aeschylus may be making to Dionysus' request. The general outlines are clear enough—and I think we can be pretty sure of the main distinctions that each of the rival poets makes.

Euripides splits hairs in riddling and confusing wordplay (*pista apista* . . .), "trust the ones you didn't trust before . . . etc." Aeschylus is more circumspect and asks (1454–56), "What is the city actually doing now? Honoring the worthy or delighting in the good-for-nothing?" Dionysus responds that it is the good-for-nothings that currently hold power—but goes on to explain that this is only because there are no worthy people left. Aeschylus sounds exasperated; but he now comes up with a peculiar demurral—he doesn't want to give his advice to the city "here and now" (1461), but would prefer to wait until he is back on earth (in Athens) to deliver it. Dionysus will not allow this: "No—send up your blessings/good things from here, now!" (1462)—and perhaps the audience recognizes that these phrases, "here and now . . . from here . . .," may refer simultaneously to the Underworld where Aeschylus and Dionysus are talking and to the Theater where they themselves are now sitting, listening, and awaiting the denouement of the play (their salvation). He is cajoled into offering his advice:

> [The city should] consider the enemy's lands its own, and
>   its own land
> The enemy's; consider [its true] resources/wealth (*poron*) to
>   be the ships;
> And consider [all other kinds of material] resources (*poron*)
>   to be no
> Resource at all (*aporian*).
>
>   (1463–65)

In an enigmatic and ambiguous Aeschylean manner (though in comic rather than tragic meter), he is recommending what had been in effect the war policy instituted twenty-five years earlier by Pericles: rely on naval strength to maintain Athenian power over the Aegean, and allow the Spartans to invade Attica (and to keep their fortified outpost at Decelea) without committing large numbers of infantry against them. (A similar policy had prevailed generations earlier too, against the Persians at Salamis—after the Athenians had evacuated their city for the enemy to occupy.) So, in winter 405, Aristophanes' Aeschylus is in favor of trusting to Athens' traditional strength and continuing the war as vigorously as possible.

Plouton interrupts once again—he is getting impatient. "Please make your decision!" (1467). Dionysus is ready:

Here is my verdict (*krisis*) on them.
I shall choose the one that my spirit (*psuchê*) wants.

The term "spirit" here (*psuchê*) is crucially important (as will be seen in chapter 6). Whereas earlier it had been Dionysus' "heart" (53–54 *kardia*) that was yearning for Euripides, we may understand now not simply that his "heart" disagrees with his "mind" as to which poet to choose, but perhaps too that his "immortal, enlightened consciousness . . ." (*psuchê*) has come into play at a deeper level. We will return to this final scene of decision-making (and the issue of Alcibiades) in chapter 7. For now, we may observe that Dionysus does—suddenly—choose Aeschylus. Euripides accuses him of breaking his oath, but Dionysus rebuffs him with three quotations absurdly adapted from Euripides' plays. The contest is over, and the celebration (*kômos*) begins.

The final scene is full of bustle and stage business, even as Euripides fumes in the background. (When does he actually depart? The text gives us no direct clue: perhaps after line 1478.) Aeschylus and Dionysus are welcomed into the palace by Plouton and Persephone (1479 "Come inside . . . and celebrate").

The Chorus sings a joyous ode of "blessing" (*makarismos*, 1482–99). Then Aeschylus, Plouton, Dionysus reenter the orchestra—along with Xanthias too, perhaps, played now by a silent actor (see chapter 7)? Preparations are made for Aeschylus and Xanthias (and Dionysus too, presumably) to wend their effortless way back to earth—to the Theater of Dionysus, obviously, where Aeschylus belongs! They are (after all) here already, and the Chorus is singing for them, here as there in Hades, along with all the powerful Underworld "spirits" (*daimones*). As the torch-lit procession departs, the whole city can look forward to a better future of "salvation" and artistic reinvigoration; Aristophanes' comedy has saved tragedy for us all.

Suggestions for Further Reading

The introductions to the editions of *Frogs* by Stanford (1963), Dover (1993), and Sommerstein (1996) all have good discussions of the formal features of the play in relation to Old Comedy in general. On the narrative and formal structure of Aristophanic comedy (in relation to Vladimir Propp's analyses of folktales), see Sifakis (1992).

For the notion of a comic (everyman) hero and his/her "great idea," see especially Whitman (1964); also Reckford (1987), and for a more sceptical account, Hubbard (1991).

·4·

Agôn Sophias[*]
Judging the Arts in Classical Greece

The Greek Contest System

Competition and contests were built into archaic and classical Greek society at every level and in many forms, some more overt than others. The desire, and social pressure, for a man to prove himself "better" than others was almost universal, and hard to resist: for in order to be, or at least to be perceived to be, an especially "good" man—or woman—and thus to be admired, respected, and important, you usually needed to outperform others. This meant, of course, that others had to be, or to appear to be, "worse, inferior." Notions of success, manliness, and honor were largely built around the desire to avoid the shame of appearing "weaker, lesser" or of allowing someone to mock or humiliate you.

Social interactions in ancient Greece accordingly have been described by some as a "zero-sum game" in which honor, prizes, and prestige (to say nothing of physical and military power) were usually achieved only at someone else's expense. This pervasive attitude of competition was equally capable of enhancing, or of ruining, social relations, as the Greeks themselves recognized:

[*]*Frogs* 882 "The greatest poetry contest in the world"

> There are two kinds of *eris* ("strife, conflict") in the world;
> One of them you'd praise when you saw it;
> But the other is reprehensible . . .
> The [better kind] . . . stirs even a lazy person to start working . . .
> Potter gets angry with potter, carpenter with carpenter;
> Resentment everywhere—beggar vs. beggar, singer vs. singer."
>
> (Hesiod *Works & Days* 11–26)

Eris is thus the spirit of conflict, strife, emulation in the world at large, a spirit that can spur people on to exceptional achievement, but all too easily can spill over into bitter hatred and outright violence. Indeed in this passage even Hesiod seems a little unsure whether the rivalry of "potter vs. potter, singer vs. singer," is entirely positive: the verbs he uses here, 25 "gets angry," 26 "begrudges, resents . . .," normally carry quite negative associations.

Greek society certainly provided numerous opportunities for fierce competition, especially between elite men: war; athletics; and (in democratic Athens, particularly) all the political processes of elections, lawsuits and jury votes, as well as "liturgies," including chorus production (*chorêgia*, see chapter 2). Institutional venues and occasions were specifically designed to channel such competitive energies into displays of more constructive and productive activity: the Greek term for such a venue/occasion was *agôn*. Originally denoting a "place where people gather together" (and thus related to *agora*, "marketplace"), *agôn* soon acquired the more particular sense of a more or less formal "contest, public competition," and hence even organized "games." Contests were held for all kinds of activities: not only athletics, but also—especially—"music," and *Mousikoi Agônes* were important components of both the annual Panathenaic Games in Athens, and the panhellenic Pythian Games at Delphi, with prizes for choral performances, for solo singing, and for instrumental performances on the *cithara* (concert lyre) or *auloi* (double-pipes).

Literary/performative competition of a more informal kind was also a common element in the symposium. In addition to the professional musicians and dancers who would often entertain the whole company, individual guests might be required to take turns singing pieces of songs, capping each others' clever imagistic comparisons, posing and answering riddles, proposing rival eulogies of people, objects, or ideas, and of course performing—and critiquing—the poetry of the past. This is the pattern followed in Plato's *Symposium*, with its quasi-competitive succession of speeches in praise of Love (including a fantastic and inspirational myth of creation offered by none other than Aristophanes). A more formal (but amusingly facetious) example of such posing and debating of literary "problems" is provided in Plato's *Protagoras*. There the famous sophist and teacher of rhetoric remarks (338e), "I myself think that for a man the greatest element of education is being expert concerning poetry," whereupon he and Socrates proceed to offer rival interpretations of a famous passage from a lyric poem of Simonides.

The traditions of iambic poetry (chapter 1) provided another context for explicit and implicit competition on "literary" topics. Mockery of the pretentions, extravagance, and bad taste of others—including poets and visual artists—had always been an important component of the invective poetry of Archilochus, Hipponax, and their successors: and parody (including burlesque epic such as *The Battle of Frogs and Mice*) is only effective if both poet and audience are fairly intimately familiar with the original that is being distorted, ridiculed, and implicitly corrected.

Throughout all these different contexts of artistic contestation and literary contradiction we can see an ongoing tension (often quite amiable, but nonetheless pervasive) between, on the one hand, the notion that there is a *right and proper way* to say and do things, a *correct* (accurate and/or morally superior) *version* of a story or social formula; and, on the other, the desire for something *new*, distinctive, provocative, *better* (and therefore in some respect *different*) that will trump previous or currently competing efforts. So one might award a prize to a rhapsode (such as Plato's Ion) for most perfectly recapturing Homer's original words, meaning, and manner; or to a dithyrambic poet who has composed a song and trained a chorus to perform a brand-new dolphin dance. Both impulses are strong—and of course the songs of the past, however innovative they may once have been, will always be regarded as more traditional than those of the present.

In *Frogs*, we are informed by the Servant of Plouton that special thrones are reserved in the Underworld for the best practitioners of each of the most highly regarded "crafts, professions" (*technai*):

> There's a law established down here,
> That from each of the crafts that are important and skillful,
> The man who's the best of all the fellow craftsmen
> Gets free lunches in the Prytaneum and sits on a throne
>   next to Plouton . . .
> Until someone else more expert at this profession (*tên
>   technên sophôteros*) arrives:
> And then he has to surrender the throne to him.
>
>   (761–67)

This is clearly recognizable as an Underworld equivalent of a well-known Athenian institution—the award of free meals in the Prytaneum [Town Hall] and/or front seats at festivals to individuals who had performed some exceptionally noteworthy deed, such as winning an Olympic victory or (very occasionally) leading an army successfully on a major campaign. In real life, as far as we know, artists and craftsmen were never in fact thus rewarded; so this Underworld "law, custom" may be a little piece of Aristophanic fun, suggesting that the fine arts at least deserved honors equivalent to those given to successful athletes and generals. The notion that prizes might be awarded to expert craftsmen in various fields would not be felt to be especially comic or peculiar, however: Greek mythology is full of all kinds of such contests, e.g., for weaving (Arachne vs. Athena/Minerva), painting (Apelles vs. Zeuxis), prophecy (Calchas vs. Mopsus), and even physical beauty (Hera, Athena, and Aphrodite, in the Judgment of Paris).

For Athenian playwrights in particular, the annual competitions at the City Dionysia and the Lenaea provided especially prestigious and well-attended competition venues; and the contest of Aeschylus vs. Euripides in *Frogs*, even though it is set in Hades, alludes constantly to the conventions of the Athenian theater, as if these must be well-known to all the inhabitants of the Underworld. And in fact the idea of a face-to-face contest between poets—which would seem a little peculiar to most modern audiences—would have been entirely familiar to Greeks everywhere. Indeed, it is hardly an exaggeration to say that most Greek poetry of the archaic and early classical period was performed and enjoyed in a directly agonistic context.

Some examples: Hesiod in the *Works & Days* tells us that he once was awarded a tripod for "having won the victory with my hymn" at the funeral of King Amphidamas (*WD* 650–62); and there is even a surviving prose narrative of *The Contest (Agôn) between Hesiod and Homer*, describing their—doubtless fictitious—encounter at a big public festival, with each poet taking turns to recite some of his own verses and then proceeding to "cap" verses begun by his rival. The eventual verdict is hotly disputed, since the majority of the audience want to give the prize to Homer's rousing war poetry, but they are overruled by the king, who favors instead Hesiod's emphasis on peace and justice. Competitions of choruses and of solo singers and instrumentalists, and in epic recitation too, were widespread, both locally and at several of the great Panhellenic or Panionian centers (Delphi, Delos); and other kinds of competitive display of "wisdom" seem also to have taken place there (especially at Olympia). Contests in poetry and music occur frequently in mythological narratives as well: e.g., Thamyris vs. the Muses (*Iliad* 2. 584–600) or the satyr Marsyas vs. Apollo (Ovid *Met.* 6. 383–400—also frequently in fifth-century Athenian literature and vase-painting; see chapter 5). One feature of the outcome of these contests is striking—the verdicts are frequently disputed and may not always end up being obviously "correct," whether because the criteria are unclear, or because the judges are unreliable or biased, or both. Seldom is an artist unanimously and uncontroversially judged the winner. We will need to bear this in mind when we come to consider Dionysus' final verdict in *Frogs*.

So the basic idea of a competition in "wisdom/poetry/verbal skills" (*agôn sophias*, 882) would not in itself strike an Athenian audience as unusual, though one taking place in the Underworld might be rather unexpected. Athenian audiences would also of course be familiar with many scenes in tragedy in which a more or less explicit contest of arguments/speeches takes place between two characters and a decision or verdict is passed; occasionally we even have an actual trial (as in Aeschylus' *Eumenides* and Euripides' lost *Palamedes*). Aristophanes' own plays likewise are often built around one or more large-scale *agôn*-scenes, in which one character seeks to convert some sceptical opponents, or two rivals debate the merits of their positions in front of a powerful "jury" of observers, with the outcome of the *agôn* often bringing about a radical shift in the trajectory of the comic plot. The process of argument and counter-argument that leads up to such moments of decision and/or reversal usually combines serious, thought-provoking argumentation with absurd trivialization, distraction, and distortion of all kinds (and sometimes a fair measure of physical slapstick humor as well).

Aristophanes and other Old Comic playwrights had indeed on several previous occasions already included poetic contests of one kind or another in their plays; and their own back-and-forth competition with one another, conducted both through these fictional narratives and through directly self-referential commentary, mainly in *parabases*, seems to have taken on a vigorous life of its own. In some cases, we know only the barest outlines or just the titles of these comedies: e.g., Aristophanes' own *Gerytades* and *Poiêsis*; Cratinus' *Archilochoi* (perhaps involving a contest between Archilochus and Homer and/or Hesiod); Pherecrates' *Crapataloi* (*Sprats*, which included a scene in which the ghost of Aeschylus appeared); Phrynichus' *Tragôidoi* or *Apeleutheroi*; Plato Comicus' *Skeuai* and *Laconians* or *Poets*. From Pherecrates' *Cheiron* we have a bit more: there survives a highly amusing speech by the female character Mousikê ("Music"), full of sexual double entendres as she complains of the disgraceful violations that have been perpetrated against her (a scene that we shall revisit in chapter 5 when we look at Aeschylus' critique of Euripides' lyrics in *Frogs*).

Phrynichus was also the author of another comedy that competed against the *Frogs* in the same Lenaean festival of 405, entitled *The Muses*. The few surviving fragments include praise of the dead

Sophocles and instructions to someone (who?) on how to vote for acquittal or condemnation. While we cannot tell from these fragments how much of the play dealt with the recently deceased playwright(s) or what kind of "trial" took place, the coincidences between this subject matter and that of *Frogs* are striking. Did Phrynichus set out purposely to compete against Aristophanes with a play on the same basic topic (or vice versa)? (If so, he will have been disappointed in the outcome—it was Aristophanes who won the prize and who was invited to restage his play a year or two later.)

Judging (*Krisis*)

The Greek term for any act of "judging" or "evaluating," whether in a law court or in a competition, is *krinô*. A "judgment" or "verdict" (noun) is *krisis* (as at *Frogs* 779, 785, 1467) and the related adjective is *kritikos* (whence English "critic, critical, criticize, criticism"), while the "standard," or "measuring rod," by which a visual assessment is made (e.g., in architecture or carpentry) is a *kritêrion*. For any competition (or trial, for that matter) it is essential for the contestants to know exactly what the criteria are by which they are being judged, and who will be the judge(s). In Greek athletic competitions, the rules and method of evaluation were usually clear, and the judges' task was easy: one person would obviously jump the farthest, cross the finish line first, or knock out his opponent. And the victor would always be glad to win. But in other competitive contexts, things might not always be so straightforward.

Tastes differ and fashions change, especially in matters artistic; so judges can disagree, for good or bad reasons. Even such apparently straightforward and objective criteria as "correctness" of linguistic usage, or metrical/musical intonation and instrumentation, might shift quite radically within a few years, then as now. Who is then authorized to judge the best poet or musician, and by what ultimate (or contingent) standards? What sort of critical language or tools of measurement are required to make accurate aesthetic and artistic judgments? (Do we need a special vocabulary of terms of the trade, even special instruments? See chapter 3, p. 74, and Fig. 1–1b) There have always been people who would prefer to keep things simple and to eschew technical analysis: "I don't know much about art, but I know what I like (and it isn't this . . .!)." The actual juries that voted in the Theater of Dionysus at the dithyramb, tragedy, and comedy competitions were apparently not composed of specialists, and as far as we know the ten judges for tragedy did not confer with one another before voting: it was presumably taken for granted that everyone knew the basic criteria of evaluation. But in the poetry competition of *Frogs*, some definitions and much disputation are required to establish the criteria, and it is soon decided that the god of drama himself shall preside and give the verdict.

Much of the fun, and of the critical interest, of *Frogs* comes from the fact that the terms and grounds for judging poetic merit are indeed so slippery, multifarious, and contestable. Just when one criterion seems to be leading us towards forming a verdict on one side or the other, a new criterion is invoked, or the participants spontaneously strike off in another direction. Even in the opening scene Heracles— no reliable judge of poetry, to be sure—has an opinion to offer when he hears Dionysus' snippets of "adventurous" Euripidean phraseology: "That's complete rubbish, and you know it!" (104). The term he uses, *kobala*, literally means "stuff to be carried away by a porter"; its associations are like our "trash, garbage," i.e., heavily colored with the class-based distinction between what discriminating people admire and what the riff-raff go for. And throughout the play, it is made clear, first, that, even if Dionysus is a divinity and the chief, most experienced patron of drama, his tastes are generally rather crude, popular, and superficial, and second, that Euripides' fans (among whom of course we have to count Dionysus himself, at least early in the play) are the lowest of the low on the social and moral scale. And yet Euripides himself claims to have advanced the interests of the lower classes by making tragedy "demo-cratic"—and in Athens such a statement should not be taken lightly.

How seriously should we take this "democratic" claim and the im-plication that Aeschylus' drama is (was) more exclusive and elitist than Euripides'? And what are we to make of Dionysus as our official— rather simple-minded, yet intermittently pretentious—judge? One school of critical interpretation of this play has argued that Dionysus himself actually gets to be educated and improved as the play goes on, and that the audience likewise is being educated along with him into a better understanding of the value of drama in general (and of Aristophanes' comedy in particular). Others see little or no sign of improvement in Dionysus' taste or judgment from start to finish: his final verdict seems just as arbitrary, unpredictable, and ill-founded as any of his previous off-the-wall assessments. Is the selection of Aeschylus over Euripides in the end the right choice? How should such a choice be decided, by anyone? (Does it really matter—or is this decision by Dionysus just one last joke on the audience?) We will consider these questions at greater length in chapter 7.

For now, let us just bear in mind that, in our own day, not only are law-court verdicts quite often controversial (and they may usually be appealed to higher authorities), but, in the case of artistic competitions, we have all seen prizes being awarded to books, films, or actors that are considered by many (at the time, or in later years) to be quite inferior. This was certainly true also for the dramatic competitions in Athens. Euripides in fact rarely won a first prize in his own lifetime (though his tragedies came to be the most popular of all from the fourth century onwards, and even in his own lifetime he was consistently awarded a chorus), and Aristophanes likewise seems to have been only moderately successful in the festival competitions (though he too was consistently given a chorus, once or even twice a year; see chapter 2). Such critical imprecisions and incongruities are exploited in *Frogs* to delicious effect, as we, the audience, find ourselves being caught up just as much in the process of evaluating the criteria—and evaluating the judge himself (Dionysus)—as in the act of choosing between these two famous playwrights.

Judging the Value(s) of Poetry

What criteria and procedures did the Greeks generally use for determining that one poet, musician, or playwright was superior to another? What did it take for someone to win an artistic contest? Who was regarded as being best qualified to judge artistic merit and quality? What should judges be looking for and evaluating, anyway? Can we even agree what poetry or drama (or fiction in general) is *for*, so as to be able to measure whether or not it has succeeded in its mission? To all these important—and still relevant—questions, *Frogs* provides some of the most provocative and sophisticated (as well as some of the silliest) answers that can be found anywhere in ancient Greek or Latin literature.

Although in the archaic and early classical periods there were certainly plenty of poets and poetic contests, no single term existed for "poetry" or "poetic composition" as such. The word *poiêtês* (literally "maker") is not found in the sense of "poet" before Herodotus, i.e., the last third of the fifth century, though this family of terms (including *poiêma* = "poem," *poiêsis* = "poetic composition") quickly established itself as standard after that and occurs quite frequently in Aristophanes' literary vocabulary. But there were other terms for "poetic composition/performance" that had been in use much longer. Two sets of terms in particular are fundamental, both of them found prominently in *Frogs*.

The first is *aeidein, aoidos* ("sing, singer"). Every schoolboy knows and knew the opening words of the *Iliad*: "**Sing**, goddess, about the wrath <of Achilles . . . >." Even though epic verse by the sixth or fifth centuries was probably chanted and no longer set to music, it was still imagined as "song"; and Hesiod and all the other hexameter poets likewise referred to themselves as "singers" (as in *WD* 26, quoted above). Other poems of the archaic period, notably those of the choral lyricists (Stesichorus, Pindar, etc.) and monodists (Alcaeus, Sappho, Anacreon, etc.) *were* in fact sung—set to melodies and accompanied by the *cithara* or aulos, often with set dance-steps as well: so "poetry" and "song" were understood as being more or less co-extensive as notions and practices. The *aeid-/aoid-* terms, contracting in the Attic dialect to *ôid-*, give rise in turn to such terms as *trag-ôidia* ("tragedy," lit. "goat-song") and *kôm-ôidia* ("comedy," lit. "revel-song"; see chapter 1), and these words of course occur frequently in Aristophanes' plays, not least in *Frogs*. Thus it is natural for Aristophanes' characters (and his audience) to think of

Aeschylus and Euripides as being in a real sense successors in a direct tradition stemming from Homer, Hesiod, and other "singers" of the distant or more recent past.

The second, equally important—though more complicated—set of terms for "poetic activity, expertise" and "artistic skill" in general, was derived from the *soph-* root. The adjective *sophos* and noun *sophia* cover a broad range, including "wisdom, expertise, cleverness, technical skill," and these *soph-* words in the Archaic period and into the fifth century comprised the standard terms, not only for mental sagacity in general, but also to denote "poet, poetry, poetic art." Not surprisingly, then, it is precisely this term that is chosen as the focus for the showdown between Aeschylus and Euripides, which is announced as being "the great contest of poetry/wisdom" (882 *agôn* **sophias** *ho megas*). Some brief discussion of the implications of (poetic) *sophia* is therefore in order here.

As the opening verse of the *Iliad* makes clear (quoted above), epic poets and many other "singers" of the archaic period liked to promote the notion that they received their poetry as a gift from the Muses (or other gods). This divine "gift of song" was more than a mere figure of speech:

> The Muses . . . plucked a bough of laurel and gave it to me as a staff,
> And breathed into me (*enepneusan*) a divine voice, so that I might celebrate
> Things that will be and things that were before;
> And they told me to hymn the race of the gods who live forever,
> And always to sing of them.
>
> (Hesiod *Theogony* 30–34)

The "staff" (*skêptron*) symbolizes the poet's authority to be heard, to be believed, and to be trusted to transmit valuable truths—in this case, the genealogies of the gods themselves. The poet's voice is derived from the very "breath" of the goddesses (the literal meaning of our word "inspiration" comes from Latin *in-spiro*, the exact equivalent of Greek *en-pneô*, as at *Theog.* 31). Later in this same poetic preface, Hesiod describes the quasi-magical power of poetry to delight an audience and make them forget their troubles (*Theog.* 98–103); and throughout the archaic period poets are presented as being the sources both of important, specialized knowledge and also of pleasurable distraction and entertainment. Their "divine voice" is something to be respected and treasured.

From our perspective, poetic *sophia* may conveniently be broken down into three broad categories, though the Greeks themselves did not always make these distinctions (and consequently tended to run into some critical inconsistencies, as we shall see): (a) knowledge; (b) moral wisdom and authority; (c) technical skill and capacity to entertain. To some degree, we might identify these with intellectual, moral, and aesthetic qualities, respectively. The best poet, ideally, should excel in all three categories. Or conversely, if you want to impugn the credentials and performance of a poet (for example, a rival in a contest), your best bet will usually be to demonstrate his shortcomings in one or more of the three areas: so (a) he tells lies and gets things wrong (names, places, genealogies, events); (b) he and his poetry are morally degenerate, and perhaps are even corrupting the community (especially the women and children . . .); (c) his poetry is inept, clumsy, and dull—improperly executed, unoriginal, and unpleasant to hear. Criticisms employing all three of these categories are exploited to the full in *Frogs*.

For category (a), the prime criterion of merit is truth and accuracy. So, for example, Homer calls on the Muses to help him recite the names of all the Greek leaders who commanded ships and troops at Troy, because "you are there and you know . . ., but we [humans] only hear about it" (*Iliad* 2. 484–93); and Hesiod asks the Muses to convey to him an accurate rendering of "the birth of the gods" (*Theogony* 33–34, 114–15).

The second category (b) requires that a poet convey good moral lessons and examples, especially by praising and honoring those who deserve it (gods and heroes; soldiers and war leaders, athletes, kings, etc.), and narrating their admirable achievements—or else perhaps, if he is an iambic or comic poet, by exposing guilty and vicious people to ridicule and blame. Poetry was also the medium for large numbers of proverbs and traditional sayings (*gnômai*), many of which proclaimed moral principles and instructions for proper behavior. Thus Homer, Hesiod, and countless lyric and elegiac poets from the archaic period (for the Athenians, Solon above all) were generally regarded not only as repositories of the great deeds of the past (their cultural heritage), but also as moral and political "teachers" to their community—especially to the young, whose education included extensive poetry recitation and participation in choral performances.

The third main aspect of poetic *sophia* was (c) technical virtuosity—the ability to tell a story in such vivid detail and with such engaging characterization that the audience would be moved to tears, excitement, laughter, even "forgetfulness of their troubles" (Hesiod *Theogony* 102). Good poetry (and music) could deeply affect people's psychological states (the Greeks called this *psychagôgia*, "mind-bending, charming of the spirit") through exceptionally skilled use of words, rhythms, melodies, and in some cases visual effects as well (dance, costumes, acting). And it was understood that such effects were pleasurable as well as emotionally and aesthetically satisfying.

How widely were these claims of poets to special authority and divine "wisdom" endorsed and accepted? It is of course impossible to tell what most people—even the poets themselves—really believed. Poets certainly tended to be granted high status in their communities, and conversely poetry was employed by rulers and governments of all political types, both as a component of festivals and other local celebrations, and as a means of spreading ideas and in some cases the personal reputations of their patrons. And the very fact that "wisdom" (*sophia*) was such a broad category made it easy, indeed entirely natural, to associate political and moral leadership with the expression of opinions in verse. In Athens, the example of the great sixth-century statesman and lawgiver, Solon, stood out above all, since much of his iambic and elegiac poetry was still available for Athenians to recite; but they were proud too of the contemporary poets who competed annually in the theater festivals (dithyrambic, tragic, and comic), according them high cultural status. We should recall, for example, that it was the poets, along with the political leaders, that Socrates says he initially approached when he began his quest in response to Apollo's oracle, expecting to find them the "wisest" of the Greeks (Plato *Apology* 22a–c).

By Aristophanes' (and Socrates') day, however, claims about the divine source and special value of poetry had come increasingly under fire from various quarters. In all three categories inroads had been made by other practitioners of *sophia* who pointed out limitations in the works of Homer, Hesiod, and the other poets as sources of knowledge, moral guidance, or even entertainment. Philosopher-scientists such as Xenophanes and Heraclitus (both writing ca. 500 BCE) had complained that poetic accounts of the Olympian gods and of various mythical creatures (centaurs, giants, etc.) were naive and silly; that is to say, even the divinely inspired Homer was often telling lies (falsehoods, fictions). Similarly (though less stridently), historians like Herodotus and (especially) Thucydides were replacing Homeric narratives about the past with prose accounts of their own, and were frequently criticizing poets for providing fantasy and tall stories rather than accurate and believable narratives. Within a generation or two of *Frogs*, Plato in turn would launch his infamous assault (*Republic* 10. 595a–607d) on the epistemological limitations of all "imitative" art. Among intellectuals such as these the truth-value of poetry, and of the arts in general, had sunk quite low.

As moral guides too, the poets were being challenged and to some degree replaced. A new type of expert educator was evolving, especially for teaching young elites in cities like Athens. Speaking (and writing) in lively and artful prose rather than verse, they claimed to teach people how to excel as citizens and as leaders: their expertise lay in teaching the "art of politics," especially through the skilled use of words—i.e., "rhetoric." Whether we choose to call them "philosophers" or "sophists," or simply "sages" (*sophoi*), their verbal expertise and psychological insights often challenged the "wisdom" and the engaging stories of the poets. In one Platonic dialogue (set ca. 440 BCE in Athens) the great sophist Protagoras half-jokingly suggests that those poets of old, Homer, Hesiod, and Simonides, were simply sophists in disguise (*Prot.* 316d), and one of his own favorite teaching techniques was to critique famous passages of poetry, showing how much wiser and more skillful he (and, in turn, his students) could be than these old-fashioned and obsolete "teachers" of the past.

These "sophists" were really the first professional literary critics, and their techniques of verbal and rhetorical analysis seem to have been directly adopted—with varying degrees of seriousness and absurdity—by Aristophanes in *Frogs*. In particular, concern for correct usage of words, word definitions and homonyms (as in *Frogs* 1124–69, especially 1153–65 on "return, come back . . ."), evaluative comparisons between poems and competitive interpretation conducted on the same passage by two rival critics, are all attested of Prodicus, Protagoras, and other sophists. Aristophanes was clearly familiar with such procedures, and from his lost play, *Banqueters* (from the early 420s), some lines are preserved in which rare Homeric words are being explained, along with technical legal expressions, very much in the style of sophistic professors. Likewise, Aristophanes and his audience are clearly familiar already with the notion of measuring words, meters, and phrases as if they were pieces of furniture or sculpture, or components of an architectural edifice, to check if they are properly "straight," "well-fitted-together," "correctly proportioned," etc., all of these terms doubtless characteristic of the new critical methods employed by the new-fangled verbal experts and educators.

In the field of musicology too, the theorist Damon of Oa was expounding radical ethical-psychological doctrines concerning the character-forming effects of different musical scales and attunements (theories which in due course came to influence Plato and others). So, for those who wished (probably only a very small minority of intellectuals and professional teachers, to be sure), it was now possible to cite a scientific justification for one's subjective musical preferences, and—perhaps more importantly—for the condemnation of unconventional musical experiments and/or the bad taste of lower-class audiences.

Both in the verbal-grammatical criticism of Protagoras and Prodicus, and in the musical theories of Damon, the emphasis on criteria of "correctness," "straightness," "uprightness," "harmony," etc. tended to carry moral-political implications as well as purely technical ones.

Likewise in *Frogs*, when Euripides describes the Spirit of older Tragedy as an obese female figure (overfed by Aeschylus and his puffed-up language) who needed to be put on a diet (*Frogs* 939–44), or when Aristophanes' rival Pherecrates brings onstage a Muse behaving like an elderly prostitute (*Cheiron* fr. 155; cf. *Frogs* 1306–28, both discussed in chapter 5), these are poetic-dramatic concretizations of aesthetic evaluations that (in later decades) would be expressed in a more specifically literary-critical vocabulary. By the time of Callimachus and Cicero these will have become purely literary metaphors (the "thin" style vs. the "inflated" style, etc.), but in the context of Athenian stage drama—in which actors and choruses appear physically before their audience, and have to move, sing, and dance before their eyes—the sound and character of the performance are intimately related to the physical appearance, vocal-choreographic agility, and elegance of the performers. So the medical procedures of diet, walks, etc. that Euripides describes (and about which Hippocratic treatises write at length) indeed came to be part of the training of actors and orators (Quintilian *Inst. Orat.* 11. 22–29).

One strategy for rescuing poetry—and music too—from attempts to load it with excessive moral, educational, and epistemological value (a strategy that also, of course, might tend to relegate such arts rather to the periphery of a philosopher's or politician's interest) was to insist that the sole purpose of these arts was to provide pleasure. Art is for art's sake, that is, for aesthetic satisfaction and delight: so truthfulness, ethical improvement, psychological purgation, etc., are more or less irrelevant. Such views are not found directly expressed before the later fifth century, and are associated above all with the names of Gorgias and Democritus (and their successors/followers), whose works unfortunately are largely lost. But we know that they were both very influential, and enough of their work survives in fragments and paraphrases for us to be able to sketch roughly what they were about—and we can tell that Aristotle in particular, in both the *Poetics* and the *Politics*, was very much aware of these theories, and to some degree incorporated them into his own ideas about mimetic art, music, education, and culture. It is likely that Aristophanes was aware of some of the theories, and as we shall see some of his characters (especially Dionysus!) might be said to draw on them from time to time, at least implicitly.

Gorgias of Leontini proposed in one of his publications (quoted by Plutarch *On the Glory of Athens* 348c) the following paradoxical views about drama and its audience: "The one who deceives is juster and more honest than the one who doesn't, while the one [sc. audience member] who is deceived is more intelligent than the one who isn't" (82 B 23 DK; cf. too the "Double Arguments" [*Dissoi Logoi*] 90 B 3.10 DK). Gorgias goes on to explain that tragedy is *supposed* to be a fiction (a "deception"), and not to present reality; hence a playwright is doing his job well if he presents a successful deception, so that the audience will buy into the illusion. An audience member who accedes to this dramatic illusion is being smart (*sophos*, "wise, intelligent"), whereas one who supposes that the characters and events on stage are real and actually happening—i.e., is not "deceived"—is actually himself stupid and "aesthetically incapable." On a slightly different wavelength, the prolific and influential materialist philosopher Democritus of Abdera (ca. 460–400 BCE?) argued that the arts in general, including music and drama, had not arisen from any original social necessity and did not provide any educational or moral benefits, but were simply sources of (optional) pleasure to those whose basic material needs were already taken care of. Plays are for fun, not instruction.

Clearly, to most modern audiences around the world (as to Aristotle when he wrote the *Poetics*), the amount of sheer pleasure provided by melodies, rhythms, colorful and surprising language, unexpected but cleverly justified twists of plot, unusual spectacle, and coordinated movements (etc.) usually comprises a significant proportion of theater's appeal—not just in staged plays, but in movies, TV, opera, rock and dance concerts, etc., as well. In fact, at the end of the *Politics* (8. 1339a–42b) Aristotle—who is by far our most articulate and thoughtful surviving source for classical Athenian attitudes to the theatrical experience—actually begins an analysis (unfortunately, never completed) of the nature of music's appeal and value to human beings, concluding that at least the following four (or five?) payoffs are all to be acknowledged: relaxation, ethical (educational) improvement, psychological excitement/release, play/fun, and mental/psychic "engagement" (*diallagê*)—whatever this last category may be thought to mean. Aristotle's ideas about the pleasures and psychic rewards of tragedy and comedy, as partially outlined in the *Poetics*, seem to assume these same "musical" payoffs, as we would expect given the strong musical and metrical component of these dramatic forms as performed in the Theater of Dionysus.

Of course, if pleasure-giving *is* the chief criterion of artistic (dramatic) excellence, then a democratic process of polling the audience (or the panel of judges) should suffice for the awarding of prizes and assessing of talent. The results of such polls, weekly talent contests, and annual top-ten lists are notoriously erratic, and often appear quite quaint in retrospect. But popularity contests *are* still contests, and there are moments in *Frogs* (as we shall see) when Dionysus seems to be operating in exactly this mode, though we certainly do not encounter in the play any explicit expression of a Democritean or Gorgianic theory of aesthetics—when Euripides remarks that Aeschylus' plays completely lack any "Aphrodite" (1045), the "charm" or sex appeal that he has in mind is rather different.

To most Athenians in Aristophanes' audience, even to many who in fact understood quite a lot about theater and the plays they watched every year, most of the latest theories, technical terms, and critical tools employed by the various experts in their discussions of poetry must often have seemed bizarre and pretentious. Some of them indeed are explicitly mocked in *Frogs*, just as they were in *Clouds* almost twenty years earlier. Yet, as we have seen, the concepts and concerns underlying these terms and tools were not entirely new: the methods of these latest experts (*sophoi, sophistai*) amounted to more of a systematizing of existing notions than a radical new departure in taste and understanding; and Aristophanes himself, whatever his own personal opinions may have been about (the moral effects of) the latest fads in intellectual, poetic, and rhetorical virtuosity, was clearly well-attuned to them and quick to adapt them to comic effect. Indeed, between the sophists and the comic poets the process of developing formal strategies and vocabularies for critiquing literary and musical performance seems to have been a two-way street. And certainly *Frogs* comprises our first and most extensive "treatise" on the criticism of poetry to survive from antiquity.

Propriety and Genre

As we have seen, poetry and drama, like "music" (*mousikê*) in general, were recognized as being a sophisticated "craft, art, skill," one that required expert manipulation of a particular medium and set of artistic tools—in this case, words combined with melody and rhythm (and, in the case of drama, costumes and choreography as well). Although originality and "adventurousness" (as at *Frogs* 99) were always appreciated, ancient audiences (like, for example, many modern aficionados of ballet or opera or jazz) were particularly attuned to issues of idiomatic correctness, formal mastery, and technical proficiency. The best poet or playwright, by definition, should thus be the one who had the best technical control of his materials: vocabulary, figures of speech, narrative and argumentative skill, rhythms, melodies (since most Greek poetry was sung), vocal timbre and articulation, and even choreography (since most lyric poetry was also accompanied by dance-steps). *poiêtikê technê* ("the art of poetry"—for which Latin uses the translation *ars poetica*) was thus a demanding, but clearly definable and even measurable, craft, with its own specific rules and techniques; and the more clearly defined these rules were—especially as to what *kind* of poem, or drama, was expected on a specific occasion, the easier it should be for judges to assess which poet (and performers) had crafted the most emotionally and aesthetically stimulating performance. That was what musical/poetic/literary criticism (*krisis*) was about, and it is certainly what Aeschylus and Euripides focus on for much of their competition in *Frogs*.

But the boundary between technical expertise and moral-political correctness can become quite fuzzy in the evaluation of the arts; and the boundary line tends to disappear completely whenever the issue arises of genre and the "proper" way for a poet to practice his craft in a traditional medium. Such "propriety" is generally determined and governed by a mixture of technical rules and moral imperatives, even though this mixture itself may remain largely undefined, nebulous, and even variable. In fact, the whole contest of *Frogs* may be said to involve a dispute over the "proper" nature and practice of tragedy—which brings us back to all three of our components of poetic "wisdom." A good poet does it right, a bad poet gets it wrong—and this right and wrong are what the judge and audience have to determine as they go along. So the "expertise," "cleverness," and "good sense" that Aristophanes keeps alluding to in his Athenian audience is as much an implicit sense of propriety—a sense of shared values and expectations as to what a good tragedy is supposed to be like—as it is a particular set of critical skills.

Overall, despite all the recent incursions into the domains of poetic *sophia* by new-fangled intellectuals of one kind or another, in Aristophanes' theatrical world—as, presumably, in everyday Athenian life—poets still clearly retained much of their traditional prestige and authority as purveyors of truth and knowledge, moral and practical benefit, and stimulating entertainment. Good poets were still expected to tell the truth (except when they were inventing brilliantly provocative falsehoods/fictions), and to produce morally edifying guidance (except when they were behaving as shameless low-lifes and degenerates, for the sake of generating laughs), And because the standard term for "training" a chorus was *didaskô*—the same word used for "teaching" in general—there was perhaps an additional level of expectation that playwrights who were "granted a chorus" by the *archôn* should actually "teach" the citizens something good and worthwhile. Such are the (under-theorized, amateurish, yet fairly wide-ranging and realistic) critical assumptions that "Aeschylus" and "Euripides" are found to agree upon and that Dionysus employs as the basis of his decision-making during the course of *Frogs*, as the principle is maintained that poets should be judged by their success or failure in "making the people in their communities better" (1009–10) through their "demonstrations" (1032) and "teaching" (1055).

So let us turn to the contest itself as it unfolds in *Frogs*.

Poetic *Krisis* (Judging) in *Frogs*

Early in the play, when Dionysus is trying to explain to Heracles his peculiar devotion to (infatuation with) the plays of Euripides, we get to see some of the criteria that he is implicitly, and often facetiously, using as the basis of his preference: "What I want/need is a really accomplished, sophisticated poet (*poiêtês dexios*)" (71). Dionysus goes on to say that by this he means a "potent poet" (96), one who can compose phrases that are "noble" (97) and "adventurous" (99), such as "sky, Zeus' bedroom," and "the foot of time" (100). Heracles reminds him of some surviving—and quite successful—tragedians, such as Sophocles' son Iophon, or Agathon, Xenocles, and "a bunch of other young whippersnappers" (89) who are even more "talkative" (91) than Euripides. But Dionysus rejects these as being mere "left-overs," flash-in-the-pan imposters:

> . . . Ruiners of the Art [of tragedy]!
> As soon as they get a chorus, they just piss once on Tragedy
> And that's it, they're finished!
>
> (93–95)

It appears from this brief exchange that Dionysus thinks of the ideal poet (Euripides) as being both daringly innovative and yet also solidly capable of maintaining the manly dignity and weight of tragic tradition. So he must be "clever, skilled, accomplished" (71 *dexios*—a term that shares several of its semantic functions with *sophos* and recurs frequently in the play overall [71, 700, 762, 1114, 1121, 1370]—and one to which we shall return), yet also "fertile, potent" (96 *gonimon*) and capable (in the terms of Dionysus' vivid metaphor) of repeatedly impregnating the Art/Muse of Tragedy, whereas the current batch of poets can barely manage a single ejaculation in their whole career, and even this may be mere "piss" rather than spunk.

This quick discussion between Dionysus and Heracles has in fact revealed in passing that not only Sophocles (also recently deceased, like Euripides), but also possibly Agathon and Iophon might well have been capable of turning out "noble" and "clever" enough plays—but for various reasons they are ruled out. Then with Dionysus' further discounting of Xenocles, Pythangelus, and the "thousands of others who are still composing tragedies, prattling away miles more glibly than Euripides" (86–91), he seems implicitly to be attributing exceptional weightiness, durability, and even "nobility" to Euripides' poetry—even despite his joke about Euripides' "stop-at-nothing, criminal character" (80) and Heracles' dismissal of those "adventurous" phrases as sheer "rubbish" (104). The audience's critical appetite has been whetted: is Euripides deserving of all this fuss (and resurrection) or not? Is he a heavyweight, or just a sensationalist?

Later, once the scene has shifted to the Underworld, it is not Dionysus but "the people, the masses" down there who actually instigate the competition, as if this is a customary and straightforward way to settle any such dispute (like a public referendum in modern American politics):

[Servant] As soon as Euripides arrived down here,
He started giving recitations of his poetry
For all the burglars and muggers and thugs
(And there's lots of these in Hades); and when they heard
His double-arguments and turns and intricacies
They went totally crazy, and thought he was the greatest
    (sophôtaton).
So he got all fired up and tried to claim the chair
That Aeschylus had been sitting on.
[Xanthias] Didn't he get pelted <with stones> for that?
[Servant] No; the masses clamored to set up a contest
As to which of them is the better at that art (tên technên
    sophôteron).
[Xanthias] You mean, the masses of criminals?
                                               (771–81)

And so, in deference to popular opinion (implicitly, the opinion of the riff-raff), Plouton has agreed:

> [Servant] He's setting up a contest (*agôna*) right away, a trial (*krisin*),
> An examination between them in their artistry (*tês technês*).
>
> (785–86)

"Contest . . . trial . . . examination": this is very much a popular and populist way of deciding things, in the Underworld as in democratic Athens itself. And as the Servant sarcastically observes, the more "worthy" group of people, that is, those who would prefer Aeschylus to retain his chair, are in a minority down there, just as they are among the current audience (782–83).

When the two playwrights appear and the contest gets under way, they readily agree, without argument, about the range of technical-aesthetic, intellectual, and moral-educational qualities that poetry in general should be expected to promote:

> [Aesch.] Answer me this: what are the qualities for which one should admire a poet?
> [Eur.] **Skillfulness** (*dexiotêtos*), and also giving **intelligent advice**,
> And because we **make people better** in their cities.
>
> (1008–10)

Once again the key term is *dexios* (here in its nominal form, *dexiotês*). I have translated it here as "skillfulness"; above I used "accomplished." Literally the word means "using the right hand <well>" (as in our own "dexterity"), but as noted above it can involve more than mere technical skill: inventiveness, boldness, perhaps even "taste." In a sense, we might say that the whole contest between Aeschylus and Euripides will be about the proper definition of *dexios poiêtês*, and Aristophanes even signals this by having the Chorus remark, in the middle of the contest (1110), that nobody need fear that this audience is too slow-witted to appreciate the "finer points" under examination, since "they are veterans . . . and they all have their little books and learn all kinds of clever things (1114, *ta dexia*)." As for the other terms that are agreed upon here, these seem more straightforward, in light of our previous discussion in this chapter: poets should give "good advice," and (thereby?) make their audiences "better people." The play here on the root *poie-* is clever and engaging: the *poiêtês* (lit. "maker") by "making" (creating, composing, crafting) good poems or plays "makes" people better. It sounds simple, and obvious. But how do poems "make people better"? Is it by presenting only positive and morally uplifting models of behavior and concealing all elements of wickedness and moral failure, even if these do actually exist in the world? Is a "good" poem/play one that contains only examples of "good" behavior? Such are precisely the tactics that Plato's Socrates will use in his attack on poetry in the *Republic* (386a–401c); and these principles are still invoked by government censors, religious zealots, and "moral majority" groups in many parts of the world today. How would Aristophanes' audience have reacted to Aeschylus' assertion? Probably a good number would have accepted it without demur, or with minimal hesitation; but this is certainly not Aristophanes' last word on the matter in *Frogs*.

In fact, Aeschylus returns to this issue of the poet as teacher and social benefactor a few lines further on:

> [Aesch.] Consider, how right from the beginning
> The noblest of the poets have always been useful and
>   beneficial:
> Orpheus showed us mystic ceremonies, and to refrain from
>   bloodshed,
> While Musaeus revealed to us oracles and cures from
>   diseases;
> Then Hesiod taught us how to work the land, the seasons
>   of the crops, ploughing;
> And as for divine Homer, where did he acquire all his
>   honor and glory,
> If not from the fact that he provided high-quality teachings
> About men's battle-formations, valorous conduct (*aretas*),
>   and weaponry?
>
>   (1030–36)

The idea that Homer was to be valued primarily—or at all—as an effective teacher of practical battle-skills would strike us nowadays as silly; but it recurs, and is apparently taken seriously, in, e.g., Plato's *Ion*, a dialogue in which a famous rhapsode's claims for the social usefulness of Homeric epic are steadily eroded under Socratic questioning until all that remains is its alleged value as instruction for generals like Agamemnon. More commonly, however, Homer and other poets were approved for providing inspiring examples of valor (Achilles, Hector . . .), endurance and quick-wittedness (Odysseus), strength (Heracles), etc.—though in due course Plato will object (e.g., in the *Republic*) to the excessive emotionalism and unreliable morality of even these heroes, as well as to the unbelievable and improper conduct of the gods as described in the epics.

If poets are to be judged for their effectiveness as teachers, then (so both Aeschylus and Euripides agree) it should be possible for them to evaluate each other's success or failure by looking closely at the moral and intellectual characteristics of the Athenian citizens who have been watching their respective plays. So Aeschylus boasts that his fellow citizens were made more valorous and militaristic by watching his plays ("breathing spears and lances . . ., their hearts six ox-hides thick," [1016–17]), while Euripides has turned them into "runaways, cheats, and riff-raff" (1014–15). Aeschylus cites his own *Seven against Thebes* as having inspired its audience to want to be brave soldiers (1019–22)—whereupon Euripides retaliates that the play would actually inspire the Thebans, who are Athens' enemies. Neither of them acknowledges that the main theme of the play is really fratricide and Eteocles' moral dilemma; instead, the naive equation of warlike subject matter with making men brave is allowed to stand. This is literal-mindedness at its most extreme, as if Athenians could only be inspired by the image of other Athenians and no audience can put itself imaginatively into a different subject position from their own. But the general notion that audiences *are* affected and even changed by the plays they watch is accepted by both, as is the idea that war and manly valor should be a suitable topic for high, serious tragedy—with Aeschylus adding the further detail (crucial to his whole case throughout the contest, and disputed by his modernistic rival) that such mighty topics require big, impressive-sounding words to be properly conveyed, i.e., the "decorum/propriety" argument.

Aeschylus' next example, *The Persians*, is chosen on similar principles, to show that he "taught <the citizens> to desire to defeat their adversaries" (1026–27). But it produces an oddly tangential reaction from Dionysus: "I certainly enjoyed it a lot when I heard the dead Darius and the chorus clap their hands together like this and say 'Iauoi!'" (1029–30). For Dionysus (sitting in the front row in the Theater, presumably) it was apparently the ghost-raising ritual and exotic choral music that had brought especial delight, rather than the reminders of military prowess. The switch from moral-political "teaching" to musical-choreographical (aesthetic) entertainment is quick and spontaneous. Is it meant to suggest that Dionysus is an irresponsible judge? Or does it just go to show that in a poetic contest *anything goes*—whatever points you can score or pleasures you can provide to the audience, you should make the most of them? Certainly we are made aware that the critical standards can shift suddenly and without warning, as they will continue to do throughout the rest of the scene.

So far, both poets have agreed that the subject matter of the plays (*Seven against Thebes, Persians*) was both factually true (in mythological/historical terms) and evocative of strong audience responses. But when Aeschylus begins to criticize Euripides for his choice of sleazy subject matter in his plays (1043ff), an interesting critical wrinkle is introduced by Euripides' response:

> [Aesch.] By Zeus, I certainly didn't keep writing about
>   whores like Phaedra and Stheneboea;
> Indeed, nobody can claim that I ever wrote about a
>   woman in love at all.
> [Eur.] Of course not! You were never touched in the
>   slightest by Aphrodite!
> [Aesch.] I should hope not! But in your case and your family,
> She [i.e., Aphrodite] sat down all too heavily right on top
>   of you;

> She turned you over completely on your ear!
> [Dion.] <to Eur.> By Zeus, that's true, you know! You
>   yourself ended up
> Being hard hit by all the bad things you were writing
>   about other people's wives.
> [Eur.] <to Aesch.> What harm are my Sthenoboeas doing
>   to the city, you scumbag?
> [Aesch.] You made noble women, the wives of noble men,
> Decide to drink hemlock [= commit suicide] in shame at
>   your Bellerophons.
> [Eur.] But wasn't that an already existing and true story
>   about Phaedra that I wrote up for the theater?
> [Aesch.] Yes, of course, it was already in existence; but a
>   poet, surely,
> Is supposed to cover up and conceal things that are really
>   wicked,
> And not bring them on stage or promote them publicly.
> Little children have a teacher (*didaskalos*) to guide them
>   and give them advice;
> But for grown-ups there are poets.
> So we really must at all costs tell them things that are really
>   good.
>
> (1043–56)

So Euripides is insisting here that his plays actually tell the truth in exposing the nasty but inescapable realities of human (especially female) behavior, while Aeschylus argues that playwrights should select carefully—even edit and self-censor—their traditional material so as to provide only good and enlightening examples to their audiences. This is a crucial issue (however flippantly introduced here) in the history of literary criticism, and of the arts in general. Should artists reveal ugliness as well as beauty, show the world in all its complexity, including evil, injustice, moral ambiguities, and corruption? Or is their task to use their art to make everything beautiful, reassuring, and uplifting? In either case, is it "truth" or "fiction" (even "lies") that they are representing in their work?

These questions about the proper objects and style of tragic representation are of course a mirror image of the concerns raised (absurdly and indirectly) in the opening lines of the play, in the repartee between Xanthias and Dionysus about their audience. Even though the discussion there is not framed as being overtly about aesthetic principles, and Dionysus has not yet said anything about his yearning for Euripides, Aristophanes' competitive dilemma has already been outlined (as we noted in chapter 1, pp. 3–4). *What is Comedy supposed to (be) like? What should its audience be expecting?* As a proper theatrical slave, Xanthias wants to make the "usual" jokes about carrying oppressive burdens, having sore shoulders, farting and shitting, and all the other set pieces for eliciting crude laughs. But his master has higher standards, and is more "sophisticated" (4 *asteion*: lit. "urbane, citified"), and regards such comic routines as cheap and nauseatingly predictable:

> [Dion.] Don't say any of those things, I beg you,
> Except when I'm ready to throw up anyway! (11)

At this point Xanthias alludes to some of Aristophanes' best-known rivals:

> Then why did I have to carry all this stuff
> If I can't do any of the things Phrynichus usually does,
> And Lycis, and Ameipsias too?
> They all carry [i.e., their characters carry] stuff in their
>   comedies!
>
> (12–15)

What Xanthias wants to "do" is what every comic poet "does/makes/writes" (*poiei*), i.e., get the audience to laugh at stock scenes, characters, and routines (in the terms of Italian Renaissance Commédia, *lazzi*). But Dionysus is eager to innovate, to avoid clichés, and to "make" something better than what those predictable old rival playwrights churn out every year. (All three of these comedians won first prizes, and Phrynichus in particular was consistently successful, perhaps more so overall than Aristophanes, though in this particular competition *Frogs* actually defeated Phrynichus' *The Muses*.) In any case this opening scene has reminded the audience genially that they, like the playwright himself, may be as inconsistent and arbitrary as they wish: they can enjoy the repetition of standard routines (a vital element in comedy, and in many other forms of art; cf. Homeric formulae and type-scenes; musical licks; poetic tropes, and commonplaces; etc.) even while they can appreciate someone who is smart and hip enough to parody and critique such old forms and provide something new, bold, and unexpected. Aristophanes—the creator of both Xanthias and Dionysus (and later, of both "Aeschylus" and "Euripides")—can give us both sources of pleasure and satisfaction, and even show them arguing with one another.

Is Aristophanes himself truly dissatisfied with "old-fashioned" comic routines? Does he expect his audience to have developed a superior, more sophisticated type of humor by now? Probably not. All of his plays demonstrate a similar blend, or alternation, of the utterly predictable and the startlingly unexpected, the gross and the subtle, the old and the new. Thus, in the *parabasis* of his revised *Clouds*, Aristophanes, via his chorus leader, had reproached the audience for their previous poor taste in not awarding first prize to the earlier version of this play:

> Spectators, I shall speak to you frankly and freely
> The truth, by Dionysus who raised and nurtured me!
> So may I win the victory, and be regarded as a skilled, good poet (*sophos*);
> Just as I previously thought that you were expert spectators (*dexious theatas*),
> And that this play was actually the smartest (*sophôtata*) of all my comedies,
> So I felt that you should be the first ones who deserved to taste it—
> And it was a play that had cost me a lot of hard work!
> But then I was defeated by a bunch of crude guys
> When I absolutely did not deserve to lose. I blame *you* for all of that,
> You supposedly clever ones (*sophois*), the ones I did all that work for!

> Even so, I shan't ever give up on [betray?] the real experts (*dexious*) among you
> ... So now this new comedy of mine, like Electra, has come before you
> Looking to find [suitably] smart and tasteful spectators (*sophois theatais*) ...
>
> (*Clouds* 518–27, 534–35)

This speech is full of metatheatrical allusions (mainly to Aeschylus' *Libation Bearers*), and continues by making a proud distinction between this new, modest, tasteful comedy and the crude antics of the poet's rivals:

> She [Electra/my play] doesn't have a leather *thing* stitched to her,
> All red at the tip and thick, to make the kids laugh,
> And she doesn't make jokes about bald men, or shake her hips in sexy dances,
> And there's no old man hitting people with his stick while he speaks his lines
> To cover up the fact that the jokes are really terrible . . .!
>
> (*Clouds* 538–43)

We have no way of knowing for certain whether or not Aristophanes' characters in this (second version of) *Clouds* did actually refrain from wearing the traditional phallus attached to their costumes—but most commentators on the play have regarded this as unlikely. You cannot have an Old Comedy (or even a New Comedy, for that matter) at Athens without that "leather thing, all red at the tip . . ."; that is part of what Dionysus has always required and what the audience expects. But the nice idea here, that "Electra," as a well-brought-up, sophisticated young lady-drama, is the "daughter" of a noble father-poet and will help him achieve victory without resorting to crude slapstick humor and sexual suggestiveness, draws the "expert, intelligent" (*dexios, sophos*) members of the audience into agreeing implicitly with the poet's higher standards of humor and literary sophistication. As in the opening of *Frogs*—and as in all of Aristophanes' plays, we might say—the audience thus find themselves being simultaneously encouraged to laugh "like little children" at the same-old, same-old jokes and crudities, while also patting themselves on the back as being "above all that," primed and ready for something intellectually and artistically more challenging. Their poet really is special and unique—even if their own track record of giving him first prize is not spotless.

During the initial buildup for the tragedians' competition (795–906), while the contestants are arriving and the chairs (and other stage machinery) being set up, the Chorus and Dionysus express their excitement at the prospect of testing and measuring exactly the words, structures, and ideas of the two poets, for their cleverness, novelty, and precision. "The <whole> musical art is going to be weighed in the balance and they'll be bringing out rulers and measuring tapes of words . . ." (797–800). The prime criterion appears to be technical skill and originality, as Euripides plans to "test the tragedies word by word" (802 *basaniein*, a term used normally either for "testing" gold and silver coins with a touchstone or, by extension, for "torturing" a slave witness who is giving testimony in court; cf. chapter 2, pp. 47–48; again 826–7 "smooth tongue, metal-detecting mouth-worker of words.)" At the same time, the anticipated confrontation is described—especially from Aeschylus' perspective—in terms more of a wrestling match or Homeric battlefield, or even a" hurricane" at sea (848), than of a civil servant's coin-testing station or artisan's workshop:

> There'll be helmet-glittering struggles of lofty-crested
>   words . . .
> He'll roar and hurl his bolted-together utterances,
> Ripping apart timbers with his gigantic blasts of breath. . . .
>   (822–25)

Decibel-level, wind-speed, and over-the-top bombast seem likely to be Aeschylus' "weapons" for the verbal contest to come: wild, destructive, uncontrollable, a far cry from the "tools of art" that the stage machinery seems built to assess.

Once the proper preliminaries have been carried out (sacrifice and prayers from all parties, 847–903), the two poets let fly at one another. Euripides begins by complaining that Aeschylus' plays contained insufficient dialogue and action: a character would sit silently on stage while the chorus sang interminably long odes; and, when the character did eventually speak, it was in language that was so far removed from ordinary speech and so pretentiously inflated and artificial that the audience could not understand any of it. They were just mystified and confused, and only enjoyed the plays because they themselves were too naive and stupid to recognize the pointlessness and emptiness of what they were watching:

> [Eur.] He hoodwinked the audience and cheated them,
> Slow-witted morons that they were back then . . .
> (909–10)

Euripides' own plays, he insists, were streamlined, quick-moving, and accessible, with characters of all social levels speaking clear, everyday language:

> [Eur.] . . . Not horse-cocks and goat-stags, like you!
> . . . No, as soon as I took over the Art (*technēn*) from you,
> All puffed-up and swollen with bombast and obese words,
> I slimmed her down immediately and took off that weight
> With a diet of neat little words, exercise, white beets,
> And juice strained from slick-talking books . . .
> And, from the very beginning of the play,
> I didn't leave any character idle: everyone spoke,
> Women, slaves, masters, girls, old women—everybody!
> . . . It was totally democratic!
> (937–51)

Predictably outraged, Aeschylus retorts that the compound adjectives and traditional epic-mythological figures in his plays are what should be expected in tragedy, whereas Euripides' everyday language and inclusion of all kinds of characters and subject matter have debased the art (950 "you deserved to die for that!"). Their disagreement about the type of language appropriate to tragedy, and the contrast between Aeschylus'"grand, inflated, fat" Art and Euripides' new model, "talkative, slim, quick," has already revealed that issues of "decorum" (what *is* the most appropriate diction for tragedy?) are deeply and inseparably implicated with questions of subject matter, audience, social class and gender, and even morality. And this is the point at which Aeschylus pins Euripides down, and gets him to agree on the moral-political-didactic role of poetry (1008–10, "making people better in their communities," discussed above).

So the ensuing episode focuses on the *proper* subject matter, *proper* language and characters, with Aeschylus insisting that his plays contained no lustful females, no kings wearing rags (1063, a reference to Euripides' *Telephus* in particular), no outspoken low-life characters (950–58, 1069–73), but plenty of war heroes and heroic conflict between men—all expressed in the language appropriate to "demigods," i.e., epic-style heroes:

> [Aesch.] Great thoughts and mentalities require equal-sized words to express them!
> And it's only right and proper for demigods to use bigger and better language,
> Just as they wear much finer and more impressive clothing than the rest of us.
>
> (1059–62)

The term here for "more impressive" has associations of "august, solemn, reverend," and captures exactly the aura of larger-than-life stateliness and dignity that is characteristic of most Greek tragedy, the heightened language, restrained meters, and measured stage movements (as compared with the knock-about antics, phalluses, broken up metrics, and colloquialisms of comedy). This is a matter of "propriety, appropriateness"—what the Romans termed *decorum*. Classical notions of literary and artistic genres were heavily conditioned by this principle: a "high" style was "fitting" for "high, noble" subjects. Tragedy is meant to be "high and mighty"—and Euripides has debased and corrupted it. In other plays Aristophanes extracts more comic mileage out of Euripides' controversial habit of having heroes or kings (e.g., Telephus) appear in his plays costumed in rags, as beggars or spies in disguise; but in *Frogs* Aeschylus's focus is mostly on the way in which he has "pimped" the art through presenting on stage "those whores, Phaedra, Stheneboea, and the others . . ." (1043–52). In Aeschylus' tragic world, there is no place at all for *erôs* and Aphrodite.

From 1119 to 1248, the debate shifts to dramatic technique: pacing, building of tension, and in particular the "prologues" (= opening scenes) of their plays. The opening lines of several of each tragedian's plays are closely examined, critiqued for repetitiousness, obscurity/ambiguity of expression, realism vs. conventionality and formalism, predictability . . . in very much the way that Hesiod and Homer are made to critique each other's lines in their (fictional) *Contest* mentioned above. The comic climax of this section comes with Aeschylus' deployment of the "little oil-bottle" (*lêkythion*): much discussed by modern critics and still a little puzzling (see further chapter 5). This episode probably involves both a play on Euripides' loss of virility (in contrast to Dionysus' claims in the opening scene) and the predictability of his rather prosaic style.

From prologues to lyrics: Aeschylus' high-flown, yet standardized choral "rhapsodies" are pitted against Euripides' evocative odes and monodies, melodically and metrically ever-shifting while also linguistically and thematically rather mundane. This segment of the play is in some respects the most virtuosic, in its brilliant parodying of the two great authors' most characteristic—or most extreme—lyric styles; and at every turn the technical and the moral issues are inextricable: what *should* tragedy *sound* like? Are Euripides' innovations to be lauded as bringing this art form up to date and opening it up to a wider cross-section of the Athenian audience? Or should we cringe at them, as corrupting the four-square and time-tested beauties of the age of Marathon? (We will have more to say about these old vs. new styles in the next chapter.)

In Conclusion: Which Criterion Prevails?

After one more round of measuring (whose words are *heavier?*, predictably won by Aeschylus with his huge words and hefty images: see Fig. 1–1b), Dionysus is still wavering as to whom to pronounce the victor. How will he ever decide? At last, for the final stages of the contest, the terms shift, to the direct measurement of each poet's political "good sense, wisdom" (*nouthesia . . . sunesis*). Which of them can impart the most useful practical advice to help the city in its present difficulties? Although each of them does continue to quote lines from his own plays in formulating such advice, the focus is very much on the city of Athens, now (Alcibiades, the War, issues of citizenship), not on aspects of tragic technique and style. In the meantime, of course, we have also heard from the Chorus (in its *parabasis*), and have been reminded once again of the sociopolitical priorities that should be guiding the city's leaders, including—implicitly—the tragedians. Thus, in the end it is a combination of practical and moral excellence that is required [*sophia* (a) and (b)], with cleverness, technical skill [*sophia* (c)] taking a back seat. We will return to examine this closing scene and Dionysus' final choice in chapter 7.

Suggestions for Further Reading

On the powers and attractions of poetry in Archaic and early Classical Greece, including the question of "truthfulness": Detienne (1996), Ferrari (1989), Walsh (1984).

On Greek poetic and musical competitions, and the competitive habit in various performance contexts, including Aristophanic comedy: Biles (2011), Griffith (1990), Lloyd (1992), Rosen (2004), Ruffell (2002), Wright (2009).

On the sophists and the practice of rhetorical and linguistic criticism in the fifth century: Ford (2002), Kerferd (1981), Richardson (1975), Tell (2011); and on Gorgias' theories about the effects of poetry and drama: Rosenmeyer (1955), Segal (1962).

On the place of *Frogs* within the "history" of ancient literary criticism (and literacy): Denniston (1927), Goldhill (1991), Hunter (2009), Lowe (1993), O'Sullivan (1992), Russell (1981), Wehrli (1946), Willi (2002).

· 5 ·

Old and New Styles in Tragedy

Aeschylus, Euripides, and the Rest

At the beginning of *Frogs* Dionysus says he is pining for a "skilled poet," one who is "potent" and full of adventurous expressions and ideas (71, 96–102; see chapter 4). Later, during their competition, Aeschylus and Euripides agree that poets should "teach" their fellow citizens and make them "better" (1030–56). At the same time, as we have observed in the previous chapter, the overriding concern throughout the contest seems to be for what is "appropriate" to the genre of tragedy: whether this art form should be fat or slim, loud and bombastic or neat and clever, elevated above the ordinary or accessible to the masses. In all of this discussion it is taken for granted that the audience are an experienced group of veteran theatergoers, "smart, sophisticated" and perhaps even "holding their little books" as they watch and judge (1110–18); so they can be relied upon to recognize what makes a good or bad tragedy. This is not a situation like that of the raw and gullible folks being outwitted and bemused by Socrates' new teaching methods in *Clouds*, for example. This audience, both the ghosts in Hades and the Athenians in the Theater, surely know what's what.

Many hundreds of Athenians, boys and men, danced and sang in choruses every year at the City Dionysia, whether in dithyrambs, tragedies, or comedies (see chapter 2). So a significant proportion of the theater audience was somewhat experienced, even expert, in recognizing and assessing various poetic and musical styles and skills, especially in regard to the choral parts—rhythms and melodies; choreography; clarity and tunefulness of singing; etc. Athenian culture in general was highly musical, and the theatergoers were probably more so than average.

Most of the audience members watching *Frogs* in 405 would surely have attended several performances of Euripides' and Sophocles' plays, since both these tragedians were regular competitors at the festivals during the years ca. 430–405. On the other hand, rather few will ever have attended an Aeschylean first performance, since Aeschylus left Athens in 457 (the year after his *Oresteia* won first prize) and died a year later in Sicily. Certainly Aristophanes himself had never done so and had never personally met Aeschylus (since he was probably not born until after 450). So it is reasonable to ask the question, whether anyone watching *Frogs* really had a good firsthand knowledge of what Aeschylean tragedy originally sounded and looked like. At *Frogs* 1026–30, Dionysus remarks how much he had enjoyed seeing and hearing the chorus performing its exotic dance in *Persians* (first performed in 472 BCE): would anyone else in the Theater at this moment (apart from Aeschylus' ghost-character) have attended that first performance?

We are told (though the evidence is far from solid) that a special decree had been passed allowing Aeschylus' plays to be revived and performed at the City Dionysia during the decades after his death, and it seems pretty clear that reperformances of tragedies and satyr-dramas by various playwrights took place, perhaps on a smaller scale, in the deme theaters, mainly during the Rural Dionysia. But we may wonder not only which plays were thus revived but also whether these reperformances kept at all strictly to the original text, let alone to the musical score and choreography. To train an *aulos* player and chorus to play, sing, and dance in a musical style that was now thirty or fifty years old might not be worth the trouble and would probably not win many prizes. Of course Aristophanes himself and a few of the more sophisticated and literate members of his audience (like Dionysus—absurdly—enjoying *Andromeda* while serving on board ship "under Cleisthenes," 48–54) had *read* many of these plays, but those written texts probably provided very little if any information about music, choreography, costuming, or staging.

Writing tragedy, like most skills and occupations in the ancient world, tended to run in families. This was true in the case of Aeschylus, whose sons, nephew, and grandnephews were all successful tragedians (Euphorion, Euaeon, Philocles, Morsimus [mentioned at *Frogs* 151], and Astydamas); true also for Sophocles (his son Iophon, cf. *Frogs* 72–78; grandson Sophocles jr.) and Euripides (a son and/or nephew Euripides jr.); also Carcinus and his sons (Xenocles, cf. *Frogs* 86; and other sons too, *Wasps* 1445ff, discussed below). It seems unlikely that any archaizing tendency or respect for tradition for its own sake would have held back any of these family members from revising and updating the plays of their parents and predecessors. Indeed, we possess at least one conspicuous example of such updating: the final scene of Aeschylus' *Seven against Thebes* as preserved in the medieval manuscript tradition has been completely rewritten so as to follow the plot-line of Sophocles' *Antigone*. We also find in our manuscripts (especially for Euripides) numerous interpolations of varying lengths, many of them apparently made by actors who wished to beef up their parts. Such revisions and adaptations were doubtless standard practice (as they were in England with regard to Shakespeare's plays) and we also have plenty of evidence that actors, musicians, and symposiasts/diners all were in the habit of performing selected snippets from their favorite plays, disregarding context, costume, and original musical setting. The Athenians had no video or audio recordings and no way of preserving past performances, so their ideas of the best, or proper, way to perform Aeschylus—or Euripides, for that matter—were bound to change constantly to suit contemporary taste.

The contest that is staged in *Frogs* is between two playwrights of different generations: thus at every turn it is a contest between old and new as well as between two of the three most famous theater artists that Athens had ever produced. Not surprisingly, Aristophanes has chosen to ignore points of similarity and continuity so as to emphasize the contrast between them, offering thereby a kind of comic commentary on the evolution of the whole art of tragedy during the fifth century. This is obviously one reason (in addition to the fact that *Frogs* was almost certainly planned and largely written before Sophocles died, so that references to his recent passing and arrival in the Underworld were only added at the last minute) why Sophocles is not included in the contest: he was in many respects an intermediate figure and his plays offered less material that was suited to extreme contrasts and ridiculous parody.

Unfortunately, we possess almost nothing of the works of Aeschylus' famous predecessors and contemporaries, Phrynichus, Pratinas, and Carcinus—all of whom enjoyed high reputations and won several victories in the tragedy competition. So it is impossible for us to determine how distinctive Aeschylus' style really was in its day. We do know that songs from Phrynichus' plays were still familiar to Athenians—especially to older and more old-fashioned people—during the later fifth century. Aristophanes' *Wasps* presents a hilarious scene in which a drunken old man sings and dances his favorite melodies (mostly those of Phrynichus) in an informal competition with the younger and hipper practitioners of the "New Music" (1445–1537); and Phrynichus is also mentioned earlier in that play in a wonderful Aristophanic portmanteau word (*Wasps* 220 *archaiomeliSidônoPhrynichêrata*, "lovely-ancient-Phrynichus'-honey-Sidon-songs . . ."; cf. *Birds* 748–50). Sidon was a wealthy (largely Phoenician) city in Syria, and it seems that eastern (Ionian, Anatolian, Levantine, Persian) themes and stylistic features were characteristic of Phrynichus' style, especially his choral lyrics. Aeschylus' *Persians* likewise has extensive choral songs in "Ionic" rhythms, lists of foreign names, exotic cries of lamentation, and even a scene of necromancy. Indeed, Athens during the careers of Phrynichus and early Aeschylus (ca. 520–470 BCE) was heavily involved with Ionian cultural forms, especially among the upper-class symposium-set: both the visual art (e.g., the so-called "Anacreontic" vases) and the literature of this period indicate that elite men's costume, sympotic music and poetry, and perhaps dance as well, all tended to favor "luxurious" eastern styles.

Aeschylus was regarded as having inherited much from Phrynichus. Thus Euripides in *Frogs* complains that Aeschylus' audience was "really slow-witted because they'd been raised by/with Phrynichus . . ." (910), while Aeschylus remarks later, "From a fine source [sc., the citharodic *nomoi* of Terpander etc., 1281–82] I took them [and added these] to a fine [repertoire],/ so that I wouldn't be seen picking [my flowers] from the same sacred meadow of the Muses as Phrynichus" (1299–1300). The implication here seems to be that Aeschylus' poetic "meadow" was right next to Phrynichus' . . . similar, but containing some choice extra blooms of its own. But, unlike Aeschylus' relatively well-preserved repertoire, it does not appear that anything more than a few songs of Phrynichus—no whole plays—were still available and in circulation by Aristophanes' time.

On the other end of the scale—the "moderns" and their latest trends in tragedy—Euripides did not by any means have the field completely to himself, since Agathon was clearly a major player too by 405 BCE. But Euripides had long been the most dominant and controversial figure (Agathon was much younger, and had only won his first victory in 416 BCE)—and of course Euripides was the one who had just died. In truth, Euripides was more of a contemporary of Sophocles than a successor: Sophocles' career began in the 460s, Euripides' in the 440s, and the two competed against one another on and off for over thirty years. But throughout Aristophanes' career it had been Euripides who had stood out as the beacon of innovative styles and controversial themes—and not only was it Euripides' plays that his comedies most persistently and brilliantly parodied, but Aristophanes himself apparently was regarded as a bit of a "Euripidizer" in his own approach to comedy—as one of Cratinus' comic characters sneeringly remarks (see chapter 1).

Knowledge about the origins and early years of tragedy must have been quite limited for Aristophanes and his contemporaries (as it is for us). Like Aristotle, they must all have been vaguely aware that tragedy had evolved out of dithyrambic choral performances, but it is very unlikely that they (or he) knew in any detail at all how Thespis, Choerilus, Phrynichus, and others had first created the *technē* that Aeschylus inherited. Even though those names of famous predecessors were known, and Thespis in particular was often credited with being the "inventor" of tragedy (whatever that might mean), the earliest whole plays and samples of tragic dialogue and speeches available for anyone to read were quite likely those of Aeschylus himself. Certainly he had been the towering genius of tragic theater during the years between the Persian Wars and the rise of the Athenian Empire in the 450s and had won more victories than any other playwright. And as "Aeschylus" remarks in *Frogs* (868–69), his plays "have not died with me" but endured for subsequent reading and reperformance. Whether or not the later generations of Athenian readers and theatergoers were aware of the stages by which Aeschylus' skills and tragic technique grew from *Persians* (472 BCE), to *Seven against Thebes* (467) and *Suppliant Women* (463?), and eventually to the consummate artistry of the *Oresteia* (458), they certainly did recognize the striking formal and stylistic differences between all of Aeschylus' plays and the plays of his great successors. That is to say, even as Greek tragedy overall remained generally quite consistent and conservative throughout the fifth century (and later) in its conventions, language, and overall structure, there were several immediately recognizable ways in which Aeschylus' plays stood out as being different and more old-fashioned than those of Sophocles and Euripides.

What are the chief differences? And which of these differences are highlighted (with due comic exaggerations and distortions) in the *Frogs* contest? First and foremost, obviously, is Aeschylus' language. Somewhat as Shakespearean or—especially—Miltonic English verse strikes most modern Anglophone speakers and readers as being both amazingly creative and bold, yet also so far removed from everyday language as to be barely intelligible unless one has studied it carefully beforehand, so does Aeschylean poetry sometimes depart strikingly from standard Attic Greek vocabulary and phraseology, and consistently uses longer words and bolder images than that of his successors. Greek epic and lyric, especially in contexts involving gods, heroes, athletic victors, etc., had always employed elevated and "augmented" language, with multiple adjectives (epithets) and longer-than-usual compound words; and for readers and audiences in later centuries such elevation and strangeness were greatly heightened by the fact that so much of that epic dialect consisted of vocabulary and spellings or dialect forms that were by now unrecognizable, even obsolete. The language of choral lyric too tended to be especially heightened and distanced from everyday speech, while also incorporating a good deal of Homeric diction, since this was felt to be appropriate for all "high" poetry (like the old-fashioned Biblical and Miltonic phraseology still found in many highfalutin' nineteenth-century English writers). Aeschylus' diction maintains many of these epic and lyric expressive mannerisms—even exaggerating them at times, with hefty polysyllabic adjectives, bold neologisms, and clusters of complex and unusual images, to a degree unique among classical authors. In his own way, Aeschylus had thus been every bit as "adventurous" in his language as Euripides is claimed to be by Dionysus in *Frogs*.

Euripides in *Frogs* makes much of these habits of Aeschylean speech, to ridiculous effect. Indeed, even before the contest gets under way, as the Chorus is preparing us for the confrontation, they characterize the Aeschylean manner vividly:

> To be sure, the mighty-thunderer will hold terrible wrath
>   within . . .
> . . . There will be glittering-helmeted struggles of
>   lofty-crested speeches . . .
> Bristling the shaggy-necked hair along his hirsute back,
> Roaring, he will hurl forth nail-riveted utterances,
> Tearing them like ships' timbers with his gigantic
>   breath-blasts!
>
> (814, 818, 821–25)

Later too they hail him: "You who first of the Greeks built up towers of august words . . ." (1024). These epic epithets, "mighty-thunderer," "glittering-helmeted" (the constant epithet for Hector in the *Iliad*), "shaggy-necked" (used of a wild boar in the *Odyssey*), and "gigantic" (lit. "earthborn"), together with the emphasis on loudness, battles, towers, and the world of nature (stormy winds, wild boars . . .), all prepare us for a mightily heroic figure of super-human size and scale. Aeschylus himself insists that his subject matter was war and courageous male achievement: "a play stuffed full of Ares [the war-god] . . . the *Seven against Thebes*" (1021); "My genius fashioned many valiant models of men, Patroclus, Teucer and the rest . . ." (1041–42); and so, he claims, the Athenian citizens who watched his plays themselves grew up to be "noble, worthy men, six-feet tall . . ., guys who breathed spears, helmets, shields . . . and hearts seven layers thick" (1014–17). And Aeschylus goes on to articulate to his despised rival exactly the aesthetic principles of decorum and the "high" style *avant la lettre*:

> It is inevitable and obligatory, you poor fool,
> That great ideas and great thoughts generate great verbal
>   expressions too.
> And in any case, it's only to be expected that heroes and
>   demigods
> Employ larger expressions than everyone else!
>
> (1058–60)

The concept of "greatness" thus embraces moral seriousness, elevated social status, and bulky, sonorous, abnormal, polysyllabic language all at once.

From Euripides' perspective in *Frogs*, this kind of language, along with its focus on war, male heroism, and sheer size for the sake of grandiosity, is not calculated to produce quick wits or "communicating like a human being" (*phrazein anthrôpeiôs*, 1058), but only thick heads and stupidity. He describes the speech-patterns of Aeschylus' plays as alternating between dead silence from major characters—"while the choruses sang strings of lyrics," because Aeschylus was too "stupid and simple-minded" to think of any clever dialogue (911–18)—and a few incomprehensible and bizarre expressions, "a dozen ox-hide thick phrases, with great big eyebrows and crests on them, weird monster-terrors that the audience couldn't understand at all" (924–26).

The imagery used to describe Aeschylus' language reminds us not only of Homeric battle scenes and similes, but also of the traditional terms for poetic inspiration and divine power: thunder and mountaintops belong to Zeus (and his mighty opponents, the Giants); breath and wind suggest the "inspiration" of the Muses, while meadows, springs, and rivers are likewise familiar haunts of the Muses and their followers. And indeed *Frogs* is the first place in Greek literature where we unmistakably encounter the opposition between two rival aesthetics of verbal composition: the "high, grand" style vs. the "thin, delicate" style (subsequently developed, through Aristotle and Theophrastus, to Callimachus and the Roman elegists, Cicero and Dionysius of Halicarnassus, and beyond). From one perspective (that of epic and the "sublime"), lofty is valued over low, grand over puny, inspired over mundane, with Aeschylus always counted among the proponents of grandeur. From the other side, the clever, intricate, delicate, and "fine-spun" is preferred over the inflated, rough, and bombastic. And some of this same contrast can be detected also in the critical sniping between (grand old, "bull-eating, wine-drinking") Cratinus and (young, clever, Euripidizing) Aristophanes (above and chapter 1, p. 19).

Elsewhere in his comedies Aristophanes tends to treat "tragic" style as being more or less homogeneous, a high-flown generic manner that can be amusingly contrasted with the speed, earthiness, and colloquialism of comedy, often for parodic effect. Differences between Aeschylus and Euripides may thus be relatively unimportant. But in *Frogs*, for the most part, the contrasts of stylistic register that are addressed are not between tragic and comic, but between Aeschylean and Euripidean tragedy, and these contrasts naturally entail some exaggeration and drawing of black-and-white oppositions rather than scrupulous accuracy and nuance. In this context, it is not surprising that Aristophanes ignores the variations in Aeschylean style (some segments of Aeschylean dialogue, and even song, can in fact be quite straightforward and direct) in order to present it as being relentlessly strange, larger than life, and at times overpowering—and almost incomprehensible. Comedy is generally granted such license to distort, exaggerate, misrepresent.

Likewise, Euripides' complaint about Aeschylus' excessive use of long silences on the part of his main characters (*Frogs* 911ff, quoted above, citing the examples of Achilles in *Myrmidons* and Niobe in *Niobe*), is probably a gross exaggeration, though it is hard for us to assess since we lack both of those plays. The evidence of *Prometheus Bound* (perhaps Aeschylean, but of disputed authorship) and of the

Cassandra scene in *Agamemnon* does indeed confirm that a character's silence could be used to powerful effect; but this is not uniquely an Aeschylean technique: Euripides actually achieves somewhat comparable, though less extreme, effects with his figures of Alcestis (veiled and silent in the final scene of *Alcestis*) and Phaedra, veiled and refusing to respond to the Nurse until the name of Hippolytus provokes her cry (*Hippolytus* 309).

In contrast to the bombastic language and larger-than-life characters of Aeschylus' plays, Euripides in *Frogs* makes much of the fact that his dramas give a voice to everyone, regardless of status or gender: "Right from the beginning, I wouldn't leave anyone idle/but the wife (or "woman," *gunê*) spoke, and the slave no less/and the master, the maiden, and old woman" (947–49). This, he claims, makes his plays more "democratic" (951), and he goes on to assert that he taught everyone—including "all these people here (954, i.e., the theater audience) how to talk . . . weigh, measure, twist their hips [sc. like a wrestler], apply the latest techniques (*technazein*), think around in circles and find evil meanings in everything . . . I'd bring in real everyday things that matter to all of us" (956–59). The implication is that in Aeschylus' plays only the upper classes, and primarily men (kings, soldiers, generals), were given voice ("like Cycnus and Memnon and the rest . . .," 963), and that for this reason only old-fashioned, militaristic men in the audience could therefore learn anything from these types on stage (965–66). This is not, of course, borne out by the evidence of Aeschylus' surviving plays. Five out of seven have female choruses; one of these consists of slaves (*Libation Bearers*), while in two others the chorus is a lower-status or disadvantaged group (*Suppliant Women, Prometheus Bound*). These choruses are all extremely articulate and expressive. Furthermore, the Nurse in *Libation Bearers* (730–82) is as low-status a character as we find anywhere in Greek tragedy; the low-class (male) Watchman of *Agamemnon* (*Ag.* 1–40) likewise makes a strong impression. So we should not accept Euripides' claim too readily here, though we might concede that his plays do contain more—and longer—scenes than Aeschylus' involving minor, low-class characters who are engaged in dialogue with other characters and are given the opportunity to express their opinions and their criticisms of others.

In one objective respect, to be sure, Euripides' plays are certainly more "democratic" and populist than Aeschylus': the consistently lower linguistic register of *all* his characters, both elites and commoners or slaves—they all do sound a bit more like ordinary people, less like epic heroes and demigods both in their speech patterns and in the greater degree of metrical license (more "resolved" short syllables) in the spoken verse line of dialogue, especially in the later plays. That is to say, while Aeschylus' dialogue generally maintains a regular twelve-syllable line, alternating light and heavy syllables ($\times - \smile - / \times - \smile - / \times - \smile - //$), Euripides often "resolves" a long syllable into two short ones and thus fits thirteen or even fourteen syllables into his trimeter (thus, e.g., $\times \smile\smile - / \times - \smile\smile / \times - \smile - //$). This latter feature, even while Euripides' meter never comes close to the degree of freedom and informality of Aristophanic dialogue verses, nonetheless does mark off Euripides' later plays aurally as being distinctively different from the norms of Aeschylean and Sophoclean tragic discourse.

As for the issue of women being represented on the tragic stage—which becomes a major factor in both the stylistic and the moral categories of evaluation as the contest proceeds, with Aeschylus complaining bitterly about Euripides' immoral females, "whores (*pornas*) like Phaedra, Stheneboea, and the rest" (1043)—here too the picture is not quite as simple and one-sided as Aristophanes presents it. When he has Aeschylus state, "Nobody knows of any woman in love that I ever created [in any of my plays]" (1044), he apparently expects us to ignore the conspicuous case of Clytaemestra in the *Oresteia* (*Ag.* 1435–36, *LB* 893); ignore too the marital love of Hypermestra for her bridegroom/husband Lynceus (a key theme in the *Danaids*, the final play of the trilogy to which *Suppliant Women* belonged); and of course Helen's adulterous elopement with Paris/Alexandros is mentioned repeatedly in *Agamemnon*. So it can hardly be maintained that Aeschylus never included "a woman in love" in any of his plays. The crucial difference is that in Euripides' plays the woman's dilemma (Phaedra's feelings for Hippolytus, her stepson; Stheneboea's for Bellerophon, who is the guest of her husband in their household) are highlighted and discussed explicitly onstage, and the tormented female lover is allowed to explain her inner feelings in detail, in a way that Aeschylus never explores for any of his female (and barely for his male) characters. Euripides' critics (including Aeschylus in this play) were apparently horrified by the sympathetic dramatization of a woman openly struggling with her feelings of desire, since such scenes implied that these feelings were deserving of serious attention, perhaps even capable of justification. (In Aristophanes' *Thesmophoriazusae*, by contrast, the women hate Euripides because his plays reveal all their guilty sexual secrets.)

In Greek society, representations of male sexuality and of gods and heroes overwhelmed by passionate feelings, often to the point of even committing serial seduction and rape, were omnipresent, and quite acceptable in tragedy as elsewhere (including, e.g., Athenian vase paintings): Heracles, Theseus, Apollo, Zeus, Agamemnon, Poseidon . . ., the list is endless. But, as in many other societies over the centuries, overt expressions in serious ("high") literature and visual art of female sexuality were another matter entirely, and this was especially true of fifth-century Athens. Respectable women were not supposed to assert themselves against men, nor to be much heard or seen in public. It is a fascinating question (and much discussed by modern critics), why Athenian tragedy throughout the fifth century focused so insistently on stories involving assertive and/or transgressive women. Yet, even here, it was clearly felt to be one thing to present a vengeful Clytaemestra or Electra, a dutiful Antigone or the cousin-hating (but again, father-respecting) daughters of Danaus, but something quite else to make an audience confront a woman whose self-assertion or transgression was fueled primarily and explicitly by sexual desire. Moral outrage was quick to assert itself whenever women were shown exhibiting any significant degree of sexual autonomy, and Athenians then, like many societies in the world today, seem to have been more shocked by such scenes than they were by depictions of even the grisliest acts of violence and mayhem (or male sexual misbehavior).

Thus war, massacres, genocide, family killings, infanticide, virgin sacrifice were all regarded as appropriate for representation in Greek tragedy (as most of them have been in the Bible and on modern TV), whereas "explicit" scenes, or even discussions, of sex were felt to violate much more seriously the audience's sense of propriety. (This is probably the reason why of all Aristophanes' plays *Thesmophoriazusae*, with its hilarious and explicit depictions of cross-dressing, sexual deviance, and gender-bending of all kinds, is the one least well represented in surviving manuscripts.) Opening up this particular (large) can of worms is certainly part of what Euripides in *Frogs* means by his reference to "everyday things that people care about" (959). In actuality, Euripides as his career progressed had begun to include "romantic" plots of a novel kind in his tragedies, most notably in his *Andromeda* (probably 413 BCE), a play in which Perseus' rescue of the beautiful Libyan princess, Andromeda, from a sea-monster, and their mutual love and marriage, had been hugely popular (and much parodied by Aristophanes, especially in *Thesmophoriazusae*). Such romantic themes had previously belonged more in satyr-dramas than in traditional tragedy; and this Euripidean innovation appears to have marked the beginning of a shift towards more serious treatments of love themes on the stage—and to the development of the New Comedy of Menander and his rivals, and ultimately to the Greek romance/novel. The divergent attitudes of Aeschylus and Euripides in *Frogs* on this issue of women and/in "love" thus seem to reflect a genuine uncertainty in critics' minds in the late fifth century as to what was and was not "proper" for serious drama.

What about Euripides' "talkativeness, chattiness" (*lalia*, 1069, cf. 91, 917, 954, 1492; also 751)? Whether or not we might think that Aeschylus has a valid point in his complaint about Euripides' shameless women and the contrast between his own militaristic, "noble," tough-guy ethos and Euripides' everyone-speaks, anything-goes "realism," one cannot disagree with the observation that Euripides' plays are unusually full of scenes of debate, accusations, self-justifications, and verbal and moral hair-splitting of all kinds, confirming both the complaints and the self-justifications presented by the two contestants concerning the rhetorical strategies and dramatic impact of Euripides' "democratic" ways of writing tragedy and his zest for ingenious argumentation. Often the debate scenes in his plays pit two ingeniously argued sets of claims against one another, so that the audience members are required to ask themselves just what standards of truth and morality should be applied (e.g., *Trojan Women, Medea, Ion, Bacchae*) as they are confronted with unexpected and disturbing conjunctions of radically contrasted moral positions without any clear indication or guarantee as to who/what is right or wrong—very much like some of the debates we encounter in the *History* of Thucydides or the sophistical teaching methods of Protagoras and Gorgias.

For some traditionalists and reactionaries, it was all too easy to point to just one side, or even one phrase, taken from such a moral debate, and to cite this as an example of Euripides' own morally degenerate views and social program, or his outright impiety. Thus they seized on the infamous line uttered by Hippolytus, when confronted by the (to him) disgusting revelation of his stepmother's lust for him: "My tongue swore, but my mind/heart (*phrên*) is unsworn" (*Hippolytus* 612; cf. *Frogs* 101–2, 1471). In its original dramatic context, this line constitutes a brief moment during which the young man is contemplating breaking his oath of silence (sworn to the Nurse) in order to denounce Phaedra's revolting immorality to his father, but twice in the course of *Frogs* it is cited as an example of Euripides' own radical and iconoclastic rejection of conventional religious practices. It was not uncommon in antiquity for authors thus to be credited and blamed for the views expressed by individual (fictional) characters in their works, without regard for the context or eventual outcome (i.e., in this case, the fact that Hippolytus decides in the end to honor his oath, doesn't reveal Phaedra's secret, and is even exiled and killed as a result); but most of us nowadays would regard this as a faulty method of artistic evaluation.

In general, Euripides' plays are full of provocative opinions, questionings of conventional piety, expressions and demonstrations of morally dubious intentions and states of mind. Any audience that is paying serious attention to the drama unfolding onstage will be quite well aware that these opinions, questionings, expressions, and demonstrations are only part of the story: they are spoken by individual characters (or the chorus), and are far from being presented as Euripides' own advice or considered judgment as to the overall meaning of his play, or the true nature of the gods, or the correct definition of right and wrong. Nonetheless Euripides' plays were clearly controversial, and he did acquire a reputation during his lifetime for being an iconoclast, a sceptic, a sophistical intellectual—even an atheist. He was frequently associated with Socrates (cf. *Frogs* 1491–92) and with peculiar new ideas about the gods (cf. 888–94); the comic poets made merciless fun of all these supposed eccentricities and improprieties.

Later biographical tradition followed the lead of the comic poets, and the "legend" of Euripides quickly grew to match—but contradict—that of the "heroic" Aeschylus and Sophocles: Euripides was supposed to have spent most of his time alone in a cave on the island of Salamis, working amid a library of books but with minimal contact with other human beings, except for his intellectual companion, Socrates. And, unlike Sophocles, who was said to be perennially "good-tempered" (*Frogs* 82) and to have served his polis with distinction, repeatedly, as an elected politician, and to have been a well-adjusted lover/playboy, with wife, mistress, and boyfriends, Euripides was reputed to have been misanthropic and misogynistic, with two failed marriages (those "shameless wives" again), partly, it was alleged, because his musical collaborator, Cephisophon, lived with him in his house and had an affair with his wife (as is intimated at *Frogs* 944, 1408, 1452–53; cf. fr. 596). As for Aeschylus, his biography emphasized instead (accurately or not, we again have no way of judging) his participation in the Battle of Marathon and lifelong devotion to the Eleusinian Mysteries. It appears that *Frogs* was actually one of the chief texts that shaped these respective portraits—however historically unreliable—of the three great tragedians.

Of all the stylistic criticisms undertaken in *Frogs*, perhaps the most discussed and least agreed-upon by modern critics is the notorious "oil-flask" episode (1197–1247). What should we make of this battle of the "prologues" and the recurrent "lost his little bottle of oil" (*lêkuthion apôlesen*)? Nobody will deny that the scene is very funny, as Aeschylus' constant interjection of this annoying little phrase reduces Euripides to impotent rage and demolishes his claim to have composed "fine opening scenes" (1197). But modern critics are far from agreeing as to why exactly "a little oil-flask" was selected as the item to be thus deployed by Aeschylus (and by Aristophanes). A *lêkythos* is a small jug (of almost any shape, it seems), and a *lêkythion* is a mini-*lêkythos* (*-ion* being a standard diminutive ending in Greek). Probably what is meant here is one of the little oil-flasks, sometimes referred to as *ariballoi* by modern archaeologists, that young Athenian men carried around with them everywhere (rather like a man's wallet, or a lady's purse in the modern era), often attached to their wrist, so they could oil themselves at and after gymnasium workouts or at other opportunities when they wanted to look their sleekest and most attractive. Perhaps the stage-character Aeschylus, who certainly would have belonged to the upper-class, gymnasium-frequenting crowd, is carrying (wearing) one of these, and actually swings it around and "assaults" Euripides and his plays with it. In any case, whether it is a physically visible or merely verbal "oil-flask," the joke seems to depend on at least four simultaneous effects:

1. the predictable and monotonous structure of Euripidean prologues, which very often open with, or at least include, a direct and rather prosaic account of the setting and story so far.
2. the trivial, everyday nature of a "little-oil-flask," implying that the terrible tragedy that is supposedly being set up in this prologue is in fact something quite humdrum and petty (like the lost rooster that is lamented in hyper-Euripidean style at 1331–63). Several of the opening speeches in Euripides' plays are delivered by low-class characters, and sometimes they are engaged in menial activities (as in *Electra*, *Ion*, etc.)—though it is true that several other prologues are delivered by deities, and also true that two of Aeschylus' surviving plays (*Agamemnon* and *Eumenides*) both begin likewise with lower-class, minor characters.

3. the sheer mechanical-comedic effect of this metrical-rhythmical-verbal repetition (like the frog-chorus' *brekekekéx koáx koáx*) is presumably enhanced by the stage antics of Euripides and Aeschylus, and perhaps (as commentators have suggested) by the audience's engagement as well, shouting out the rhythmic *lēkuthion apōlesen* in unison with Aeschylus, when he gives them the cue.
4. the "oil-flask" is obviously a male attribute (most explicitly so at Aristophanes' *Thesmophoriazusae* 139–40 "Why an oil-flask (*lēkuthos*) and a bra . . .? It's like having a looking-glass and a sword . . .!)," and Euripides is thus represented as repeatedly "losing" his poetic virility—picking up on the earlier reference to the need for "a potent poet, a tragedian with balls" (96–98). Several critics have gone further and suggested that the "oil-flask" has a phallic reference, and that some stage business with the bottle and/or the costume phallus took place here. Some confusion, however, (at least for modern readers) is caused by the alternation between the *loss* of the *lēkythion* (as in the recurrent phrase) and Dionysus' remarks that the *lēkythion* "will blow mightily" (1221), that Aeschylus has "attached" the *lēkythos* to these prologues (1234), and that "it grows the way sties grow on people's eyes" (1247). It seems perhaps that the Euripidean heroes have all "lost" what they are supposed to have, but that Euripides is also being beset by an unwanted outcrop of "flasks," phallic and otherwise, being hurled at him by his opponent.

Lyrics and Music

Of all the stylistic contrasts, critiques, and parodies of the old and new tragedians that we encounter in *Frogs*, the most striking and memorable involve their musical (lyric) characteristics. This is itself a valuable reminder of what it was like to attend the theater in classical Athens and what audiences most valued and enjoyed. Although Aristotle in the *Poetics* (mid-fourth century) argues that story line, characterization, ideas, and language (in decreasing order) are really the most important components of a good tragedy, with the musical and visual dimensions ranked fifth and sixth (out of six), he also acknowledges that popular taste ranks these differently: spectacle and music appeal very strongly to the emotions of an audience and often eclipse the more refined and cerebral effects that he himself analyzes so thoughtfully in the main body of his theoretical work. As we noted, Phrynichus' songs were still well known (and loved by some) in Aristophanes' day; and we are told too that Euripides' choral odes came to be memorized by hundreds of his contemporaries and were in demand by theater lovers all over the Mediterranean (e.g., Sicily in 413; Plutarch *Nicias* 29, *Lysander* 15.3). The fact that we ourselves have lost virtually all the music and choreography of fifth-century tragedy and possess only the written texts should not mislead us into thinking that the words were all that mattered, or were even the chief reason for many to attend the theater at all. Greek tragedy, and comedy too, was musical theater.

Although choral songs in tragedy tended to become shorter during the course of the fifth century, and the extent and complexity of actors' roles became correspondingly greater (especially after the introduction in the 440s of a separate prize for actors at the City Dionysia), we should be careful not to slip into thinking that this meant a major reduction in the amount or quality of the music and singing that the audience could look forward to in tragic performances. Tragedy did not become more "prosaic" or any less musical (in the way that, for example, European tragedy of the nineteenth century became generally more bourgeois and "realistic" in its language and plots than its Elizabethan and neoclassical predecessors). On the contrary, Euripides was a central and pioneering figure in the musical revolution that swept through Athens during the later fifth century, and his plays offered a wide range of highly original, imaginative, and sometimes exotic vocal, instrumental, and choreographic forms. His music was thus no less important than Aeschylus' music had been for the impact and popularity of his plays, but it was very different. And Aristophanes makes the most of these differences in *Frogs*, to fascinating and hilarious effect.

Greek tragedy had evolved out of group songs associated with the dithyramb, that is, choral performances honoring Dionysus. The choral lyric component of early tragedy had thus been central. Both Phrynichus and Aeschylus were credited with making significant innovations of their own, though, as we noted above, it is impossible (since so much is lost) to judge in any detail how the evolution of tragic form took place during the decades before Aeschylus' earliest surviving plays. But the evidence of *Frogs* is important, and probably somewhat reliable, on this question. Not only does the play inform us, plausibly enough, that Phrynichus had a significant contribution to make (1298–1300, discussed above), but the offhand remark by Euripides that many of Aeschylus' choral songs followed closely the patterns of citharodic *nomoi* (1282)—that is to say, choral songs performed to the *cithara* (concert lyre) in the tradition of Terpander, Olympus, and the other founding fathers of Greek choral lyric—confirms that the rhythms and structures of many of Aeschylus' choral odes adhere quite closely to a venerable Panhellenic performance tradition.

In certain key respects, tragedy had developed its own unique choral conventions—notably strophic pairing ("responsion" of stanzas, strophe to antistrophe), with each successive pair composed in a different metrical-musical shape (AA BB CC, etc.), rather than recurrent triads (AAB AAB, etc.) or metrically identical stanzas repeated over and over (AAAA, etc.), which were the standard forms for nontheatrical lyrics. This meant that tragedians could vary their meter and music much more extensively and fluidly than previous lyric poets could, and thus could draw at will on a huge repertoire of already existing styles and traditions of prayers, dirges, heroic narratives, wedding songs, magic spells, hymns, etc., by adopting elements of their rhythms and language (and probably choreography too) according to the dramatic context and shifting emotional moods of each play.

Aeschylus must have been a major contributor to the development of this repertoire of tragic lyric styles. The six or seven Aeschylean plays that we possess in their entirety (*Prometheus Bound* may be inauthentic; it certainly presents very different lyric forms from the other six plays) exhibit quite a wide range of metrical elements and stanzaic patterns, some of which are found also in Sophocles and/or Euripides, while others seem to be distinctive and peculiar to Aeschylus' own musical style. As we might expect, it is some of the latter that are singled out for comment and parody in *Frogs*. Indeed, Euripides complains that all Aeschylus' songs sound the same: "I'll show that he is a rotten songwriter/ and always composes the same thing over and over" (1249–50); "I'll cut down all his songs into one [pattern]" (1162); and he proceeds to quote passages from eight separate plays that exhibit the same metrical pattern. These include the famous (to us, and apparently to Aeschylus' audience too) opening lines of the mighty choral song at *Agamemnon* 104ff (104, 108–111 are quoted), along with seven other quotations in identical rhythm taken from plays that we have lost. (We depend on the scholiast to this *Frogs* passage for identification of the plays they come from.)

The rhythm of all these lines from the different plays is indeed identical: heavily dactylic (i.e., runs of long-short-short syllables –˘˘ –˘˘), sometimes introduced by an iambic five-syllable phrase (short-long-short-long-long = ˘–˘––). The sense of repetitiveness is absurdly exaggerated by the use of an identical verbal refrain in alternating lines, in similar meter. The first pair of lines quoted (from *Myrmidons*, fragment 132) goes as follows, in very literal translation:

> Achilles of Phthia, why, hearing the man-slaying
> O! O! beating/chopping, do you not approach to help?
>
> (1264–65)

The phrase "O! O! beating . . ." (*iê kopon* . . .), which does belong properly with the address to Achilles in fr. 132, is repeated over and over (1265, 1267, 1271, 1275, 1277) following lines from other plays with which it makes no sense at all. This is not, of course, an authentic replication of actual Aeschylean practice, but an absurd compression and exaggeration of the more subtle refrain technique that we do find—strikingly employed—in *Agamemnon*, where each of the first three stanzas of this choral song ends, "Sing woe, woe! But may the good prevail!" (*Ag.* 121, 139, 159). In the *Frogs* parody, the effect of monotonously repeated rhythm combined with garbled sense—and an insistent emphasis on inarticulate cries (*iê* . . .!) and the "beating, chopping" of the clash of weapons at the battlefront—results in a ludicrous impression of rhythmical and repetitive violence, devoid of sense, predictable and ponderous.

Key to the overall effect, too, is the fact that the dactylic rhythm (similar, but not identical to that of the Homeric dactylic hexameter) apparently follows closely the cadences of archaic "citharodic nomes [songs, tunes]" (1281–82). Citharodes were professional singers and/or composers of elaborate narrative poems performed to the accompaniment of the *cithara* (i.e., the large concert lyre with deep sounding-box, double neck and bridge) at venues such as the Pythian and Panathenaic Games. Famous early citharodes included the semi-legendary Terpander, Alcman, and—an especially strong influence on Aeschylus, it seems—Stesichorus of Himera (South Italy; mid/late sixth century). Surviving quotations from Stesichorus' work, including bits of a lyric *Oresteia*, and further papyrus fragments of a long poem about Tiresias and the family of Oedipus, reveal that his poems were regularly composed in just this kind of dactylic lyric meter; furthermore, ancient commentators remarked that "after Homer and Hesiod, Stesichorus . . . was the poet that the tragedians most borrowed from. . . ." So Aristophanes' parody here is well directed at a feature of Aeschylus' most typical (and old-fashioned) tendencies.

An extra ingredient is added in the middle of this segment of Euripides' critique—and this actually is the moment at which "citharodic tunes" are explicitly mentioned, so it is not entirely clear whether the (garbled) quotations of 1264–80 are meant to sound rhythmically very much the same as what follows (1285–97) or whether a significant adjustment takes place. The basic rhythm of the dactylic lines quoted and mocked in 1285ff remains almost identical (including *Ag.* 108–11), but the lines are now interspersed with a fresh and even more bizarre "refrain," a recurrent onomatopoeic phrase written in our manuscripts as

PHLATT *o* THRATT *o* PHLATT *o* THRAT

The rhythm of this phrase is cretic rather than dactylic (i.e., built out of alternating long and single-short syllables, rather than long-short-short): $-\smile-\smile-$ (= *tum-ti-tum-ti-tum-ti-tum*). This rhythm, and especially this precise metrical unit, recurs constantly throughout the *Oresteia*, and may be regarded as being every bit as distinctive and characteristic of Aeschylus' lyrics as the dactylic runs. But nowhere does Aeschylus in fact combine or alternate these two rhythms as Euripides makes him do here; so some scholars have argued that the *phlattothrattophlattothrat* phrase is intended here, not as a sung verbal-metrical pattern, but as a rhythmic strumming of chords on the *cithara* itself between vocal phrases. Yet the instrument accompanying choral song in tragedy—and comedy too—was almost always the *auloi* (double-pipe), not the *cithara* or any other kind of stringed instrument; so it is hard to see how the actor or *aulêtês* here could have imitated the sound of a *cithara* being strummed. The lack of stage directions and written musical notation makes our interpretation very uncertain.

In any case, the "Aeschylean" choral verse lines that are cobbled together here (and actually performed by a solo singer, i.e., the actor playing Euripides), even while they make no verbal sense at all in this combination, do provide some authentic-sounding Aeschylean rhythms and mannerisms, with the regularity of rhythm and structure emphasizing and exaggerating Aeschylus' regularity of strophic correspondence and refrains. We may note too that the few surviving lyric lines of Phrynichus tend to reflect similar metrical patterns: mostly dactylic, again like the stanzas of Alcman and Stesichorus, those old-style choral lyricists.

What about Euripides' songs? The rhythmical as well as verbal characteristics of the lyrics in Euripides' surviving plays set them apart quite distinctively from Aeschylus', as the plays' meters clearly indicate. Not only does Euripides tend to use a different repertoire of metrical types, but—even more significantly, especially for Aristophanes' parody techniques—he assigns many of his most striking and distinctive lyric passages to solo actors, rather than to the chorus, and is also quick (particularly in his later plays) to abandon strophic pairing in favor of "free," non-strophic stanzas of unpredictable metrical character. He also introduces much more vocal and instrumental bravura (repeated single words, unusual metrical resolutions, etc.; see p. 125) even into those standard meters that he shares with Aeschylus. And the tiny scraps of musically notated Euripidean lyric texts that survive on papyrus (from the third century BCE) confirm that vocal melismas (single verbal syllables extended over several different notes in the melody) were also employed, just as the parody of Euripides' lyrics in *Frogs* indicates (see below, pp. 147–48). All of these tendencies form part of a decisive shift in the structure and character of Greek drama during the later fifth century about which a number of (later) classical sources inform us—as well as Aristophanes himself, of course.

The parodies of choral and solo lyric in *Frogs* involve meter (rhythm), melody, vocalizing technique, and choreography all at once—as we should expect, given the nature of Greek musical performance. Our medieval manuscript texts of tragedy and comedy provide us only with the bare words, however. From these texts we can deduce (from the verbal meter) which lines are to be spoken in dialogue, which chanted (recitative), and which sung (lyrics), but nothing further about the actual melodies, nor any direct evidence as to the vocal timbres, speed, and pitch of delivery, etc. Likewise, the choreography is completely lacking. These deficiencies are very unfortunate since so many of the most vivid and amusing effects in *Frogs* obviously depend on precisely those aspects of the performance. Nonetheless, there is a certain amount that we can do to fill in those missing elements, from our knowledge of Greek music history of the fifth and fourth century (including the musical papyri) as well as our careful reading of the relevant passages of *Frogs* itself.

The musical instruments, tunings, modes, and techniques of performance that the Greeks had developed by the fifth century had mostly been adopted originally from Anatolian regions, especially Phrygia and Caria (also perhaps Thrace), and thus they were derived ultimately from much older Mesopotamian traditions (Sumerian, Babylonian, Hurrian; also Hittite and Minoan): the music-styles of the Eastern Mediterranean and Anatolian regions probably all sounded fairly similar, and Athens had not apparently played a significant role in the development of "Greek" music as such, as compared with Lesbos, the Ionian cities, Crete, or even Sparta. But the later fifth century witnessed major developments and controversies about new styles in theater music and about the growing professionalization of pipe-playing and solo singing as well. Athens, with its huge annual festivals of dithyrambic and dramatic performances, seems to have comprised the central venue for these fierce and high-stakes "culture wars"—wars that obviously lie at the heart of the contest between Aeschylus and Euripides in *Frogs*.

In Aeschylus' day, and still probably during the early career of Euripides, Athenian theater performance was almost completely citizen-based and amateur. Not only was it required that members of all the choruses at the City Dionysia be Athenian citizens or sons of citizens (a rule that persisted, as far as we can tell, into later centuries), but it was usual for the playwright himself to take one of the acting roles, while also being responsible for composing all the music and choreography.

This rule did not apply to the pipe-player, however. All the choral performances at the festival, dithyrambs as well as dramas (and comedies at the Lenaea too, presumably), were accompanied by the double-pipes (*auloi*). The piper (*aulêtês*) probably stood or sat in the middle of the orchestra (see Figures 1–1a and b), and was treated for dramatic purposes as if he was not there at all; but the instrumental accompaniment was clearly a very significant component of the overall sound and emotional impact of the sung portions of the plays, and there are references made to the sound of the *auloi* in several choral and monodic songs in our surviving tragedies and satyr-plays. Archaeologists and music historians have traced a remarkable evolution—or revolution—during the later fifth century in *aulos* construction and capability, proceeding in tandem with radical developments in Greek theories and practices of musical modes and tunings that we find referred to in literary texts as well. The *auloi* of Aeschylus' day were simple in design, and their limited numbers of bored holes allowed only five or six basic notes to be played accurately and easily (rather like a modern recorder or Indian flute). At this period it was also conventional—indeed, more or less required—for each particular tune or song for strings or pipe to be composed within one set tuning of a given pair of tetrachords (or *harmonia*, usually translated nowadays as "mode" or "tuning"): thus "Lydian," "Phrygian," "Dorian," etc., each with a different range of legitimate notes spanning (usually) a bit less than an octave and emphasizing the intervals of the fifth, fourth, and second, along with one or two designated subsidiary whole-tones and half-tones and (in some tunings) quarter-tones (microtones) as well. (These subsidiary tunings within the tetrachord were the so-called enharmonic, chromatic, and diatonic, the details of which need not concern us here. A particular melody might thus be composed in "enharmonic Phrygian," or "diatonic Phrygian," or "diatonic Dorian," etc.: the options were very numerous.) A given strophic pair of lyrics (or whole song composed monostrophically or triadically) would thus at this period always have to be played and sung in the same *harmonia* and tuning; indeed, it would be very difficult for an aulete (or citharist) to play accurately notes that were not part of the pre-assigned "scale" and melody. Then, if a new melody, composed in a different *harmonia*, were called for, the aulete would need to switch and use a different instrument (while a citharist would likewise have to retune his strings).

But, as the fifth century proceeded, new technical improvements were made to the aulos—including movable keys and rotating sleeves, not unlike those used for modern clarinets, saxophones, flutes, etc.—which enabled a skilled aulete to play in any *harmonia* on one and the same instrument, and thus to modulate from one type of melody to another without needing to pause to switch to another pair of *auloi*. Manipulating these keys took skill and practice (just as mastering the saxophone or oboe takes more practice than a recorder or pennywhistle). Thus, by the later fifth century a professional aulete could play far more complicated melodies than an amateur; and it is during this period that we find the emergence of star auletes such as the family of Pronomos (from Thebes), who become much in demand in Athens and elsewhere for dithyrambic and dramatic competitions.

This was also precisely the same period that the prize for acting was instituted at the City Dionysia. So both pipe-playing and acting by now had become professional occupations—a process that was doubtless accelerated in due course by the growing proliferation of theatrical venues and performance opportunities outside Athens. No longer did playwrights act in their own tragedies: they could rely instead on big-voiced, fully trained vocalists with exceptional physical and gestural skills (who would also presumably specialize in effective use of masks). Their vocal-melodic range and agility would be much greater than those of an ordinary (amateur) chorus singer or gentleman lyre singer at a symposium. In some cases, playwrights also began to make use of professional collaborators in their musical composition: so Euripides and Cephisophon apparently worked as a team, as is repeatedly mentioned in *Frogs* (944, 1408, 1452–53).

Evidence of these developments in the professionalization of tragic performance can be detected quite clearly in the texts of Euripides' surviving plays, as the actors and aulete are given increasingly complicated assignments while the contributions of the chorus generally shrink. So whereas Aeschylus regularly punctuates the situational crises of his plays with lengthy choral odes in which the morality and emotional consequences faced by individual characters are explored in tightly structured sequences of strophic pairs ("strings of lyrics . . .," as Euripides sneers at *Frogs* 914–15), Euripides has much shorter choral songs, with the individual characters themselves often bursting into song instead, thereby raising the emotional temperature rather as European opera and modern Bollywood movies do. Furthermore, both the choral songs and the actors' monodies in Euripides (especially in his later plays) are often quite loosely constructed and non-strophic, with the metrical (and presumably musical) character shifting quite freely as the song progresses. Music is of course intrinsically a highly expressive medium, and semi-musical modes of vocalizing (lamentation, ghost-raising, binding spells) had already sometimes been included in earlier tragedy. These forms were continued by Sophocles and Euripides, but now with the addition of the more elaborate solo songs (*monôdiai*, "monodies") for which Euripides and his actors came to be so well known and admired. It is these "monodies" that Aristophanes seizes upon for his most extreme and grotesque parodies in *Frogs*.

The most successful musical-lyric innovators of this era, Melanippides, Cinesias, Phrynis, Timotheus, Philoxenus, and others (mostly non-Athenians), were the focus of much controversy, to judge from mention made both by contemporaries (especially Aristophanes) and by later generations of Greek music historians and music theorists. Their dithyrambs and nomes (*nomoi*) were admired by thousands—and bitterly criticized by a few, whose criticisms in some cases survive (especially Plato's). But fairly quickly, i.e., by the mid-fourth century, the "revolution" was over, it seems: this "New Music" had triumphed, and had become mainstream. Timotheus, for example, was now a household name, his songs read and sung everywhere; and subsequent music theorists (Aristoxenus, et al.) all took for granted the tunings and melodies of this kind of music with no further anxiety about its potential to cause moral degeneration and laxity. Yet, by a strange twist of cultural history, it is Plato's—and Aristophanes'!—complaints about the "degenerate" new dithyrambists and the "perverted" nature of their new music that have carried the day with most classical scholars, and the standard accounts of Greek drama and musical history all still tend to read as if these virtuosos were a pernicious, undisciplined, flashy bunch of shallow bubble-gum artists, undermining the simple purity and authentic beauty of the true "classical" style.

At the center of this late fifth-century musical revolution in Athens we find the two tragic poets Euripides and Agathon. Indeed, the whole movement came to be known collectively as "theater music," since dithyramb, tragedy, and satyr-drama (all Dionysian music forms, of course, favoring the *auloi* over the *cithara*) were the most prominent and influential venues. Modern critics have usually labeled it instead "the New Music," and have (mistakenly) tended to connect it primarily or exclusively with dithyramb and other nondramatic forms. Thus they have felt free to hold those abovementioned dithyrambists (several of them mocked by Aristophanes: e.g., Cinesias, Melanippides, etc.) responsible for the alleged "decadence" and decline of Greek music from the glory days of the fifth century, while exonerating Sophocles completely and regarding even Euripides as more of a follower (or victim) than a leader in these new directions. But the evidence speaks otherwise—and Aristophanes' own lyrics likewise show clear signs of adherence to the new styles, even as some of his characters repeatedly poke fun at Cinesias (as at *Frogs* 153, 366, 1437), Agathon (prominently in the opening scene of *Thesmophoriazusae*), and Euripides himself for their "dithyrambic" excesses.

The chief characteristics of this new musical style were its multiplicity, irregularity, and versatility—melodies could shift quickly from one meter and mode to another, with composers often preferring to spin out extended astrophic (i.e., non-repeating) songs that flowed seamlessly and unpredictably from one metrical-musical character to another, without pairing stanzas into strophic or triadic structures and without sticking to a single fixed and familiar mode or pattern. Admirers of this fluidity and versatility referred to it as "intricacy, variability" (*poikilia*—a strongly favorable aesthetic term in Greek); traditionalists sneered at the "multi-noted-ness" (*poluchordia*) and "ant-like wanderings" (or "ant-hill complexity"?)—these phrases occur at *Thesmophoriazusae* 100) of the *aulos* melodies—and of course its wild popularity and exciting (even, some alleged, sexually stimulating) effects on large audiences. In the minds of some snobs, including anti-democrats such as Plato, it seems to have been precisely the fact that this music was so popular with the masses that most offended them and confirmed its debased and degenerate character.

Aeschylus' parody of Euripidean lyrics in *Frogs* is one of the play's high spots (cf. the equally brilliant parody of Agathon's songs at *Thesmophoriazusae* 95–145). First we are presented with a stanza of mock-choral song, accompanied by a "Muse" dancing with castanets (1309–23), and then follows a monody (1330–63). Even for us, lacking the original music completely and with only a sketchy knowledge of the metrical and choreographical mannerisms that are being reproduced in this exaggerated form, the self-referential antics and verbal incongruities of the two songs are not hard to follow. In the first song, as in the earlier parodies of Aeschylean lyric, we have a mixture of actual passages from Euripides' plays (mainly his lost *Hypsipyle*) chaotically jumbled up with other snippets, whereas in the monody, all of the verses seem to be new and ludicrously untragic—yet still quite close to the Euripidean manner, as is the extravagant metrical character of both passages.

Aeschylus introduces multiple grounds for complaint during this passage (1301–63). First, in contrast to Aeschylus, whose songs are characterized as being "all the same" (and highly traditional, derived from the bee-meadows of Phrynichus), Euripides' songs are said to "get their honey from absolutely everywhere—"porn-songs (or "songs-for-sale," 1301 *pornôidiôn*), Melêtus' drinking-songs, pipe-tunes, and laments and dances from Caria . . ." (1301–03). Like a prostitute, and unlike the well brought up (and presumably monogamous) Muse of his tragic predecessors, Euripides' female spirit of inspiration buys and sells her sweet goods indiscriminately. So this music is "foreign" (non-Greek, Asian); it is performed by professionals (i.e., "for sale" and no longer the province of gentleman amateurs); and it is gendered distinctly female (unlike Aeschylus' more manly songs—this Muse appears to belong to a world similar to that of the dancer depicted in Fig. 5–1b).

Aeschylus thinks for a moment that he might play some of Euripides' tunes on a lyre (1306–07), just as Euripides did (or pretended to do) in parodying Aeschylus' style of *cithara*-strumming at 1284ff. But he quickly abandons that idea in favor of calling onstage "that girl who plays percussion with little bits of pottery . . . Hey, come here, Muse of Euripides! You're exactly the right accompanist [for me] to sing these songs to!" (1306–07). By "little bits of pottery" (*ostraka*) Aeschylus sneeringly means hand-percussion, i.e., castanets (*krotala*), which were a long-standing component of various forms of Greek choral and solo performance by women (especially in Dionysian and Cybelean contexts).

The "Muse" immediately appears, and Dionysus remarks, "This Muse—she certainly wasn't one to do Aeolic tricks, for sure!" This line has been much discussed, and agreement has still not been reached among scholars as to what is meant. Nor are interpreters agreed what this "Muse" should look like as she appears on stage: sexy, exotic, gorgeous (like Agathon in *Thesmophoriazusae*)? or old, ugly, and disgusting? In 1307, ". . . do Aeolic tricks" is my translation

Figure 5–1. Two examples of Dionysian music, as represented in Athenian vase-painting of the fifth century.
(a) Dionysus plays a *barbitos* (lyre) while two satyrs dance and play *krotala* (castanets).

Interior of Red-figure kylix-cup by the Brygos Painter, ca. 480 BCE (ARV^2 371,14: Cab. Méd. Inv. 575). Drawing by Elizabeth Wahle.

for the Greek *elesbiazen*, which literally means "(she) used to do (the) Lesbos-things," which here must involve at least two common meanings in Greek (but probably not a third). The first, surface meaning, in the context of musical-metrical discussion such as this, must be "perform/sing in the meters and style of the poets of Lesbos, i.e., Alcaeus and Sappho and their tradition (later represented

Figure 5–1.(b) A young man plays the *auloi* (double-pipes), presumably at a symposium, while a woman dances with *krotala* (castanets).
Red-figure Athenian kylix-cup by Epictetus (*ARV*² 72,16), ca. 500 BCE (London E38, 1843,1103.9). Photo courtesy of the Trustees of the British Museum.

by Catullus and Horace in Rome); and in fact the choral lyrics that follow are in that Aeolic manner, while also containing a number of highly "Euripidean" licenses and resolutions. So perhaps this "Muse" in her versions of "Aeolic" song is not performing like a true inhabitant of Lesbos, but more like a modern Carian or Athenian professional? The other well-known meaning of "lesbianizing" in Greek culture was sexual, referring to women who performed skillful fellation (blow-jobs); so some scholars have argued that Aeschylus here is referring to the old age and ugliness of this "Muse" and insisting that she could never even have been a desirable prostitute. But this seems contrary to the logic of this whole passage, in which Euripides' wanton Muse is being accused of collecting "honey" from all over the world, presumably with a view to sweetening her offerings to all comers. So it seems more likely that the comment means that her appearance and movements here indicate that she was more of an "Asian" dancer, less of a "Lesbian" cock-sucker. (As for the third possible meaning of *elesbiazen*—there would seem to be no sense to be made here of a "lesbian" implication, which in any case at this date seems not to have been prominent in references to women from that island.)

But whichever interpretation we give to this line, and whether we take the Muse to be old or young, attractive or hideous, it is in any case crucial that she is female. The notion of the "art" of tragedy, or a "Muse," or "Music" itself, being a feminine companion or sexual plaything of the male poet, thus both a source of his inspiration and the object of his control—possibly even a sex object to be pandered to others—runs deep in this play, and is a recurrent theme in Greek (and Roman) culture at large. (It was clearly a major theme also of Cratinus' *Pytinê* [421 BCE]; see chapter 1.) By contrast, no comments or innuendoes are made in *Frogs* about Aeschylus' wife or family (or any mistress): the legitimacy of his Athenianness and of his poetry is taken for granted. The notion that Euripides had a *ménage à trois* with his composer, Cephisophon, consorted with a foreign dancing-Muse, and presented whorish heroines on the stage in his tragedies calls into question both his moral and his political respectability, just as such accusations do in the case of (allegedly) foreign-born populist politicians such as Cleophon (680–82). This happens again at the end of the song of the "Muse," as Aeschylus points to the "foot" or "leg" (1322–23 *poda*) of the dancing Muse, and scoffs at Euripides, "When *you* are composing/making (*poiôn*) stuff like that,/ do you have the nerve to find fault with *my* songs/limbs (*melê*),/ as you make your songs/ move your limbs (*melopoiôn*) in (or "with") the Twelve Tricks of Cyrene?" Cyrene was the name of a famous, expensive courtesan in late fifth-century Athens, whose beauty and "moves/tricks" were frequently alluded to by Aristophanes and others. (Cyrene was also the name of a Greek city in Libya, exotic and wealthy.)

In a similar comic turn, Aristophanes' contemporary and rival, Pherecrates, in his *Cheiron* (fr. 155, a substantial fragment of which survives in quotation), had introduced Music (*Mousikê*) as a character onstage who complains that she has been sexually molested by a series of leading practitioners of the New Music. She refers first to the fast-and-loose switching back and forth of lyric modes by the dithyrambist Cinesias, as he "composed ill-tuned bendings in his strophes . . . so that you couldn't tell his left from his right," and then Phrynes "bending and twisting . . . with twelve tunings (*harmonias*) on five strings," and finally Timotheus, who "completely ruined [her] with his twelve strings"—a striking echo of the "twelve-position-tricks of Cyrene" mentioned in *Frogs* (1323 *dôdekamêchanon*): in both cases the reference must be to the multistring instrumentation, quick modulations, and technical versatility of these innovative dithyrambists, with all their connotations of sexual promiscuity and professionalization.

The choral ode in *Frogs* (1309–23) is not only thoroughly Euripidean in its adventurously resolved aeolic meters (1322 ". . . that *foot* of mine"), but is also full of language and images characteristic of dithyrambic and late-Euripidean choral self-referentiality. The New Music and its choruses frequently make mention of "dolphins," of "leaping, circling, whirling" movements and configurations, and of the paraphernalia of Dionysian costume, props, and dance. So here we find "halcyons . . . the pipe-loving dolphin leaping at the ship's prow . . ." (a passage taken from Eur. *Electra* 435–37), the "curling tendril, pain-stopping joy of the grape . . ." (1321), and also the in-and-out intricate movements of the "singing shuttle" (1316; in contrast to Aeschylus' straight-ahead "rope-winding from Marathon," 1296–97). The swift, sweeping and leaping, circular movement of dithyrambic choreography made sharp contrast with the rectilinear and more angular movement of older-style choruses; and this mannerism is very much evident in Euripides, as signaled, e.g., by the Greek root *heli-* ("winding, spiraling, curling"; esp. *heilissô* = "I whirl, spin," 1314, 1349).

The most deliciously Euripidean/New Musical feature of all, in Aristophanes' brilliant take-off, involves the musical delivery of this very word, on both of its occurrences: *eieieieilissete* (1314), *eieieieilissousa* (1349)—the repeated *ei*-syllable in the manuscripts must represent here a musical melisma, i.e., several melodic notes sung in succession for this one syllable. This is not normal practice in earlier Greek lyric meters (since it was a basic principle that each syllable should receive just one note in the melody), but it is one that we can actually observe in the tiny scraps of musical notation that survive on papyrus from lyrics by Euripides (from his *Orestes*). Clearly, in such passages the music (both instrumental and vocal) has become more important than the words in determining the melody and rhythm—a matter about which traditionalists complained bitterly.

The monody in other respects too is perfectly (absurdly) hyper-Euripidean. It is sung by a lower-class character; it concerns mundane, domestic activities (the loss of a rooster . . .); and it is replete with repeated words which perform more of a musical than a semantic function: 1352 "flew away, flew away"; 1353 "miseries, miseries"; 1354 "tears, tears"; 1355 "I shed, I shed." Any modern listener could quickly find similar examples of repetition, and of the extreme subordination of words to music, in the operas of Mozart and Puccini, or the songs of James Brown and Marvin Gaye. Aristophanes doubtless is not seriously critiquing Euripides' poetic technique; he is rather presenting an exaggerated, over-the-top version of a Euripidean pop song—including "Cretan" companions (1356–58, in a quotation from Euripides' *Cretans*, fr. 471) and puppies, who are collectively asked to "circle around . . . all over the house," together with Dictynna, Hecate, and all the magical forces of the East, in a final dithyrambic extravaganza of song and swirling movement.

The songs are over (1363 "Stop your songs, both of you, right away!" exclaims Dionysus). Neither has defeated the other; but each has presented a hilarious and observant pastiche of all that is most distinctive, most entertaining, and most absurd in his rival's musical style. Aristophanes himself has displayed his intimate knowledge of musical traditions, both old and new, and his ability to replicate and make fun of the musical-choral history of Athenian theater from its very beginnings (Phrynichus, or even earlier, the "citharodic nomes") to its latest and most sensational innovations. Old and new, the best and the worst. Dionysus enjoys it all, and apparently still reserves judgment as to which kind is really the "best." So how will he finally decide?

Suggestions for Further Reading

On the development of tragic style and forms during the fifth century: Battezzato (2009); Herington (1985); Jens (1971); Scott (1984); Stanford (1942).

On actors and acting (and singing) technique: Easterling and Hall (2002).

On Greek music and music theory, especially fifth-century musical innovations: Anderson (1966); Barker (1984, 1989); Comotti (1989); Power (2010); West (1992). On Euripides in relation to the "New/Theater Music" of the late fifth century, see Csapo (2000b); also Csapo (2003, 2004). On Aristophanes' lyric style, and his attitude to Euripides and new trends in tragedy and comedy: Bakola (2010); L. Parker (1997).

· 6 ·

Underworld and Afterlife

Dionysus and Greek Fantasies of Salvation

Frogs is about art and politics: about good vs. bad tragedy, old vs. new, the value of the arts in general, the city of Athens and anxieties about its future. But it is also about the possibilities and nature of the afterlife; about salvation, personal and collective; about immortality even, of some kind: what happens after death, and the prospect of escaping or re-emerging from the darkness of the Underworld into a state of renewed "living" in blessed light and eternal joy. And at the heart of all of these issues we encounter—of course—the figure of Dionysus: enigmatic, transformative, theatrical. In this chapter we shall explore the ways in which Dionysus' quest to retrieve a poet from the Underworld (originally, Euripides; but, in the end, Aeschylus) exemplifies and enacts—but also extracts humor from—processes of initiation and ideas of personal and collective salvation that were well known to most of Aristophanes' audience, even while they might be also to some degree secret and not fully acknowledged by the city's religious institutions.

The theme of "salvation" (in Greek, *sôtêria*) operates on several different levels in *Frogs*. Not only is the play about saving the city from military and political disaster and salvaging (reclaiming) tragedy from decline and decadence, but the whole plot is built around the possibility of retrieving a deserving ghost from subterranean existence and restoring it (him) to a place of honor and glory within the community where he used to live; and also, more broadly, around the idea that some people—but not all—may be "saved" from misery and oblivion after death, if only they know the proper formula and can prepare themselves properly. Salvation is within our (comic) grasp.

Any discussion of Greek religious attitudes, behaviors, and beliefs, of ideas about the soul and life after death, and—especially— about Dionysus, is inevitably going to be provisional, contradictory, and confusing. Religion itself is a notoriously nebulous and elusive concept, and one that is quite differently defined and practiced in different cultures. The Greeks had no word for "religion," yet by our standards, and in our terms, religious activities and concerns occupied a great deal of their attention. Many modern scholars would prefer to employ the plural ("religions"), and they would insist also that "the Greeks" overall were quite disparate and inconsistent in terms of their beliefs and practices regarding the gods. Local differences were certainly very great, and there is all too much that is not known about Greek mind-sets and religious cults. But for fifth-century Athens in particular we are, all things considered, rather well informed—and this is to no small degree thanks to the plays of Aristophanes.

In particular, *Frogs* is one of the earliest, best preserved, and most important texts that we possess concerning the Eleusinian (and other) Mysteries, Athenian ideas and cults of Dionysus, Orphic doctrines and initiation, and even mainstream Athenian ideas concerning life (or existence of some kind) after death. At the same time, *Frogs* is obviously a comedy, designed like all of Aristophanes' plays to provide fantastic and absurd situations and to distort the familiar procedures and expectations of everyday life ("reality") for comic, theatrical effect. The play's "theology" and "eschatology" are hardly likely to be any more coherent, nor necessarily any more seriously intended as a viable prescription for living, than are, e.g., the ideas about relations between men and women that we find presented in *Thesmophoriazusae*, *Lysistrata*, and *Assemblywomen*, or notions about the distribution of resources in *Wealth*. And, to add to our difficulties (i.e., the challenge of interpreting appropriately the full range of "religious" and "spiritual" issues that fill the play), the fact that Dionysus, the play's main character, is himself patron divinity of comedy and of the Athenian theater introduces a self-referential and circular dynamic into any interpretation of the play, so as to make it both all the more engaging and yet (for those who seek tidy and consistent answers to big questions) inevitably quite frustrating.

In this chapter, we will begin with (i) a brief sketch of relevant aspects of Athenian religious practice and belief, along with (ii) a reminder of the standard views of the Underworld and the afterlife that would be familiar to most of Aristophanes' audience. Then we will discuss (iii) the nature of the various mystery cults that were in existence by this time around Greece, offering guarantees of some kind of enhanced existence after death, i.e., "salvation," if not outright immortality—most notably, of course, the Eleusinian Mysteries; and (iv) the meaning and impact of "Dionysus/Bacchus/Iacchus" in general within Athenian society, and especially in the Theater. With these preliminary surveys in place, (v) we can look more closely at *Frogs* itself, examining the behavior and significance of the two Choruses (frogs and Initiates), Heracles the successful immortalized hero, Xanthias the slave, and, above all, Dionysus (both as god and as comic hero) and Aeschylus the poet as revitalized/immortal culture hero. We will also find ourselves considering Athens itself as a city "saved" and "reborn," and exploring the audience's sense of their salvation through the recovery of a renewed art of tragedy.

(i) Athenian Religion (and Old Comedy)

The classical Greek world was full of gods, spirits, superhuman forces of all kinds. Every human activity potentially involved divine agencies that might help or hinder the outcome: battle, weaving, a sea-voyage, deliberating in assembly, cursing or blessing one's enemies or friends, making music—all of these would be more likely to be successful with the favor and help of (a) god(s). On the large scale, the Olympian divinities, Zeus, Apollo, Athena, and the others, were celebrated citywide with temples and annual ceremonies as well as by individual households, while poets composed innumerable hymns and stories in their honor. On a lower level, more specifically local and/or personal deities were recognized, whose shrines and sacred places might be encountered regularly in one's daily activities and journeys (a fountain, a mountain peak, a doorway . . .): *theoi* and *daimones* were everywhere.

These divinities were mostly imagined as being very much like human beings in their behavior and attitudes—yet radically different in being ageless and immortal, and in possessing much greater power, including (in most cases) physical strength and capability, and also knowledge (if not necessarily wisdom), as compared with mere mortals. In general, a god's concerns and motivations for getting involved in the world are not essentially different from a human's concerns: i.e., to win respect and honor, to help their own friends, allies, and family members (*philoi*), often by doing harm to the enemies of those friends and allies, and to enjoy the comforts and pleasures of food, drink, sex, good company, and entertainment (the arts).

Beliefs?

"Did the Greeks believe in their gods?"—a much asked and largely unanswerable question. In fifth-century Athens there was no Credo, no Bar Mitzvah or catechism or official priestly dogma/orthodoxy; indeed, there was very little systematic theology apart from eccentric theories argued by Socrates and a few pre-Socratic intellectuals, such as Xenophanes, Anaxagoras, and Prodicus. What each Athenian actually believed about the gods, about the creation of the world and of humans, about life after death, etc., was largely his or her own business—and was almost certainly in most cases quite muddled and incoherent. Of course, everyone was familiar with the gods of Hesiod and Homer, together with all their genealogies and myths; familiar too with local notions of Athena-Protector-of-the-City (Athena *Polias*), Athena-the-Maiden (Athena *Parthenos*), and all that these titles entailed. But everyone knew also that the gods of epic and tragedy were distinctly "literary" constructions, and that many aspects of their behavior were not to be taken at face value as representations of how these gods and goddesses operated in actual everyday life.

Yet these various gods and their sensational miracles, big and small, obviously did command some level of belief among many listeners and audience members. An overriding faith persisted that some kind of divine powers must be controlling the outcome of human (and meteorological and biological . . .) events—and furthermore that these powers must (surely?) be concerned to some degree with justice, human well-being, and favoring those who showed them proper devotion and respect. How else to explain the defeat of the Persians at Marathon, at Salamis, and at Plataea, along with countless other successes and surprising turns of events on both the large and the small scale? On a different wavelength: how to explain unpredictable fluctuations of an individual's feelings—raging sexual desire, sudden panic, vicious sibling hatred, life-threatening fever and unexpected recovery, drunkenness, musical and choreographic ecstasy—except through the presence or influence of (respectively) Aphrodite/Eros, Pan (or Phobos), Eris, Apollo, Dionysus—and again Dionysus, and the Muses? The shiver of horror (Erinys, Atê), the glow of confidence and joy at victory (Nikê, Apollo Paian), a girl's or young woman's bursting sense of vigor and independence (Artemis, Persephone-Korê)—all of these seem to transport a person out of their normal, mundane state into something different, to transform them for a while into someone else, to empower (or diminish) them uncontrollably, even miraculously. That is what the divine spirit does, to be sure—and since the Greeks did not know about hormones and adrenalin, testosterone and estrogen, endorphins and dopamine (nor about sugars, yeasts, and alcohol), to them any sudden mood swings, feelings of inspiration or depression or bliss (as well as the transformation of grapes into wine, with its resultant psychotropic effects) and innumerable other such emotional/mental/physiological alterations, all called for some kind of supernatural explanation—and cure, or invitation. The "gods" are indeed everywhere in our lives, whatever names we may give to them.

Aristophanes' audience undoubtedly represented a broad cross-section of Athenian society, including both traditional-minded peasants and highly sophisticated intellectuals (see chapter 2). All of them will have known well the gods and goddesses of Homer's epics and tragedy. Quite a large number, perhaps as many as a third or even a half, will themselves also have been initiates of the Eleusinian Mysteries (which will be discussed in the next section). They will all also have been fully aware that in Comedy the gods (like other elites) may be represented as behaving in very undignified, even scurrilous and nasty ways. In the *Birds*, for example, or *Wealth*, Aristophanes' audience is expected to feel quite comfortable watching the gods (including even Zeus himself) behave in utterly disreputable, foolish, and incompetent ways as humans outwit and outmaneuver them, without any negative consequences. This is all part of comic fantasy-making.

Of all the divinities and mythic heroes who were thus ludicrously portrayed, Heracles was clearly the favorite, as we find him constantly showing up as the central hero-character both in Comedy and in satyr-drama. He is usually represented as a gluttonous, heavy-drinking, womanizing thick-head—the epitome, one might say, of shameless, aggressive, pleasure-seeking, *kômos*-celebrating masculinity (the "comic hero"). Of course Heracles is also a rare example of a mortal man who conquered death, both in the sense that he visited the Underworld (wrestled with Thanatos [Death], captured Cerberus, retrieved Pirithous, Alcestis, etc.), and also in his final apotheosis and ascension to Mt. Olympus, where he married Hebe and joined the other immortal gods. The fact that throughout the first half of *Frogs* Dionysus is wearing the Heraclean lion-skin (he only discards it—presumably—after he enters Plouton's palace, before the poetic contest begins) and in the opening scenes is so concerned to obtain Heracles' advice about visiting the Underworld, reminds us constantly (and reminds some of Plouton's attendants too) of this illustrious, violent precedent. Heracles is everyone's paradigm, negative as well as positive, for what Dionysus and Xanthias are attempting.

It is common in the modern world, though by no means universal, for people to want and expect their god(s) to be perfectly good and benevolent—not only strong, but also just, kind, and loving. It is reassuring to convince oneself that the world (or universe) is governed by one or more all-powerful entities that intend the best for humankind—or at least for their own followers and favorites (e.g., a particular nation or people, pious worshippers, etc.). But many cultures of the world have not seen, and do not see, things this way. While they may be deeply sensitive to the majesty of creation, to the amazing regularity yet multiplicity of natural phenomena, and even to the inspirational or terrifying presence and effects of superhuman forces in the world, it has not seemed likely to them either that just one person ("father," "king," "lord," or whoever) was in charge of absolutely everything, or that any person(s)-in-charge (divine force, energy, spirit . . .) would regard this universe as existing primarily for the benefit of humans. Instead, given the complexity and competing interests observable in both human affairs and the nonhuman world ("nature," or "the cosmos"), it has seemed more believable that gods are plural and that looking out for the benefit of humans was only one of their concerns. Mesopotamian religion, South Asian Hinduism, East Asian Buddhism, and archaic-classical Greek polytheism would all (in their different ways) seem to share such basic tenets.

By Aristophanes' time—which was also the time of the aging Socrates and Democritus, and of young Plato—there were indeed some Greeks who liked to insist that god(s) must be entirely good, rational, and (ultimately) benevolent, and that myths and cults that represented divinities as behaving like less-than-perfect, selfish human beings were misguided and even impious. This is not the place to map the processes through which Greek intellectuals began to modify traditional ideas about multiple, quasi-anthropomorphic, competing gods, so as to insist on the justice, omniscience, and perfectness of the divine (and increasingly too on the idea of a single "god" or divine principle, sometimes identified with Zeus, or with a notion of "intelligence" or "providence"). But such optimistic and simplistic views of omniscient and omnipotent divine philanthropy (endorsed in due course by Platonists, Stoics, and several types of Christians, in much the same terms) were by no means mainstream as yet: most of Aristophanes' audience members would have been more inclined to think of Zeus and the other Olympian deities as being more limited in their capacities and motivations. While it was believed (and hoped) that on the whole the gods, especially Zeus, might be expected to prefer that peace, harmony, and goodwill prevail as widely as possible, it was also recognized that such social hardships as war, hunger, disease, slavery, the dominance of men over women, and inequities of wealth were all normal and probably inescapable. In any case Aristophanic Comedy, for all its delight in exploring new and unconventional ideas, is not the most likely medium in which to find sustained theological argument. But we do find in our play some interesting and important instances (some of them presented in quite a frivolous manner) of the collision between different religious views and variant strands of cult practice.

Cult Practices

In general, the cults of Dionysus are particularly difficult for modern scholars to disentangle and interpret: Where? What? How many? Who participated (men *and* women, separately or together? slaves too? metics?)? But we do know quite a bit about the biggest annual civic festivals for Dionysus in Athens (or Attica at large) during the fifth century. These were, in chronological order: the Rural Dionysia (December/January); the Lenaea (January/February); the Anthesteria (often referred to as *Choes* = "Jugs, Beakers," or as *Dionysos en Limnais* "in the Marshes" [February/March]); and the City Dionysia (= "Great" Dionysia [March/April]). All of these festivals (as well as the Eleusinian Mysteries, which also involve Dionysian elements, as we shall see in the next section) are directly or indirectly alluded to in the course of *Frogs*.

Aristophanes' plays all received their first performance at the dramatic festivals of either the Lenaea (as *Frogs* did) or the City Dionysia, and internal references both to the conventions of the Theater and to these festival occasions are common in Old Comedy. In this play, however, the frog chorus is also heard reminding itself—and us—of another major Dionysian festival, the Anthesteria:

Marshy, muddy children of the streams,
Let's call out loudly, along with the reed-pipes,

> Our sweet-sounding hymn of praise, *KOAX KOAX!*,
> Which we sang in honor of the Nysaean son of Zeus,
> Dionysus in the Marshes (*en Limnais*),
> At the time when the hung-over band of celebrants at the
>   holy Festival of Pots
> Comes through my sacred precinct.
>
>   (211–19)

These are (presumably) not living frogs, but frog-ghosts, because they are in the Underworld: so they are remembering songs that they sang when alive, songs that are still sung every year by their living descendants during the Anthesteria. This three-day festival was one of the most warmly celebrated events of the Athenian calendar, and although many details are obscure to us (and disputed by scholars), we can reconstruct the main outlines. On the first day, the new wine was opened (*Pithoigia* = "cask-opening"). On the second day (*Choes* = "beakers, cups"), every Athenian man, city-wide, was expected to drink a separate pitcher-full of wine in silence (rather than, as usual, sharing wine from a mixing-bowl, and conversing); this was supposedly in commemoration of Orestes' arrival as a refugee in Athens after killing his mother. On the final (third) day, "Pots" of cereal (219 *Chutrois*) were prepared for Hermes Chthonios and for the dead, and a large procession (218 *kraipalokômos*, the "hung-over band") took the participants to an old, largely disused sanctuary of Dionysus "in the Marshes" (217), which was apparently opened up just for this one day of the year; there the croaking of the local frogs was experienced as a kind of additional accompaniment and supplementary, natural celebration of the god, part of the "soundscape" of that occasion. So the underworld ghost-frogs can call those Marshes "[our] own sacred precinct" (219), and Aristophanes' whole play is named after them, brief though their participation is.

All of this is a perfect example of the nature of Greek choral/festival performance, i.e., the fact that a chorus on any particular occasion sings both as *this* group of individuals, here and now, and as the annual, *eternal* chorus of this deity, this location, this festival, representing a continuing tradition within the community. Often they will explicitly recall the moment or event or person that first brought about the creation of this festive tradition. This frog chorus is also a good example of the way in which mythology (Orestes), nature and seasonal change (marshes, frogs), human social entertainment (drinking, music), and celebration of the power of god (Dionysus, son of Zeus) are combined in specific locations (i.e., processing from one sanctuary to another, along a designated sacred route through "the Marshes"), on a designated day, to build community. Thus the god is honored and the inhabitants of Attica at large (animal as well as human) reestablish their relationship with him, while also defining who does and who does not belong in this community, and on what terms.

Such dynamics of inclusion, recapturing of the past, and performance of community are endemic to the Theater of Dionysus; and it is typical of Old Comedy especially that in this scene a genuine and highly valued religious event (the Anthesteria) is vividly recalled and simultaneously parodied (by an animal chorus!), in the presence of the very god it celebrates—a god who the singers do not even realize is right there next to them, observing, even as the audience watch him (impersonated by a human actor) enjoy the "performance" of his worship, in a play that itself comprises part of his annual festival in his own Theater. So we have three tiers/levels of performance: a human chorus singing in a Comedy in the Theater of Dionysus, who are impersonating/mimicking a chorus of frog-ghosts in Hades, who are recalling and reenacting the frog songs heard every year around the Marshes. And at all three levels Dionysus himself is "present" to watch and listen—even to join in. There is even evidence (mainly late sixth-century vase paintings, unfortunately, which could be interpreted otherwise) that at some point during the annual Anthesteria celebrations in Athens a statue of Dionysus was transported in procession on a ship-cart, i.e., a wheeled wagon built up to resemble a boat—in which case the rowing episode in *Frogs* would acquire additional humorous and cultural point.

(ii) Hades, the Afterlife, and the Underworld

What happens to us after we die? Do we simply and completely cease to exist, or does some bit of us (a soul, a personality, a replica of our mortal existence) live on somewhere, somehow? The Greeks of the archaic and classical period never developed a precise, comprehensive, and universally accepted set of beliefs about this (very important) topic. On the whole, they seem to have been less preoccupied/concerned with preparations for the afterlife than, e.g., the Egyptians or (later) the Christians. But there were nonetheless a number of ritual practices that were widely shared among fifth-century Athenians, along with general beliefs about the afterlife that seem to have been more or less taken for granted; so we shall begin by surveying these in relation to the action of *Frogs*. The more particular rituals and beliefs of specific groups, such as Eleusinian initiates and Orphics, will be considered in the next section.

In the Homeric poems, a person's "soul" or "life-breath" (*psychê*) is often described as leaving his body at the moment of death and flitting off unhappily down to Hades: e.g., ". . . at once the life spirit/fled from his limbs, and the hateful darkness closed in about him . . ." (*Iliad* 16. 606–7; trans. Lattimore). These "life-spirits, souls, shades" were imagined as being small and shadowy, almost voiceless or able merely to twitter meaninglessly, and largely devoid of consciousness, though in dreams they might sometimes appear and talk to living people. Vase paintings of the archaic period sometimes show a tiny, winged replica of a warrior flying out of the dying man's mouth and/or being escorted to the Underworld by Hermes, one of whose epithets is indeed *psychopompos*, "escorter-of-souls" (see Fig. 6–1).

In addition to *psychê*, another Homeric term for these little "afterlife" figures is *eidôlon* ("image, replica"); and in the *Nekuia* of the *Odyssey* (literally, the "Corpse-Episode," Book 11), when Odysseus wants to consult the dead prophet Teiresias, we find both terms being used of the spirits of the dead (*psychai* and *eidôla*). In this epic account of a hero's quest to the land of the dead, situated at the far

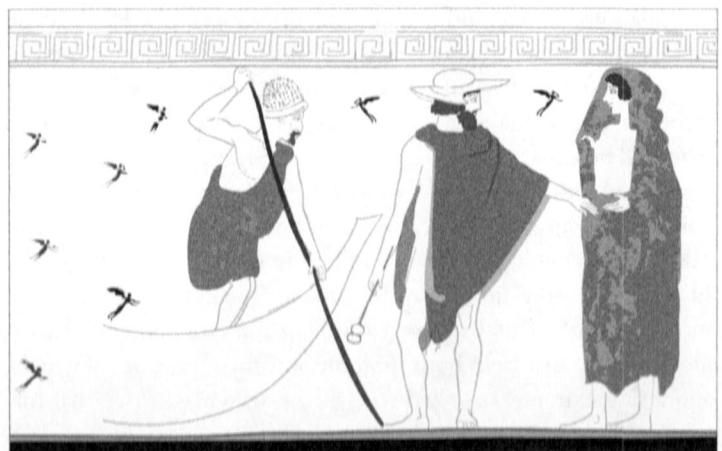

Figure 6–1. Charon, ferryman of souls, with Hermes and a dead woman.
Attic white-ground lekythos, fifth century BCE (ARV^2 846,193). National Museum, Athens ANM 1926. Drawing by Elizabeth Wahle.

western edge of the world next to Ocean, "where the sun never shines" (11. 13–22), the setting unobtrusively shifts as the narrative proceeds: what begins as a process of necromancy, with Odysseus digging a pit at ground level, filling it with blood, awaiting the arrival of the spirits *en masse*, and then inviting them one by one to drink the blood so that they can temporarily recover their wits and speak with him, soon becomes an actual visit to the Underworld: "Then I saw xxx . . . and then I saw yyy . . .," including the tormented figures of Tantalus, Tityus, Sisyphus, and others, all being punished (presumably) deep down in the depths of Tartarus.

In the *Odyssey*, then, there is some ambiguity as to whether the Land of the Dead is far off to the West (but more or less at ground level), or deep underground—i.e., an "Underworld." By the fifth century, the Underworld version seems to have become prevalent: this chthonian realm is ruled over by Zeus' brother Hades, sometimes known instead as Plouton, together with his queen, Persephone, Daughter (*Korē*) of Demeter. The geography of this Underworld was not by any means clearly demarcated or fixed in fifth-century Greek imaginations, though others subsequently (especially Plato, Vergil, and Dante) developed a topography that became somewhat canonical: a descent (via Avernus or Acheron) and river-crossing (Styx, or Acheron, plus Lethê and its waters of forgetfulness) on a ferryboat managed by Charon, with a destination consisting of segregated areas established for different kinds of soul; a panel of three judges, Aeacus, Minos, and Rhadamanthus, assesses the souls, with the wholly virtuous (very few) going off to a life of bliss in the Isles of the Blessed or Elysian Fields, the normal, ordinary souls (i.e., of people who led moderately good or bad lives) dwelling for ever more in a dark, gloomy place that lacks both sunshine and any source of enjoyment, and a few extremely wicked souls being sentenced to eternal torment in deepest Tartarus (a kind of Hell). This geography/eschatology does not seem to have been clearly established nor much discussed, however, before Plato (notably in the "myths" at the end of his *Gorgias, Phaedo*, and *Republic*—which are not entirely consistent among themselves). For Aristophanes' audience the expectations were very open-ended, as the fifth-century procedures for burial and observance of the dead in Athens demonstrate.

Burial and the Dead

The evidence concerning such procedures comes in many forms. So, in addition to the literary and visual sources we have been considering, we need also to take account of the available evidence for "real life" practices concerning the dead, such as burial rituals, tomb-offerings and hero cult, gravestones, epitaphs and other memorials, incubation and dream-cures, even magic and necromancy. Aristophanic comedy, for all its elements of fantasy and absurdity and all its allusions to Homeric and other literary traditions, never loses sight of the social realities most familiar to its Athenian audience.

In Homer's world, the dead are usually cremated and only their bones and/or ashes get to be buried: a clean, hot, and very dry experience. In most classical Greek contexts, however, inhumation had become the usual practice: after the body had been washed and "laid out" to be mourned at home (*prothesis*), it was "carried out" in a torch-lit procession (*ekphora*) through the street(s) to the public graveyard and consigned to the ground: a dark, dank residence for a slowly decaying corpse. It is no wonder the world of the dead was imagined as being (for most) "all darkness and mud" (*Frogs* 273), or even "mud and eternal shit" (145–51; cf. Plato *Phaedo* 111d–e, 113a–b). Over the grave a tombstone might be erected, with perhaps an inscription and some kind of memorial image or symbol. Offerings might subsequently be brought to the tomb on special days: libations of water, milk, or wine might be poured, cakes offered, locks of hair or garlands of flowers placed on the tombstone; prayers might be uttered. All of these suggest that the spirit of the dead person was felt to be somehow aware and capable of receiving and appreciating such offerings and messages (communications), and possibly even responding in some way.

The most conspicuous example of this belief is hero cult. Individuals whose ancestry or achievements marked them out as superior and distinguished—thus god-like—could be recognized after their deaths by being heroized: their tombs would be specially honored, prayers would be addressed to them (as Agamemnon is addressed by his children in Aeschylus' *Oresteia*; cf. *Frogs* 1126–28), and there might even be a local or polis-wide festival to honor their memory. Aeschylus himself, after he died in Gela (Sicily) was honored with hero cult; and later tradition (perhaps not entirely trustworthy) recorded that Sophocles was heroized at Athens as *Dexios* ("Receiver, Welcomer") because of his role in introducing the cult of Asclepius to the city. Other poets too were honored with prominent hero cults: Hesiod, Archilochus, Pindar, and many others. In these cases at least, it was obviously believed (by some, at some level) that a degree of consciousness persisted, or could be summoned up, in the great man after death, along with some kind of power and continuing concern for the community to which he had belonged. This is something stronger, to be sure, than the memorialization of Shakespeare at Stratford, or Goethe at Weimar.

But these matters (about the dead) are still more complicated. It is not easy to draw a clear line between formal hero cult, informal tending of a tomb by the dead person's family, and outright magic and necromancy, whether amateur or professional. Honoring the tomb of a hero and requesting his protection for the community is not an entirely different operation from routinely visiting the tomb of a less exalted loved one or ancestor/parent, making offerings and praying for "wealth and health." So magical and necromantic rituals tend to be built around these routines, with the client perhaps also sleeping at the tomb overnight in the hope of being visited by a dream, or employing a professional incantation-specialist to assist in persuading—or compelling—the dead spirit to provide healing or some other kind of help.

When King Saul consults the dead prophet Samuel through the Medium ("Witch") of Endor (I *Samuel* 28), or King Darius is conjured up from the Underworld in Aeschylus' *Persians* by the incantations of the chorus in order to provide advice about Persia's future, how different is this from seeking (as in *Frogs*) actually to bring a dead man back permanently to reside on earth? The distinction is rather fine, but it does seem crucial—at least in real life, if not in drama. In a dream or a magical/necromantic ritual, the dreamer's partially out-of-body mental state, or the songs and special powers of the medium/magician, may bring about a temporary alteration in the status quo, such that spirits can cross boundaries and reenter communication with the living. This is what the Greeks sometimes termed *goêteia* ("sorcery") and associated generally with the Thracians or Persians rather than with homegrown Greek religious observance. But this activity is always brief and transitory: it lasts only as long as the dream or spell is effective, and the spirits must always return "below" when that effect is over. Raising the dead and bringing them completely back to life, however, is another matter. In myth, Asclepius and Orpheus both attempted this, but neither in the end succeeded. It is forbidden. So Dionysus' journey in *Frogs* is an especially bold and unusual, almost subversive, quest, resembling Heracles' retrieval of Cerberus (and Pirithous, and Alcestis) in previous hero-myths rather than such fact-finding visits as those of Odysseus and Aeneas. But we note that Plouton and the other "powers under the earth" (1529) are quite willing to release Aeschylus—Dionysus does not have to fight for this privilege; indeed, Plouton has assisted in setting up the contest that would bring this about (784–86) and he volunteers his permission again at 1415–16.

But there are plenty of uncertainties surrounding Aeschylus' "return" to Athens in *Frogs*, as is to be expected. (After all, Aristophanes is not composing a theological or eschatological treatise.) Are we to imagine (at the end of *Frogs*) that Aeschylus, once he has given his salutary "advice" to the Athenians (1009, 1420, 1501–22) will take up permanent residence there again as a normal human being? (If so, will he compose new tragedies . . .? in what style . . .?) More likely, the audience understands that he will be present as a hero, a spirit residing among them, guiding them and influencing young and impressionable tragedians to compose better plays. But of course such speculations are idle: Aeschylus is not actually going to return to Athens, in any shape or form. This is a comedy. Yet Old Comedy allows (requires) its audience to enter a world in which actual ritual practice and the wildest fantasies can blend in the most delicious ways: an oneiric (dream-like) and Dionysian world.

Aristophanes was not the first comic playwright to dramatize a heroic quest to the Underworld and/or the recalling of one or more spirits of the dead to visit the Athenian here and now. We know of at least four famous and popular comedies by his rivals along those lines, but the details of staging—and of setting—are not by any means clear to us for any of them. About the plot and characters of Cratinus' *Archilochoi* (*The Archilochuses*) we know very little, except that Archilochus seems to have participated (probably successfully) in an *agôn* against Homer (and probably Hesiod as well; cf. Diogenes Laertius 1.12): where this confrontation took place we cannot tell. Much more survives (mostly on papyrus) of Cratinus' *Ploutoi* (*Wealth-gods*, from the 430s), enough to tell us that the chorus were the "wealth-giving spirits" mentioned by Hesiod (*WD* 122–26) as the remnants of Cronus' reign on earth, who (in Cratinus' play) had been relegated to an existence underground, haunting human beings and rewarding or punishing them from there, but have now been released and apparently arrive in the upper air of their own volition, rather than because anyone else has gone down to fetch them.

An especially highly acclaimed comedy, it seems, was Eupolis' *Dêmoi* (*Demes*, from 417 or possibly 412 BCE), in which four famous Athenian politicians came back up from the Underworld to help the city in its current distress: Solon, Aristides, Miltiades, and Pericles (see chapter 1). It has usually been assumed that this play involved scenes set in the Underworld, like *Frogs*. But it is equally possible that some kind of necromantic operation was conducted to conjure these dead souls up from below (like Darius in Aeschylus' *Persians*), in which case the action may all have taken place above ground, in Athens. In none of these four plays, then, is it certain, or even very likely, that an actual visit to the Underworld was staged: this may have been an innovation by Aristophanes in *Frogs*. Likewise in Aristophanes' own (lost) *Gerytades*, an embassy was sent by living poets in Athens to consult the great dead poets below, but it does not appear that any Underworld scenes were staged.

The Underworld Geography of Frogs

This geography is of course imaginary, and is not intended to be systematically accurate or precise. The itinerary that we witness being followed by Dionysus and Xanthias is not entirely self-consistent, and was certainly not intended to be realistic; Aristophanic comedy never is. But it seems that for the most part these two adventurers follow a path that had become fairly standard both in Greek literature and in the popular imagination. First, they have to be transported on the ferryboat of Charon across a "River" or "Lake." Normally the crossing entails Charon using a pole to propel the boat (see Fig. 6–1). But in this case the lake is "bottomless" (136 *abusson*) so that Dionysus has to row, a modification that highlights the theme of naval service, topically of great significance for this play. Does he use one oar, like a crewman on a trireme (see Fig. 6–2a and b), or two, like the rower in a rowboat (see Fig. 1–1a)?

Staging would make this instantly clear, but the text does not. Once across the water, in many accounts of the Underworld (as noted above) the souls are "judged," usually by Minos, Rhadamanthus, and Aeacus; and sometimes there are quite separate regions designated for the very good, the so-so, and the very evil. But the only "judgment" that we hear about in *Frogs* is the special competition between the two poets, though we do get a sense that perhaps different areas of the Underworld are occupied by different kinds of people, since the Mystic Initiates enjoy daylight and pleasant meadows that others do not.

Figure 6-2. An Athenian trireme (warship).
(a) Replica of a trireme, *Olympias*, proceeding under oar-power with sails furled (approaching Tolo, Greece, August 1990).
Photo courtesy of The Trireme Trust.
(b) Interior of the trireme, showing cramped arrangement of the three banks of rowers (whence the term "trireme").
Photo courtesy of Rosie Randolph and The Trireme Trust.
This full-scale trireme replica was researched and designed by John Coates and John Morrison, and was commissioned into the Greek navy in 1987. The crew in these photos were members of the Greek navy, together with British and American students.

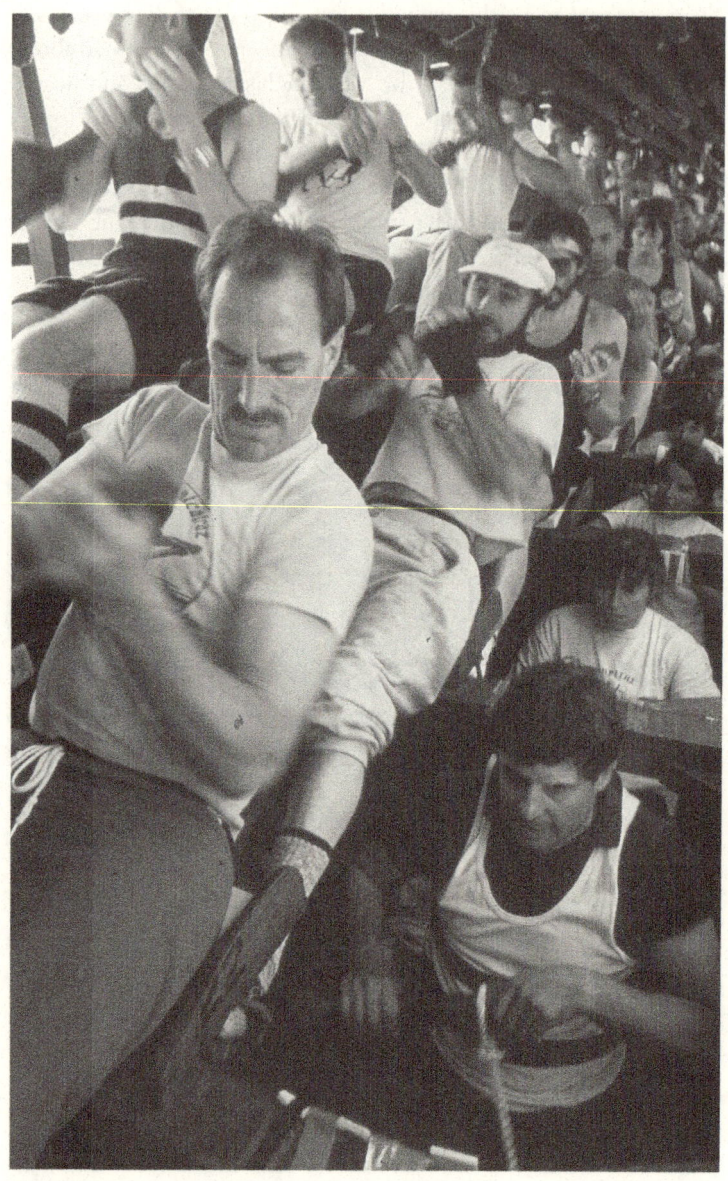

Figure 6–2. (*continued*)

Dionysus in the *Frogs*, despite his divine nature and literary sophistication, seems quite ignorant of the geography that he is going to encounter down below. At 117–19 he asks Heracles—a veteran of Underworld journeys—"Which is the quickest road for me to get down into Hades?" After several jokes (120–35 "a rope" . . . "hemlock" . . . "jump off a tower"), Dionysus reframes his request: "(136) (I want to go) on the path that *you* took down there!," and Heracles warns him that this involves "a long boat-ride . . . across a huge, bottomless lake." So where exactly is this lake? (Bodies of water often feature prominently in tales of heroic quest and "rebirth," from Gilgamesh to Odysseus to baptized Christians.) How to find it and access it for living people? It turns out to be quite close by, so that, after an unsuccessful attempt to pay a passing funeral cortege to transport them there (167–76), Xanthias agrees that they can manage to walk on their own:

> [Dion.] That jerk [= the corpse] thinks he's so high-and-mighty!
> [Xan.] To heck with him. I'll just walk there myself!
> [Dion.] You're a noble and worthy man, to be sure. Let's go then, to the ferryboat.
>
> (177–79)

All of this, of course, is largely a matter of stage conventions and dramatic convenience. Just as Dionysus' residing in Athens with a human slave (Xanthias) and their being able to walk to Heracles' house—which likewise seems to be located on an Athenian street, not too far away—makes no mythological sense but is necessary for the plot and staging, so too Heracles' house must be close to the boarding-place for Charon's ferry, and the "vast lake" must be small enough that Dionysus can row across it in just a few minutes—while Xanthias somehow manages to run round it on foot and meet them on the other side (while still alive!); see Fig. 1–1a. Likewise it is convenient that once the crossing of the Lake is completed the Mystic Initiates and Plouton's palace, along with the "thrones" on which the masters of the various *technai* sit, all happen to be "quite close by—right next to the road . . ." (155–63). And, at the end of the play, it seems that the procession that is "escorting" Aeschylus "back up to the light" (1525, 1529) includes both the chorus of Initiates and some "guardian spirits" (*daimones*) of the Underworld itself: as they walk, they pray for "a good journey" (1528, in lyric verses adapted from Aeschylus' own *Glaucus of Potniae*, fr. 36.5–6)—and it is as though they are entering the Theater of Dionysus itself in procession (an exit that is also an entrance)—though at 1480 there had been mention of "sailing away." No ferryboat seems to be needed now, no Lake, no long road past Heracles' house, etc. They are *here* already. (And where is poor Xanthias? No mention! Like the proverbial "donkey at the Mysteries" (159), and the stage donkey of the opening scene, he is apparently not needed once the serious business of poetic evaluation and communal salvation gets under way. Or perhaps he is just taken for granted here, like most slaves, most of the time: see chapter 7).

After Dionysus climbs out of the ferryboat (270ff), he looks around and calls for Xanthias—who soon appears, having apparently run all the way around the edge of the Lake. This has meant trudging through the "mud and darkness" (272) in which the souls of nastier and less than virtuous people apparently reside ("father-beaters and oath-breakers," 273–74; just as Heracles had described at 146–51). Then the two of them, again as Heracles had predicted, supposedly encounter various terrifying monsters (142–43 "snakes and terrifying wild beasts")—though these are not visible onstage and we may suspect that they are purely Xanthias' invention to torment and humiliate his boss (especially Empousa, a mythical underworld creature who changes her shape and devours the unwary [278–310]). Apparently this is what the Underworld is like for most of its inhabitants: dark, smelly, messy, and terrifying. But Heracles has advised Dionysus to seek out the Initiates (154–63), and that is what he does. Attracted to, and then guided by the heavenly smells (roasting pork), torches, and music (312–15, 337–38), Dionysus and Xanthias are able to make their way to the area in which that cheerful band is singing and dancing, and they thus escape the terrors to which other Underworld-dwellers are subjected, and arrive at the dwelling (palace?) of Persephone (Pherephatta in Athenian spelling) and Plouton/Hades. At least, this is what the audience must logically infer is happening, though the scene is necessarily staged in such a way that it has to be the Chorus who actually arrive (enter) while the two visitors keep quiet onstage, awaiting them (315, 321–22).

We should probably not worry too much as to whether, in this comical world, the various people who are encountered in the Underworld—most notably the chorus of Mystic Initiates, and the two tragedians—are made of flesh and blood or are mere insubstantial shades. (But we may enjoy the references to "criminals, father-beaters . . ."—as well as at one point the whole Theater audience (276 "Ah yes, now I see them . . . !")—as being lost souls, i.e., those unsaved and unsavable; likewise of course those incorrigible lovers of Euripides.) Despite its exotic, dark, and distant character, this theatrical Underworld in many respects exhibits the same social arrangements and living conditions as real-life Athens, including a love of pork and wine.

When Dionysus and Xanthias arrive at Plouton's palace, they knock (tentatively) at the door . . . and a fierce-looking Doorkeeper accosts them, immediately announcing that he will have "Heracles" arrested and punished for his previous acts of violence, especially his removal of the watchdog Cerberus (464–78). Dionysus shits himself with fear (479–90) while the Doorkeeper (identified by some medieval manuscripts as "Aeacus"—but probably erroneously, he is really just an anonymous slave; cf. 467–69) runs back inside, returning at 605 with two assistants and summoning three Scythian policemen to add further support (607–9). So Xanthias (who is now wearing the "Heracles" costume) is caught and tied up. The misunderstanding, that this is "Heracles" returning for another visit to the Underworld, along with the double impersonation involved between Dionysus and Xanthias, once again produces a flurry of comic business: on the one hand, the Doorkeeper and also a pair of angry innkeepers (Plathanê and her friend) who remember Heracles' shameless stealing of food and abusing of their staff seek the most extreme punishments, while in between an attractive young serving-girl invites "Heracles" to enjoy their best delicacies and her own sexual favors. Later (753ff), after the misunderstandings about identity have finally been cleared up, Dionysus and Xanthias get to be entertained in properly royal-divine style by King Plouton (737ff, 1478ff). The Underworld thus appears as just another little town or petty kingdom such as Heracles or any mythical hero—or real-life Athenian—might encounter on his travels. Likewise, the grim but hilarious scene of torture and inquiry as to the true identity of god and slave (605–72) is obviously based on domestic and judicial realities known well at firsthand by Aristophanes' audience.

(iii) Mysteries and Initiation

On many different levels, *Frogs* is about recovery and salvation, including the mysterious power of initiation, or a "rite of passage" of some kind, to provide a better future, for all or for some, after death. Initiation rituals, like rites of passage in general, have been extensively discussed by historians of classical Greek culture in recent decades, with wildly varying conclusions being drawn. There are four main areas of discussion, or four types of "initiation rite," that command our attention—and unfortunately many modern discussions do not distinguish carefully enough between them:

1. Age-group rituals (as in Arnold Van Gennep's *rites de passage*), particularly institutionalized procedures for adolescents to mark or effect their transition into fully qualified adult status within a community.
2. Mystery religions such as the Eleusinian Mysteries, along with other cult practices, especially Orphic texts and burial procedures, and perhaps other kinds of Bacchic ceremonies too, in which an individual went through some kind of ritual test or training (sometimes imagined as a "rebirth" and salvation) and was then accepted into a group (*thiasos*, or *orgeôn*) whose members anticipated a passage to a better life for their souls after death.
3. Myths of "eternal return" (*nostos*), usually taking the form of a hero's descent (*katabasis*) to the Underworld (or else a voyage to

the ends of the earth), a struggle against monsters or Death or some other obstructive threat, and a triumphant "return" to the upper world (*anodos*) where prosperity and other benefits (often including marriage) would be awaiting.
4. Rejuvenation rituals associated with seasonal fertility ceremonies, phallic celebrations and/or the Great Mother, magic spells—and comedy.

The Greek term for most of these various "rites" would usually be simply *teletai* (literally "things/ceremonies duly completed") or *orgia* ("doings, acts"). Both of these terms reflect the fact that a ritual, to be effective, must involve its participants in *saying and doing* something distinctive and efficacious: thus both "ritual action" and "speech acts" are involved. When such rites are secret and not to be divulged to outsiders, they may be known as *mustêria* ("mysteries, secret rites"), from the verb *mueô* = "I close (my eyes/mouth)," the idea being that only the initiates (*mustai*, or *memuêmenoi*) may "see" the secret objects and doings or "open" their mouths and ears to speak and hear the sacred words. For those who are not initiated and not properly prepared for initiation (because they are too unclean, too ignorant, of the wrong age-group or status, or whatever), the rule must be *euphêmein* ("keep silent!" lit. "speak <only> words of good omen") and "stand aside, stay away!" as at *Frogs* 354.

An "initiation" is literally a "beginning" (Latin *initium*), and an initiation ritual properly implies the start of a new and perhaps better life. As with several other "rites of passage" that mark a crucial transition from one status to another, initiation brings a person into a new, special community: initiates share an experience, participation in a peculiar ceremony, access to a particular body of knowledge and entitlements, and (in some sense) a common social status. The question whether, in archaic and classical Greek initiation rituals, adolescent rites of passage and age-group ceremonies were widespread and important or relatively restricted, localized, and of minor significance, continues to be debated by scholars. We do not need to resolve it here. But there is no disagreement about the great popularity and significance of the Eleusinian Mysteries—especially for Athenian citizens, of course, male and female alike, but also for all the other residents of Attica, including metics and slaves. It is estimated that as many as one-third or even one-half of the whole population (male and female) may have been initiates. Other mystery cults seem to have been popular as well, though it is impossible to measure their scale or impact: Sabazius and Attis, the Great Mother (Cybele/Kubaba), the Thracian goddess Bendis, and above all Bacchus/Dionysus in various guises. Many of these cults too allowed women to participate; some included slaves.

Several of these non-Olympian and/or Bacchic rituals were incorporated during the fifth century into the civic festival calendar of the Attic demes and Athenian polis: most notably, the Great Mother and Bendis. Other cults remained more private, and often quite small-scale. In general, as far as we can tell, participation in mystery cult or Dionysian/Orphic rituals was not very exclusive or restrictive: "initiates" could and did participate fully in other religious activities as well, including the major cults and festivals of the polis, and it was rare for issues of dogma or sacred practice to cause a crisis of conscience or conflict of commitment.

Three of the four categories of "initiation rites" that we outlined above are encountered in the *Frogs*, in forms that make the ritual structures, ideas, and behaviors explicit and obvious enough for the original audience definitely to recognize them and to realize their significance. Type (1), the adolescent/age-group "rites of passage" that are the best known, perhaps, to modern readers and anthropologists at large, is not really present in *Frogs*—unless we are to see Dionysus himself as an adolescent seeking to "come of age," which seems (to me, and to many) too much of a stretch. But obviously type (3), the narrative structure of "descent and return" (with repeated references to Heracles, and less explicit ones to Persephone and Orpheus), is central to the whole play, and we shall come back to this in a moment. Equally obvious is the importance of type (4), since both the beginning and the ending of the play set the audience up expressly to anticipate a move towards the "salvation" of tragedy and of Athens, in a form that comprises both a rescue from danger and a rejuvenation and reconstitution after a depressing period of decline, corruption, and near-collapse.

As for type (2), the Mysteries and other rituals of rebirth and salvation, our play is remarkably explicit (and informative!) about these matters. The Chorus are referred to repeatedly as Mystic Initiates (158, 318, 336, 370, 456, cf. Aeschylus at 887), and they allude rather specifically to the Eleusinian Mysteries by using the same imagery and following the same celebratory procedures. Several additional "mystic" elements also are featured, belonging to a broader (not specifically Eleusinian) phenomenon of "Orphic" and Bacchic ideas and texts that were available all over the Mediterranean and Black Sea, offering guidance towards a more blessed afterlife. So, we need to look briefly into all of these, to try to situate ourselves within the same frame of reference as Aristophanes' original audience.

Initiation and the Eleusinian Mysteries

Eleusis was one of the largest towns in Attica, at its northwest edge, 12 miles/20 km from the city-center of Athens. For several centuries it had been the center of a cult of Demeter and Persephone (aka Korê, her "Daughter"). This "mystery" cult was connected with the myth of Persephone's involuntary "descent" (*katabasis*) into the Underworld and victorious "return/ascent" (*anodos*) to the light of day and her Mother's embrace; and this story (most famously narrated in the "Homeric" *Hymn to Demeter*) of the conquest of death and darkness (i.e., escape from Hades) and return to a permanent, better existence among a like-minded community of spirits of light and cheerfulness, comprises the core of the religion of the Two Goddesses. At the same time, the fact that Pherephatta/Persephone/Kore (in the myth) has been raped and married by Hades, and continues to rule intermittently as his Queen and as Mistress of the Underworld, means that her say-so and approval, together with those of her Mother, Demeter, are of unique value for dead spirits. In combination, these "Two Goddesses" thus provide a life-affirming bridge between the world of the dead and the world of nature, life, and fertility. Of course, there are many famous Greek *katabasis* stories, including those of Heracles, Theseus, and Orpheus; but Persephone's is the most famous, inspirational, and formative of all—as well as being the most imitated in such scenes as Aristophanes' onstage reclamation of the goddess of Peace (in *Peace*)—and the Eleusinian Mysteries were by far the biggest and most inclusive of all Greek mystery cults.

The Eleusinian Mysteries were celebrated every year, involving hundreds, even thousands, of *mystai*, men and women, accompanied by torches, pipes (*auloi*), singing and dancing, as they made their way along the Sacred Road from Athens to the sanctuary of Demeter at Eleusis. From time to time they would engage in obscene joking and ritual abuse of (perhaps also from?) the onlookers and each other. Those about to be initiated wore old, even tattered, clothing, apparently because their garments were to be ritually offered to the goddesses at the sanctuary after the ceremony was completed—a feature that is mentioned at *Frogs* 404–12 (and doubtless reflected in the costuming of the Chorus), and that also seems to have served to emphasize the egalitarian, nonelitist character of the occasion. It was not expensive to be an Initiate (unlike, e.g., visits to the Delphic Oracle, or membership in certain other fancy cults).

When they arrived at the Eleusinion, only those who had previously been fully initiated were allowed entrance to the "inner sanctuary" (*adyton*). They would celebrate an "all-night festivity" (*pannuchis*, as mentioned at *Frogs* 371, 446). The priests and heralds who controlled the sanctuary also presided over the events that took place at the initiation ceremonies—and this is the part that unfortunately remains largely secret. All we know is that those being newly initiated entered a darkened room (the *telestêrion*) where they were subjected to startling, alarming, and exciting sights and sounds, including (apparently) sudden bright lights: all of these would be the "things/acts" of the goddess (*erga, drômena, orgia*; at *Hymn Hom. Dem.* 476 "the doing of sacred things . . . and rites" are mentioned); they would drink a special potion; and finally they would emerge as *epoptai* ("the ones-who-have-seen"), i.e., as fully initiated (*memuêmenoi*).

The words and "doings" of the Eleusinan rituals were thus a kind of "drama," apparently based on (mimicking?) Demeter's wanderings and searching, and Kore's descent and return. Outsiders could neither participate nor watch. Of the "insiders," some presumably "watched" as the new initiates (novices) went through the ordeal of sights, sounds, and terrors that was conducted by the professional priests (*hierophantai*). Overall, the annual "ceremonies of completion" (*teletai*) produced an extensive, ongoing community of *Mystai*, men and women of all statuses, ages, and social classes, who would continue to lead their lives in the years ahead in the awareness that a better life was awaiting them after they died. How much difference this awareness made to most, or any of them, during the rest of their lives, we cannot judge. Did they live in constant rapture and faith in an eternal bliss lying ahead? Probably not. But some degree of enhanced comfort at the prospect of death was presumably achieved (a bit like a modern life insurance policy), as well as the reassurance and solidarity of membership in a like-minded community of "those who had seen" and "those who knew."

There was a particular emotional (religious) anxiety and tension surrounding the Eleusinian Mysteries during the years 415–05. The Mysteries had long been of huge cultural significance for all Athenians, even those who were not initiates. For not only was this a widely renowned spiritual-religious phenomenon in its own right, but it was also regarded as a spectacular token of Athens' cultural superiority, since it was Attica that Demeter had chosen as the first place to receive her gift of grains to human beings, and thus to begin the processes of agriculture and civilization in general. But since the year 415 two crises had intervened. First was the scandal concerning Alcibiades and his friends, who were accused of violating the Mysteries by performing them privately in their homes. Then, after the Spartan fort had been built at Decelea (see chapter 2), the annual procession to Eleusis and the celebration there of full-scale Mysteries had to be suspended, since the proximity of Spartan troops made this too dangerous. There had been just one year of respite and renewal at Eleusis during that period—thanks to none other than Alcibiades. After his recall to Athens in 407, he had organized a large-scale military escort for the procession so that the festival could take place. So the notorious turncoat/traitor, who had himself been prosecuted for mutilating the Herms and perhaps for violating the Mysteries too, had—as so often—also won (back) the hearts of many of the Athenians by a brilliant and patriotic intervention, in this case one of a directly "religious" character. No wonder Alcibiades looms so large in the final judgment scene of our play (see chapter 7).

Other Mystai: Orphic Texts for the Afterlife

Apart from the Eleusinian Mysteries, which were a polis-sponsored, large-scale, annual event, and very much an Athenian source of pride, we need to consider also some of the smaller and more scattered cults of Dionysus, Persephone, and the afterlife that are known to have existed all over the Mediterranean world in the fifth century, and that are usually classified by scholars as "Orphic" (though that term is notoriously unsatisfactory—either too vague, or too specific). Over the last 100 years or so, a number of graves have been discovered in very diverse locations (several in South Italy and Sicily; others in Thessaly and Crete) that have yielded small gold-foil tablets (or "leaves," *lamellae*), written in Greek during the fifth to the third century, buried with the deceased person, and clearly intended to contribute to this person's future existence after death. The texts that they contain are highly formulaic; several of them are almost identical to one another, though interesting variations do also occur. Written in verse, these tablets operate almost like passports or a Rough Guide to the Underworld, giving directions as to which road to follow down there, which water to drink or avoid, which guide or protector to seek out, etc. The dead person's soul is supposed to achieve "salvation" thereby, and to "travel the sacred road (*hieran hodon*) along which other glorious initiates and Bacchants go." Some of these texts mention Persephone, others "the King <of the Underworld>" as the person who will dictate the soul's future happiness; and in general we can conclude that to members of these cult communities death is a rebirth, thanks to the "release" provided by "Bakkhios" (i.e., Dionysus). The soul will be hailed as "blessed" (*olbios*) and "fortunate" (*eudaimôn*), and/or even as "a god" (*theos*), as it walks along the sacred road and/or meadow in the company of other "blessed ones," called *bakkhoi* and *mustai*, who include both men and women. There is also a striking emphasis in several texts on the intelligence, understanding, and reliance on memory that are expected of these blessed souls after death.

Another small cluster of Dionysian/Orphic/salvationist texts comes from the very northern-most edge of the "Greek" world: Olbia, on the Black Sea (in modern Ukraine). Inscribed bone-chips, apparently written in the late fifth century for use in funerary contexts, have been found, containing brief, strikingly dualistic juxtapositions of personified entities:

LIFE DEATH LIFE (BIOS THANATOS BIOS)
  PEACE WAR TRUTH LIE (EIRÊNÊ POLEMOS ALÊTHEIA PSEUDOS)
  BODY SOUL (SÔMA PSUCHÊ)

Also written on some of them were the divine/heroic names of Dionysus and Orpheus (*ORPHIK- DION-*). These polarities, reminiscent of some of Heraclitus' riddling paradoxes, find resonances in the (absurd, yet not quite pointless) remarks of Dionysus in *Frogs* as he parodies famous lines of Euripides: "Who knows if life is death . . . and breathing is dining . . .?" (1477–78.)

Scholarly opinions differ as to what exactly "Orphic" literature and beliefs amounted to in the late fifth century: how unified, consistent, and faith-based the theology and cosmology of Orphic texts and their readers may have been; what Orpheus himself was supposed to have contributed, as sage and musician; and especially, how "Dionysus" fits in with Orpheus' supposedly Apollo-derived poetry and medical-purificatory rituals. We need not engage with this debate here. But we can nowadays assert with confidence (as scholars fifty or even twenty years ago could not) that Dionysian religion did indeed overlap in several dimensions and many different contexts with beliefs and practices concerned with mystery and purification rituals, Eleusis, and preparations for the afterlife. And, in particular, it is by now agreed by all modern scholars that "Iacchus," the divinity addressed by the Initiate Chorus in *Frogs*, and also the divinity whose statue was carried in procession during the Great Eleusinian festival, is indeed identical to (or is a version/aspect/associate of) Dionysus/Bacchus.

Turning back to *Frogs*, we can see that the elaborate, lively arrival-song (*parodos*) of the Chorus of Initiates (*Frogs* 316–459), while certainly not a direct copy of anything that would have been actually sung by anyone at Eleusis—since that would violate the code of secrecy and would be highly impious—is nonetheless unmistakably "Eleusinian" in its imagery and self-referential description (while also reminding us at several points of the songs of Euripides' Bacchant chorus, composed just a year or two earlier).

> [XANTHIAS] I hear the breath of pipes!
> [DIONYSUS] Me too, and the most mystic (*mustikôtatê*)
>   smell of torches
>   has just now breathed itself into me. . . .
> [CHORUS, *in the distance*] Iacchus! Iacchus!
> [XANTHIAS] That's just what it is, master. The initiated
>   ones (*memuêmenoi*)
>   Are playing around here somewhere—
>   The ones he [Heracles] told us about.
>   They're singing their Iacchus-hymn, the one that
>   Diagoras composed.
>
>   (313–20)

The joke here is that Diagoras was a notorious atheist who was actually prosecuted for desecrating the Mysteries, which of course immediately lets Aristophanes (the author) off any potential hook of himself "revealing the Mysteries," by alerting the audience that what follows will be a parody—however respectful and inspirational—rather than a direct replication of Eleusinian language and procedure.

So what do we find in the "Hymn to Iacchus" that follows? What can it tell us about Eleusinian-Dionysian Mystery cult and belief? And how does it contribute to the overall dynamics and meaning of this play?

Iacchus is said to "dwell here" (325) and is invited to "come and dance in this meadow . . . among the fellow-*thiasos*-members . . . in the holy choral group of initiates" (326–36). The god himself is imagined as joining in the dance, along with his chorus: "You yourself lead our young dancers to the flowery water-meadow . . .!" (350–52), ". . . our fellow-journeyer in this choral-dance" (396). The god is a luminous "star" (as in some of the Orphic *lamellae* mentioned above): "carrying flaming torches . . . light-bringing star of our nocturnal ritual (*teletês*), as the meadow is lit up by the flame" (340–44). So this is a nighttime ceremony, like the Eleusinian *pannuchis*. The "meadow" is conventional in Greek poetry for a joyous place of fertility, fun, and life (as with the "Elysian Fields"), in contrast to the "mud" and darkness that fills most of Hades, or the "parched rock" that has to be passed on the way (194). Furthermore, as in Euripides' *Bacchae* (Cadmus and Tiresias at *Ba*. 201–9, 322–24), this mystic dancing is transformative; it rejuvenates the old and brings them forgetfulness of pains and troubles: "Old men's knees are leaping, and they shake off pains and lengthy years . . ." (345–48). To all the initiates Dionysus gives limitless energy: "Show how you complete the long road without toil or fatigue . . . be my escort!" (401–3), they sing, a reminder, presumably, of the journey along the Sacred Road to Eleusis itself.

In addition to repeatedly invoking Iacchus, the Chorus calls on "Demeter" (383, 385, addressing her also as "Queen" [383], and on a female "Savior" [379–81]—who may be Athena, or Persephone). In any case, the close association of Demeter-Persephone and Dionysus-Iacchus is explicit. Indeed, the chorus credit Iacchus with being the founder of this choral celebration for her: "Iacchus, the one who invented this most sweet festival song, come here, accompany (us) to the goddess . . ." (398–400). He is almost their chorus leader, it seems—their own poet-producer, thus bringing Aristophanes himself into close alignment with the god.

Only the virtuous may participate in the initiate choral singing (354–71): all others will be excluded and/or mocked; especially we may note the "joking and mocking" that is invited at 372–74, as they proceed towards the "flowery meadows." Whether this is a reference to (adaptation of) the *gephurismos* ritual that took place on the journey from central Athens to Eleusis, as men sitting on "bridges" (*gephuroi*) uttered ritual insults at the passing procession, or to some other Dionysian or Demetrian convention, in either case the procedure adds to the pervasive sense that this mystic community embraces everyone who is well-meaning and good, and only rejects those beyond the social pale. As in Euripides' *Bacchae*, the Chorus congratulates the humble and lowly as against the high-and-mighty, and describes the simple wisdom of pure and pious commitment to god. That way blessedness lies, if the god is Dionysus.

Purity and Virtue

It is standard practice—and belief—in ancient mystery cults of all kinds that admission is restricted to those who are ritually "pure, clean" (Greek *katharos*; as at 355 "anyone who isn't pure of thought . . ."; opposite to *miaros*, "polluted, unclean," 466, 571, 1472); and usually that they must belong to certain definite social categories and adhere to prescribed behaviors (which may of course vary from one religion to the next). In *Frogs*, the audience is given multiple reminders as to who may and may not be included in the sacred rites of Dionysus/Demeter/the upcoming poetic contest, with extensive and amusing lists of the various malefactors and misfits who must be excluded (354–72; cf. 146–51). But it is clear throughout that membership of the choral group—and of the potentially "savable" community of good and well-meaning Athenians—is not meant to be especially narrow or restrictive. "We" in the audience are—almost all of us—savable, and we are made to feel that the songs and judgments that we are witnessing will draw us into unity and lead us in the direction of that common salvation.

Indeed it is striking (as also in Euripides' *Bacchae*, esp. 395–401, 417–32, 1002–10) how warmly the chorus remind the audience that this god is open to all, that he is not a snob, not biased towards the rich and famous, but oriented towards the shared enjoyment of life's pleasures (music, dance, wine, sex) and towards liberating everyone from pain and misery, however impecunious a person might be:

> You are the one who designed—to make people laugh, but also to save expense—
> The split sandal and shirt-with-a-hole-in-it.
> And you invented the idea
> That [sc. people/we all] could play and dance free, without having to pay for it.
> . . . On us alone the sun shines and we have holy light,
> We who are initiated (*memuêmetha*) and who led a pious life
> With regard to strangers and all ordinary/regular people (*idiôtas*).
>
> (*Frogs* 404–8, 454–59)

In *Frogs*, to be sure, not only do we have a Chorus of Mystic Initiates singing for Iacchus, with their sundry invitations to a life (or afterlife) of light, purity and bliss, but we encounter also a community of singing swan-frogs, waters that must be crossed (if not actually imbibed), wine to be drunk (and even pork to be cooked and eaten), and a pervasive sense of rebirth and intellectual/moral/existential recovery for all. All of this seems to be an alternative, ritual-based way to achieve what other Aristophanic heroes win for themselves through bold individual action (Dicaeopolis in *Acharnians*, Pisetaerus in *Birds*, Trygaeus in *Peace*, etc.): peace, prosperity, feasting, sex, happiness. There are several ways to be "born again": through correct ritual behavior, through music and dance—or through comic drama. In *Frogs*, we experience all of these, thanks to the multiple aspects of Dionysus.

So now it is time to look at this god more closely—in general, and how he is represented in our play.

(iv) Dionysus—in General, and in *Frogs*

He is of course an impossible divinity to define or to delimit, a god of paradoxes, contradictions, and transformations. Son of Zeus and (in most traditions) of a mortal mother, Semele (though sometimes, especially in Orphic contexts, his mother is considered to be Persephone), he exhibits at times a vulnerability, even near-mortality, that is not found among the other Olympians. Thus he is said to have been pursued by an angry Thessalian king, Lycurgus, to the point where "in terror" he jumped into the sea to hide there under the protection of Thetis (Homer *Iliad* 6. 130–40); and in another strand of tradition Dionysus-Zagreus was torn to pieces by the evil, violent Titans and had to be reconstituted and revivified (by Persephone?)—while the Titans were duly destroyed by Zeus and their blood mixed with earth to form the human race. (The similarity of several of these stories concerning Dionysus-Bacchus-Zagreus to other Near Eastern myths of a "dying" male god, often son of "God-the-Father," who returns to life and brings about renewed fertility and happiness, or even "saves" humankind entirely, has often been noted: Egyptian Osiris, Phrygian/Carian Adonis, Canaanite Jesus, etc.)

Throughout the nineteenth and much of the twentieth century, scholars usually regarded "Dionysus" as an Eastern divinity who had been adopted by the Greeks relatively late in their history—a view based partly on the very small role assigned to him in the Homeric and Hesiodic poems (where he does not appear to be an Olympian god at all), as compared with his great prominence in literature, art, and cult from the sixth century onwards. This entailed taking fairly literally the account provided at the beginning of Euripides' *Bacchae*, a play in which the chorus are Anatolian women who are following their "lord" into Greece to bring these new rituals to every city in the land, beginning with Thebes. Their songs assert—and demonstrate—that both the musical instruments (reed pipes and drums) and these holy purifications are all derived from the Great Mother, Cybele, in Phrygia (78–82, 130–34), whence Dionysus and the satyrs took them and brought them to Greece. Aurally, visually, and choreographically, this therefore appears to be an "Asian" cult (*Ba.* 152–59); and the Theban king in that play, Pentheus, sees the Stranger (Dionysus himself, disguised as a human priest) as an effeminate, luxury-loving foreigner, arrests and shackles him, and tries to suppress this novel and decadent religious cult completely. His resistance to Dionysus of course fails, and he is torn to pieces by the maenads; the "new" cult triumphs and is spread throughout Greece. Many of the nineteenth- and early twentieth-century "readings" of Dionysus linked this whole process with seasonal fertility ritual, and also with the origins of drama, with tragedy representing the wintry "death" of the hero and comedy enacting a spring-like "rebirth" or rejuvenation and recovery.

But in fact Dionysus was *not* a late importation from the East. Worship of Dionysus appears to to have been as long-established among the Hellenes as that of any of the other Olympian deities—and his name, mythology, and cult locations establish him as more "originally" Greek than, for example, Aphrodite or Apollo. The name *Di-wo-nu-so* is found on Linear B tablets from Bronze Age Pylos and Thebes; and of course his traditional place of conception—and premature "birth"—is and always was Thebes. The story of Dionysus subsequently being sewn into Zeus' thigh, reborn in Crete or Phrygia, and triumphantly "arriving/returning" to the cities of mainland Greece (beginning with Thebes) is regularly recounted as a tale of foolish resistance overcome. The locals (or some of them) at first fear or disbelieve his divine powers but are eventually persuaded and compelled to welcome him—to their everlasting benefit.

To modern audiences and readers, this "resistance-and-reception" myth (another feature of Dionysian religion that resembles/anticipates Christianity) is best known from Euripides' *Bacchae*. But Aristophanes' audience would not have had the opportunity yet to see this play—for it was not produced in Athens until a couple of years after Euripides' death, by his son. They would, however, have been well aware of other stories of Dionysus' victimization and subsequent triumph, especially the local story of the arrival of wine and Dionysus for the first time in Attica. A number of vivid Black-Figure Attic vase paintings from the sixth and early fifth century illustrate the story (a poignant one indeed): Icarius, an Attic farmer, had learned about wine from Dionysus himself, and well-meaningly introduced it to his local village; his inebriated fellow demesmen became alarmed at the bizarre effects, accused him of poisoning them, and tore him to pieces. When they recovered (next morning) and learned a bit more about how wine works, they were very apologetic and made Icarius a local culture "hero": a kind of martyr to the faith, one might say—a wine-drinking faith that obviously continued to be central to Athenian life as it was elsewhere throughout Greece.

Also widely familiar to Athenians was the "Homeric" *Hymn to Dionysus*, a hexameter poem (probably composed in the sixth century) which narrates an attempt by an arrogant and greedy pirate captain to kidnap the young Dionysus (whom he mistakes for a wealthy nobleman) and ransom him. The young god quickly releases himself from his bonds, transforms himself into a lion, and devours the captain, while the rest of the crew leap overboard in terror and turn into dolphins and the ship itself sprouts ivy and grapevines from the mast and rigging. The steersman alone, who had noted some godlike qualities in their passenger and advised the captain against the kidnapping, ends up being rewarded by the god, who makes him "all-blessed" (54). The story adds to the repertoire of elements connecting Dionysus to boats and the sea, and also contains significant resonances with the story of Arion, another musical genius captured by pirates who escapes—this time by jumping overboard and riding to land on a dolphin's back. He too eventually exacts full revenge on his former captors while also being credited with introducing all kinds of new songs into Corinth and Greece at large.

So, we recognize a definite pattern: Dionysus (or wine, or wild maenadic dance) is first rejected and scorned; he himself or his human representative is insulted, perhaps tied up, imprisoned, or even killed; then the god appears in his true power and majesty, proves his divinity, and punishes his former opponents, while "liberating" the rest of the community and rewarding them with the benefits of wine, dance, blessedness (and perhaps life after death?) for the future. Continuing rituals celebrate this victory and "release from death/pain," whence the epithets of Dionysus *Lusios* ("Liberator") and *Eleutherios* ("Dionysus the Free"; cf. Latin *Liber*), as we find also among some of the Orphic *lamellae*.

Many other roles and acts performed by Dionysus are recorded in literature and art: his versatility knows almost no bounds. He can be imagined as youthful or mature (unbearded or bearded), superpotent and phallic (associated especially with the bull) or effeminate and cross-dressing (as in the *Bacchae*, and note his saffron-dyed cloak in *Frogs*), wild and out-of-control (like his maenads) or calm, serene, and controlling. (See Fig. 5-1a, where Dionysus is depicted bearded, luxuriously but not effeminately dressed, and looking skyward—as if to suggest an other-worldly psychic state—yet calmly playing a seven-string lyre (*barbitos*), while his satyrs dance excitedly and play the castanets (*krotala*) amid vine tendrils and captured animals.) He can even be imagined as the wine itself that is poured and drunk by mortals: "It is he, born a god, that is poured out [in libations] (*spendetai*) to the gods,/ and so because of him humans receive blessings [from them]," as Teiresias explains to the sceptical Pentheus (Eur. *Ba.* 284–85; cf. 278–80). Hence in calling himself "Son of Wine-Jug" (*Stamnion, Frogs* 22) Aristophanes' Dionysus is not being entirely facetious.

Of Dionysus it is more true than of any other of the Greek divinities that he is imagined as being physically present when celebrations are taking place: his "presence" (*parousia*) can be palpable, sensed by the dancers and singers and thus a further source of energy and inspiration for them. He may even be felt to enter their bodies and souls/minds (via the wine and music, especially), and conversely he may cause them to depart from their normal selves and "become" someone or something else (= *ekstasis*, "ecstasy," literally "standing outside [oneself]"). The state of feeling "god-inside" oneself (*en-theos*) comes to be known in Greek as *enthousiasmos* (whence our "enthusiasm"), and in some of the Orphic *lamellae* the initiates actually become the god, are known as Bakkhoi, and seem to acquire some new status of quasi-divinity.

So, just as Dionysus himself goes through many changes, so does he work wonderful transformations in others. Altered states are his trademark, whether through the psychotropic effects of wine, the exhilaration and emotional effect of dance and music, the donning of a mask and costume, or a combination of all of these. He is also closely associated with Aphrodite and the joys of sex. (So it is not out of character for Dionysus in *Frogs* to show immediate signs of interest whenever the prospect arises of pretty women and the possibilities of erotic activity: 290–92, 503–48.) This capacity to transform oneself, to feel different, to experience a new and mind-expanding, life-enhancing existence, is central to Dionysian celebration. Athenian sympotic vase paintings—as well as the satyr-dramas that accompanied each trilogy of tragedies at the festival—frequently depict satyrs dancing, blowing pipes, and sexually aroused—a vivid symbol of the effects experienced by young men when they are temporarily transformed by wine and music into something half-animal, half-god. And, on these same vases, "maenads" regularly are shown too: female nymphs or women dancing with wild abandon (yet not indecorously), free of the usual constraints of domesticity and male control. These effects of Dionysian celebration and presence may be temporary, when we "play" and enjoy music, dance, and drinking; or they can be eternal—as in the acquisition of an Orphic or Eleusinian passport to a better life in the Underworld. And the capacity for Dionysian transformation is central also to the activity of theater, especially a theater which uses masks, music, and dance, and treasures the elements of disguise, impersonation, and "make-believe" as Aristophanes' comedy does (and the tragedy of Aeschylus and Euripides, too). *Frogs* draws on all of these dynamics in swift and tumultuous succession, and in combination.

It seems that the best example in Old Comedy of Dionysus himself actually being cast as a dramatic character (apart from *Frogs*) is Cratinus' very popular and successful *Dionysalexandros* (probably from the 430s). Some substantial fragments of this play survive—most notably a papyrus containing a fairly detailed plot-summary (*hypothesis*). From these we know that the play, whose chorus were apparently satyrs, involved an extensive spoof on the beginning of the Trojan War, with Dionysus filling much of the role of Paris/Alexandros (hence the play's title); so it is he who is appointed to judge the beauty contest of the three goddesses, and he who goes to Sparta and abducts Helen. The play also apparently included some virulent criticism of Pericles as a warmonger, as often in Cratinus' plays. Although the mythological content and time-frame of *Dionysalexandros* were obviously quite different from those of *Frogs*, the play does offer some interesting precedents and parallels as to how Dionysus might behave in an Attic comedy, intervening in "history" (mythology) in a way that is scurrilous, opportunistic, and yet ultimately inconsequential (since in the end it is Paris' decision to keep Helen that causes the Trojan War, not Dionysus' initial abduction of her).

Dionysus at Athens

The fact that Dionysus comes from so many places (Thebes, Phrygia, Eleutherae; like Jesus, born in Nazareth or Bethlehem, and ultimately arriving in Jerusalem), has several possible parentages, and can do many different things for different people, makes his appeal especially strong to the disenfranchised and the newly arrived, and to other "subaltern" groups. There are always elements in his cult (as in that of the Great Mother, with which it has many features in common) that can be adopted for "countercultural" purposes (wild women, drunkenness, experimental musical styles, etc.); and it seems that Bacchic groups often met at the margins and borders of a region, outside the city walls. In certain respects this seems to make Dionysian cult quite apolitical, if "political" is understood to mean the things formally conducted by the (men of the) polis in the Assembly, army, and law courts. At the same time much of what he brings to a community—including theater—is unambiguously beneficial and unifying to the collective social body, and hence of apparent benefit to the polis as a whole, even while it is difficult to imagine co-opting the phenomenon "Dionysus" into any kind of formal, political program in terms of decrees and decisions of the Assembly. So—unless you are a repressive, sexist bigot like Pentheus (or the Roman Senate contemplating the Bacchanalia, Livy 39.14)—Dionysus the Liberator should present no threat to anyone.

Apart from the big, state-organized festivals that we have discussed already, Dionysus can be (and perhaps is most appropriately) worshipped privately, in a *thiasos* (a "sacred band, group") of like-minded friends, whether for the benefits he provides in the here and now or as some kind of preparation for a better afterlife (as we saw earlier). There is reason to think that such private cults and afterlife arrangements may have been particularly popular with women. At the same time, symposium culture—primarily a male, urban phenomenon—by definition involved constant demonstrations of commitment to the god of wine, sex, and music (as Pentheus' herdsman-messenger remarks in the *Bacchae* [769–74]; and see too Fig. 5–1b). So, even while some of the most vivid and memorable depictions in myth of Dionysian worship appear to contrast the wild and abandoned mountain-roaming and all-night dancing of the bacchants and satyrs with the sober institutions of the polis, such as the army, the walls of the city, and male hierarchies of authority, in practice it is quite clear that Dionysian cult was well integrated into polis calendars and local communities all over Greece, including Athens.

One last—crucial—question remains to be asked about our play's enigmatic "hero": should we see him as a "stranger" coming from abroad to bring the new gifts that will enlighten and save the community (as in the *Bacchae* and the myth of Icarius)? Or is he regarded as a permanent resident of Attica (whether citizen or metic)? For the most part, we see him in *Frogs* behaving as a local, that is, an Athenian through-and-through, and an expert, home-grown lover of theater. He (claims to have) fought as a hoplite *epibatês* ("marine") on a trireme at Arginusae; he knows the names of all the politicians and can make rude jokes about some of them—not at all like a newcomer in town or foreign visitor; and he owns a slave, Xanthias (see chapter 3). Dionysus and Xanthias, just as much as Aeschylus and Euripides, appear to be as Athenian as can be.

It has been argued eloquently and at length by some that the play is designed overall as a playful—yet seriously intended and recognizable—rite of passage or initiation process for Dionysus himself, with the hero making the long journey into the "liminal region" of Hades (and simultaneously into the Theater of Athens), donning various peculiar garments (especially Heracles' lion-skin; but also of course his own distinctive and effeminate saffron robe, the *krokôtos*), undergoing various terrors and ordeals (including flogging and loss/switching of identity with Heracles and Xanthias, and even the rowing ordeal vs. the singing frogs), before finally emerging, transformed and empowered, into a new status and function as the rejuvenated and rejuvenating spirit of Athenian tragedy or of the city itself. There is much that is appealing about such a reading, and it illuminates several otherwise confusing elements in the play. Yet it is hard to see Dionysus at the end of the play as exhibiting any credible signs of new insight or vigor: he seems to be just as crass and frivolous as he was at the beginning. Certainly he has assisted at the rejuvenation of drama through his comic manipulation of the poetry-judging as well as his amiable interactions with Plouton and the Chorus; but it is really to the returning Aeschylus, not to Dionysus, that everyone is looking in the final scene to provide the seminal energy, "understanding," and "advice" that might save the city.

That is not to say that we should not keep in mind this notion of a rite of passage or initiation ritual successfully performed by and for Dionysus: his *katabasis* and *anodos* during the course of the play, his journey of "eternal return," especially if understood in conjunction with all those other Dionysian myths and rituals concerning life after death, surely add resonances of solemn religiosity as well as absurd frivolity to the drama, as his grossly unheroic conduct and general incompetence are constantly flaunted in contrast with the famous examples of Heracles, Persephone, and other braver and more accomplished predecessors. Yes, Dionysus does succeed in providing "salvation" for the city and for all those sitting in the audience. But he does this as the epitome of comedy, more than as a newly initiated hero.

(v) *Frogs* and Comic Salvation/Rebirth

It is time now to try to sum up the meaning of these multiple eschatological, ritual, salvationist, Dionysiac, Eleusinian, and other "religious" elements that we have found in *Frogs*, and to decide what we should make of them in their context—i.e., in a comic drama performed in the Theater of Dionysus, in the daylight, by masked actors and chorus, in front of an audience whose varying degrees of familiarity with and commitment to the numerous cults, beliefs, and festivals (and previous "literary" versions, too) we have been surveying in this chapter. Fundamental critical issues are at stake here, extending far beyond just this one play, since our understanding of the aesthetic as well as the historical and sociological impact of Greek drama in general depends greatly on our assessment of just these kinds of immediate, contingent audience experiences. And certainly *Frogs*, along with the *Bacchae*, is one of the most exciting and richly rewarding sites imaginable for excavating these issues of Dionysian ritual and salvationist drama.

One (somewhat reductive and minimalist) way to treat the Dionysian and eschatological features of *Frogs* (and many other Greek dramas too) is to regard them simply as examples of the single basic story pattern ("myth") of a hero's quest: travel, struggle, near-death, and return—a basic, perhaps universal, narrative structure. If we do so, we need also to acknowledge that this story pattern seems to provide an extraordinarily strong—and apparently consistent— emotional-psychological appeal to readers and theatergoers of many different types and from many different cultures. So we should perhaps ask the further question, how closely is this basic storyline tied to the religious beliefs, ritual practices, and social organization of each of the particular cultures in which it is found? Or should we *not* ask this? Are we instead to regard it as a "universal" human story that appeals to everyone, wherever they live and whatever their status? A further question: is this story best understood as an allegory of "everyman"—or "everywoman"—finding his/her way in the world and coming into his/her own in their individual life-quest, or as a heroic/divine tale of a special, divinely chosen individual whose sufferings and achievements are exceptional and salutary for everyone else?

Myths do not contain fixed and stable meanings but always continue to evolve with the societies for which they are being told. So, however universal a story may inherently be, each telling of it always (also) needs to be read or heard in context, as a particular manifestation and interpretation of that story. Some anthropologically-minded critics of Greek literature have tried (too hard, doubtless) to identify one basic narrative or one central ritual as being the master key to the culture as a whole: so, in interpreting instances of the "myth of return" and various *katabasis* stories, they have sought to identify all of them solely with *rites de passage*, even with specific coming-of-age rituals. But whereas such an interpretation works well for such figures as Orestes, Neoptolemus, Persephone, Gilgamesh, and even Heracles—and perhaps even for Pentheus, Hippolytus, Achilles, Iphigenia, and Antigone as well (if we take these as models of tragic "failure" in the *rite de passage*), it falls short in many other cases.

Modes of analysis that are focused specifically on adolescent *rites de passage* are not of much use for interpreting the stories of Odysseus or Aeneas (both mature, married men with children before their respective epics begin). Nor do they work at all, I think, for Dionysus (let alone Aeschylus!) in our play. Dionysus has been around for ages (whether we imagine him as mature and bearded, or as clean-shaven and youthful—both of these styles of representation being common in Athenian art and literature); and he does not, I should say, pass into a recognizably new status during the course of *Frogs*. Some critics, it is true, have emphasized the significance of his "passage" from being a Euripides-lover at the beginning of the play to an enlightened (i.e., more mature?) Aeschylus-lover at the end, with all the Eleusinian associations of the latter also contributing to his newly initiated state. And it is true that we have seen him temporarily adopt a peculiar (mixed-feminine and animalistic) costume, and thus assume a new identity; enter a liminal space; descend into the Underworld (*katabasis*); cross a body of water; knock on a door and request admittance; face numerous trials and terrors (including temporary loss of identity and reduction to servile status); be abused, insulted, physically hurt (including being whipped and threatened with being "torn apart," 474 *diasparaxei*); witness bright light amid the mud and darkness; meet and be hospitably received by the King and Queen of the Dead; and finally return in triumph to a renewed and improved existence back in the upper world. All of these features might indeed seem to reproduce much of what we might expect to find in an "initiation" process.

Perhaps too, Dionysus' acquisition of the techniques (and endurance) of rowing in the fleet and his increasing focus on the political and moral well-being of Athens, rather than (merely) the latest fads in theater-making, should be considered significant indicators of a new maturity. His comfortable familiarity with Plouton and Persephone, and his celebratory feast in their house, likewise confirm his special status as a superior and blessed being (and his last words in the play are actually his acceptance of their dinner-invitation, 1479–81). On the other hand, we are given no real sense in these late scenes of the play that Dionysus has actually become a "citizen," nor that he has really acquired much new wisdom or authority: his conduct of the final stages of the contest seems just as muddled and flippant as ever (see chapter 7). He seems in this respect to resemble a Pisetaerus (*Birds*) or Dicaeopolis (*Acharnians*), or even a Strepsiades (*Clouds*), all three of them mature citizens and self-made men rather than a Neoptolemus or Orestes, adolescents achieving their "passage" to manhood, social integration with the adult community, and/or preparation for marriage. Or, perhaps most of all, his achievement has resembled that of the mythical Heracles in retrieving Alcestis or Pirithous, i.e., acting as the heroic savior of others (in this case, Aeschylus and Athens), rather than seeking his own passage to manhood. Certainly there is no evidence that Dionysus' future status will be markedly different from what it was before the play began, and in the final lines of the play he actually has little to say and little attention is paid to him: the focus instead is on Aeschylus.

Does *Aeschylus* fit the bill better, for a rite of passage or initiation? Not really. He is old already, and long dead; and he is brought back to life at the end precisely because of what he already was when previously living, not because he has become something new. After many years of relegation to the obscurity of the Underworld, he has, it is true, undergone a rigorous series of tests and ordeals against a "monstrous" opponent, under the watchful scrutiny and final assessment of both Dionysus and the rulers of Hades—including Persephone herself; his language and characters have been "tested," "weighed," "tortured" (802, 1121, 1123, 1367), etc., and he has been found to be morally cleaner and finer than his rival, so that he is allowed to proceed back up to the light, blessed and escorted by "divine spirits of the dead,"

Mystic Initiates, and Dionysus himself. To that extent, it may be granted, he has entered a new life (however (im)permanent it may be—for in the final scene, his "return" to Athens seems perhaps to involve some mixed feelings on his part, and he actually keeps open the possibility of returning one day to his throne in Hades. Sophocles will occupy it for him in the meantime and Plouton will make sure that Euripides doesn't try again to usurp it, 1515–23). But there is no sign that Aeschylus has been "purified" or reeducated through his sojourn in the Underworld, nor that the contest/ordeal has brought him into a higher state of consciousness or new authority. (He has been louder, more assertive, more self-righteous than his opponent throughout the contest but hardly more intelligent or observant.) On the contrary, the whole point of his return to Athens seems to be that he is just the same as ever: he has acquired no new revelation or special knowledge during the contest; he just remains true to himself, which is exactly what Athens apparently wants—good old Aeschylus!

Perhaps most fatal to the overall plausibility of this particular notion of a dramatic *rite de passage* is the fact that actual adolescent rituals of passage are not very strongly attested in fifth-century Athens, and certainly not in relation to the City Dionysia or Lenaea, the festivals at which *Frogs* and almost all our surviving Greek dramas were performed. And if we try to broaden our definition of "rite of passage" or "initiation" a little, in an effort to find an actual Greek (ideally, Athenian) ritual that does correspond well to the larger mythic pattern of "return" and/or *katabasis*, we inevitably find both too much and too little: too much, in the sense that almost any ritual, if creatively and selectively analyzed, can be found to involve some kind of "initiatory" experience, a "liminal" space or state, special costumes, words, gestures, actions, and ordeals, and finally a transition to a new or renewed state of reintegration with and of community. Such a "ritual process" can be identified in a Christian baptism or Mass, for sure, but also in a football game, graduation ceremony, or rock concert. An interpretive master key that is so adaptable and ready-for-all, even if true, might seem to be of rather limited value in explaining any particular performance or work of literature. Thus the payoff of such ritual readings ends up being "too little" to be helpful.

But this does not mean that we should cease to pay any attention to obvious ritual processes and religiously significant story patterns encountered in Athenian drama. When these elements are prominent, even in some cases highlighted in specific, detailed, and unmistakable forms, it would be foolish to ignore or downplay them. And, in the case of *Frogs*, the ritual elements are especially—flamboyantly—conspicuous: they jump out at us at every turn, verbally, spatially, visually, and performatively. Whereas in some dramas critics have had to dig deep or stretch definitions implausibly to find the elements of "ritual" that they seek, *Frogs* advertises itself from start to finish as being *all about Dionysus* and his various rituals, all about the Underworld and the afterlife, all about salvation. So we are not in danger of reading in ideas that the author and his original audience would not have been aware of.

The difficulty lies, however, in determining just how closely and literally to try to "read" these rituals in the comedy, how coherent a message to try to construct out of them, and how single-mindedly to seek to interpret this message (or bundle of ritual elements) amid everything (else) going on in the play; or, it might be said, how "seriously" to take the "religious" elements in this comic context. There probably is *not* a simple answer to these questions, and it may well be the case that some members of the original audience recognized more of these elements than others, and perhaps some also took them more seriously than others.

(Tentative) Conclusions

So let us wind up now by attempting to draw some more general conclusions about ritual, initiation, and the *Frogs*. First of all, it is relevant to remind ourselves that Attic (Old) Comedy itself originated "from the phallic [songs]" (see chapter 1), that the plays were presented at wintertime and springtime festivals of Dionysus, and that (again, as we observed in chapter 1) themes of rejuvenation and salvation, both personal and collective, as well as various elements of ritual language and behavior, continued to be prominent in them (e.g., masks, cross-dressing, animal choruses, phalluses, *parabasis*, *kômos*). In our play, as we watch an actor impersonate Dionysus impersonating Heracles in an attempt to "reenact" that hero's former venture by making an actual *katabasis* of his own, and as we witness a Chorus of Initiates singing about their blissful state after death while we also hear about the contrastingly miserable life for others in the Underworld, with Dionysus seeking persistently (with Plouton's help) to recover a lost soul and bring him back to save Athens, we cannot fail to recognize that we ourselves, by our presence in the Theater as "spectators," are indeed participating in an extended ritual quest or rite. The same Greek words for "spectacle" (*thea*) and "viewing" (*theaomai*) are employed both for "religious pilgrimage, festival " (*theôria*), and for the "theater" (*theatron*). Whether, or in what sense (literal, metaphorical), this rite of "watching" itself amounts to an "initiation" may be just a matter of definition.

We still face the awkward question: if this play is enacting or mimicking some kind of initiation, *who* is it that is being initiated? *Who* is being reborn, rejuvenated, saved? In terms of the characters of the play itself, we have already discussed two of the leading candidates in some detail, (i) Dionysus and (ii) Aeschylus: the former certainly is the one who (along with Xanthias) undergoes a journey to the Underworld, faces challenges and ordeals, and survives, while the latter is the one who is actually "saved" by being resurrected and restored to the light above. But, as we observed above, neither fits the bill of a ritual initiate at all well. To be sure, (iii) the Chorus of Initiates also is "saved," and has been even further enlightened and inspired during the play by the prospect of the great Aeschylus earning his return to the light of day (1482ff "blessed man . . .," *makarios anêr*, etc.). But these Initiates had already achieved a state of blessedness and salvation through separate rituals completed long before the play began, and for years have been enjoying brilliant illumination, songs and dances, even pork and wine. So, although at the end they begin to escort Aeschylus out of the *orchestra* (= the Underworld) back down/up the side-entrance and into Dionysus' precinct here in Athens (offstage, but visible to the audience), we can assume that they really have no wish to return to a mortal life back on earth and are remaining down below, eternally rejoicing. (So they address Aeschylus as "going away . . . back to his home . . .," 1486, 1528.) Likewise (iv) the frog chorus: their ever-renewable song will always be available for Athenians to hear in the vicinity of Dionysus' (other) sanctuary in the Marshes, just as their underworld ghost-song was heard at the verge of the Lake, reminding them and us of annual Bacchic festivities and of the seasonal reunion of animal, human, and divine. They do not need to be reborn or "saved."

What about (v) Xanthias? Poor Xanthias! He began the play so sympathetically, and seemed to embody so vividly and concretely the essence of the suffering ritual victim: slave and donkey, carrying the burdens of the world, abused, tortured, patiently enduring all, assisting his master and carrying out all his duties, if not entirely willingly or uncomplainingly, at least conscientiously and successfully. But he remains a victim, a slave, and seems finally to lapse into the status of forgotten man. Even if he does have moments when he impersonates a hero (Heracles) and a god (Dionysus), he does not in the end get to be saved: he is not fully integrated among the Mystic Initiates; and he cannot look forward to a new life as a citizen. Salvation and liberation apparently extend only so far? (But see chapter 7).

On a more abstract level, perhaps it is (vi) the Art of Tragedy (*technê, tragôedia, Mousa*) that has been rejuvenated, purified, and transformed? Is "she" the one—along with the spirit of Comedy (*kômôedia*) as well (these are all feminine nouns in Greek)—that has been "saved," or at least reinvigorated and (re)educated by the play we have witnessed? When the Initiates first arrive, they declare that among those banned from their celebrations are the ones "who [were] never initiated in the Bacchic rites of bull-eating Cratinus' tongue" (357); so implicitly the one(s) blessed must all be somehow disciples of that late, great comedian. These must surely include Aristophanes himself. We will return to this issue in chapter 7.

Putting all of these together, perhaps it really is (vii) the audience (= "Athens?" yes and no, or not exactly, if by "Athens" we mean exclusively the political entity of male citizens) that experiences the most complete rebirth and rejuvenation during the course of the play. As they/we witness this spectacle of *katabasis* and *anodos*, of heroic triumph over death, recuperation of lost loved-ones, and mystic salvation enacted before them, the "viewers" (2 *hoi theômenoi*) are brought through song, dance, torches, moral homilies, and even the "presence" of the god Dionysus himself, to experience a powerful sense of solidarity and (potential) social harmony. After contemplating the anxieties of loss, death, darkness, defeat, and conflict of all kinds, they find themselves included finally in a ceremony that promises to restore the vigor of their favorite art forms (tragedy—and comedy) while also reminding them of the strength and potential of their own citizen body and social institutions. Whatever their political opinions and status, all of them/us can feel that a victory—or at least, a respite from trouble—has been achieved. Not quite everyone is to be included in the celebration of renewal, of course: nasty politicians and inept playwrights will be kept "in the darkness and mud" of disgrace and ignominy. Salvation must be earned, or at least deserved: it cannot be taken for granted and bestowed on absolutely everyone. Good art requires serious work, "skill," and "understanding." But Dionysus can rest assured: this is a community that treasures him and his theatrical gifts, and one that in return is uniquely fortunate to be blessed with his favor and the prospect of eternal comic life.

Suggestions for Further Reading

On Greek (especially Athenian) religion and ideas about the gods in general, see Burkert (1977/1985); Feeney (1991); Parker (1996); Versnel (1990, 1993); and especially Parker (2005). On Greek ideas about death, the underworld, and the afterlife, see Johnston (1999); Ogden (2001); Vermeule (1979); on mystery cults, especially the Eleusinian Mysteries and Orphic texts, see Burkert (1987); Clinton (1992); Foley (1994); Graf and Johnston (2007). On Dionysus and Bacchic rituals, see Carpenter and Faraone (1993); Cole (2007); Henrichs (1982); Segal (1997); Seaford (1981, 2006).

On initiation rites and myths of rebirth, see Calame (1998); for more sceptical views, Dodd and Faraone (2003). On ritual elements in *Frogs*, see Bowie (1993); Edmonds (2004); Foley (1980); Lada-Richards (1999); Padilla (1992).

· 7 ·

Dionysus' Verdict and the Ending/Message of the Play

The ending of *Frogs* seems at first glance to be simple and to present an obvious message: Aeschylus has won, and the values of "old-style" politics and art have been reaffirmed. The new-fangled experiments of Euripidean music and dramaturgy, and the political excesses of Cleophon and his demagogic cronies, are to be rejected in favor of the styles and behaviors of the good old days. But this would be a misreading of the play and would give a false, or at least oversimplified, impression of the mood and impact of the closing scene, as experienced both by ancient and by modern audiences.

The prevailing mood generated by the closing scene is one of reunification and community, not of rejection or vindictiveness. It is true that Euripides has been defeated and is excluded from the celebratory feasting and final procession (the *kômos*); true too that reference continues to be made to undesirable elements within Athenian society that need to be eliminated—utopia has not yet been achieved, to be sure. (And the War is still continuing.) But there has been a gradual convergence of critical outlooks, a process of increasing unanimity and good will at all levels (gods and humans, living and dead, artists and initiates, performers and audience) that seems to transcend the previous squabbling and contradictions. In this brief chapter, we will look at the ways in which the issues of the play are finally wrapped up and brought to a resolution. I hope thereby to draw together some of our discussions from previous chapters concerning the judging of the arts, the possibilities of personal and communal salvation, and the relationship between politics and performance, and to draw some conclusions about the enduring appeal of this Aristophanic masterpiece.

Dionysus' Verdict

After several rounds of fierce competition, with the most recent one involving an unequivocal demonstration (three times over) of Aeschylus' superior "weightiness" in the scales (1364–1410), Dionysus still has not announced his verdict as to which tragedian is better. Instead, quite suddenly and unexpectedly, he calls a halt to the whole competition, expressing his indecision, or refusal to continue, in strikingly conciliatory and warm-hearted terms:

> [Dion.] Both these men are dear to me. I shall not judge between them,
> 'cause I don't want to make an enemy of either.
> I think one of them is a great, wise poet, and the other one
> —gives me great pleasure.
>
> (1411–13)

Since antiquity, scholars have argued about which poet is meant in each case. A majority have insisted that Aeschylus must be the one judged to be "a great, wise poet" (1412 *sophon*; see chapter 4, pp. 99–100), and that Dionysus is implicitly conceding victory to him, even while acknowledging his own inability to give up his long-standing love for the "delights, pleasures" (1413 *hēdomai*) of Euripidean drama. Others have insisted that the implications of *sophos* here point rather to Euripides. Of course, in production it could have been made quite clear by means of simple gestures who was meant—but we may note that Dionysus does not say "this one" and "that one," as he normally would if he were pointing; it appears that he is being deliberately vague.

As we observed in chapter 3, there can be no doubt in anyone's mind by this point that Aeschylus has really defeated Euripides in the contest: by virtually every single criterion, he has emerged with the more devastating critiques, has occupied the higher moral ground, and has had the last word (indeed, the second speaker in an Aristophanic *agôn* almost always wins); and the latest three rounds of weighing the verses on the scales seem to have been conclusive. Dionysus' interruption of the process is thus both unexpected and, to some degree, an apparent reprieve for Euripides. But of course it also seems to stop the play in its tracks and return the plot to square one. What now?

The next few lines provide the vital impetus for moving the drama forward into its final phase, by combining the two—hitherto somewhat contradictory—motifs: Dionysus' quest to rescue his favorite poet from the dead, and the contest between the two dead poets for the throne of tragedy in the Underworld. Appropriately, it is Plouton who brings this about, with the first words he has spoken in the play:

> [Plouton] In that case [sc. if you won't judge], you'll accomplish nothing
>   of what you came here for!
> [Dion.] And if I do judge?
> [Plouton] Then you can take one of them back home with you,
> Whichever one you choose. Then your journey
>   Won't have been in vain.
> [Dion.] My blessings on you and thank you!
>
>   (1414–17)

Plouton, King of the Underworld (and presumably speaking here with the silent approval of Persephone, who stands beside him) is the ideal source of sage advice, reminding the impulsive, impatient Dionysus of his long-term mission and (we might say) of his ultimate purpose as god of theater. It is only now, after this intervention, that Dionysus articulates fully what this mission is supposed to be:

> [Dion.] OK, you two: listen up now!
>   I came down here to fetch a poet. Why? So that

> The city can be saved and can keep on having its
>   drama festivals.
> So, whichever one of you is going to give some
>   useful advice to the city, That's the one I think
>   I'll take back with me.
>
> (1417–21)

In 1418, the expression that Dionysus uses, "having drama festivals," could more literally be translated "conduct choruses" (*tous chorous agêi*), which would include dithyramb as well as tragedy and comedy—all the civic musical/poetic productions for which *chorêgoi* were responsible. The city's "salvation" seems thus to involve two separate but overlapping requirements: its basic survival in a period of dire crisis (above all, in the War), and its cultural health and integrity (above all, in its Dionysian festivals). The two are linked by the fact (well established by this point in the play) that the citizen body that conducts war and makes political choices and the theater-makers and audiences who "conduct choruses" and judge poets are broadly speaking one and the same. And so the "good advice" that is to be the criterion applied for the final scene of judging will implicitly apply to both, though the main focus is on political and social issues—starting with Alcibiades.

At the time of the play's original production, this question will indeed have been on every Athenian's mind: whether or not to recall their most brilliant and charismatic military genius and political lightning rod, and entrust him with their hopes for finally pulling off a decisive victory in the War against Sparta (see chapter 2). It is not unusual to find the denouement of an Aristophanic play thus directly linked to an immediately topical public issue. That was expected of Old Comedy, and constituted much of its appeal. This would mean, of course, that within months or even weeks of the first performance the "relevance" of the play was likely to be somewhat diminished, since circumstances will have changed (in a way that did not thus affect tragedy or satyr-play). In this case, we are told that the immediately topical "message" of *Frogs* was very well received, with Aristophanes being awarded not only first prize but also a special crown and an official invitation to produce the play again (see chapter 8). Furthermore, in the months that followed, several of the main items of policy recommended in these late scenes were apparently adopted by the Athenians: Cleophon was disgraced, and citizenship was restored to those who had been disenfranchised after 411. But the result was not military or political salvation for Athens. Instead, quite soon (following the disastrous battle at Aegospotami) the War was lost and the city had been occupied by Spartan forces. Alcibiades was assassinated abroad without ever having returned to Athens. (We do not know at what point amid all of this the second performance of *Frogs* was held, nor how extensively Aristophanes may have rewritten it for that occasion; see chapter 3.)

So the longer-term popularity of our play obviously could not depend on its specific answer to the question, "What to do about Alcibiades?," any more than the enduring appeal of previous plays by Aristophanes had depended on their "answers" to the Cleon question (*Wasps*, *Knights*), the peace-with-Sparta question (*Acharnians*, *Peace*, *Lysistrata*), or even the Socrates question (*Clouds*). On the other hand, in each case the specific question did also involve issues that were of more than merely temporary and local concern, and that therefore might continue to resonate with later generations. So in *Frogs* we see the large and more universal issue raised here, whether the city should be looking to a charismatic leader to "save" it, one whose record of practical success as well as his genetic pedigree and good looks might inspire many to think of him as definitively superior to others; or instead, should it rely on the collective good sense of its most trusted citizens, the "useful, worthy" ones, for the best way out of political and military crisis? This is a difficult choice faced by many communities—especially the dilemma of how heavily to count a brilliant leader's moral flaws if his/her political talents are exceptional. (This is a question that also much exercised Thucydides in his analysis of Athens' rise and fall during the course of the fifth century; Plato too.)

Aristophanes does not really present a clear-cut answer to this immediate Alcibiades-question, but the discussion that takes place at this point in the play seems basically to recommend reinstating him into the city's favor:

> [Dion.] First of all, then: what opinion do you each have
> About Alcibiades? The city is in labor, and having a
> hard time with it!
> . . . It yearns for him, it hates him, it wants to have
> him back. . . .
>
> (1422–25)

In what follows, it is not absolutely certain which poet gives which response. But most editors assign the first (negative) answer to Euripides ("I hate a citizen who is slow to help his country but quick to harm it . . .," 1427–29), with Aeschylus providing a more positive response that appears to allude, in quasi-oracular fashion, to an image used in his own *Oresteia* (Aesch. *Ag.* 716–36):

> It is best not to nurture a lion cub in a city; but if you do,
> Once it is full grown, you'd better serve its needs!
> (1431–32; also Plutarch *Life of Alcibiades* 16.2, cf. 2.2)

Although, as Dionysus remarks, this response is a bit enigmatic, reminding us not only of the ghastly murders in the House of Atreus but also of various other more recent historical figures—politicians and tyrants—whose birth and rise to power had been famously likened to the growth of a lion (Cypselus of Corinth, Pericles, Cleon . . .)—clearly Aeschylus' recommendation here is more positive: Athens should make the most of what their lion, Alcibiades, has to offer, despite his dangerous nature. Thus, in the *Oresteia*, lion-like Orestes does commit family murder, like his father and his mother; but he succeeds in restoring political stability and the proper succession, while the usurper Aegisthus by contrast is described as a "cowardly wolf," good for nothing (*Ag.* 1224, 1258–59.) In Aristophanes' Athens, the other politicians of the day who have been running the city during Alcibiades' absence—several of whom have previously been ridiculed in the play for their slippery ways, their dubious parentage, or their cowardice—can likewise hardly measure up. (Cleon had claimed to be the "watchdog" of the city, much to Aristophanes' contempt: *Knights* 1017–34, *Wasps* 894ff, 1031–32, *Peace* 313–15.)

Why might Aeschylus here favor Alcibiades, for all his faults? Presumably the real-life Aeschylus' strong associations with Eleusis would be understood to be influencing him so as to recommend reinstatement of the man whose bold and generous intervention in 407 had enabled the Mysteries to be held again on a grand scale after a hiatus of six years (chapter 6). Dionysus moves on without apparently dwelling on this topic further (though the Greek text is in a confused state at this point), and no explicit reference to Eleusis or the Mysteries is made; but as in previous rounds of the competition, we may sense that Aeschylus' response has trumped Euripides', and presumably the pro-Alcibiades members of the audience (probably a majority) will have noticed this too.

But this specific "political" question turns out not to be the ultimate test. The "wisdom, understanding" that is sought in the ideal poet involves broader concerns, and Dionysus' last test-question is more open-ended:

> [Dion.] Each of you, give one piece of advice (*gnômên*)
>   about the city,
>   As to how you think it can best achieve salvation
>   (*sôtêrian*)."
>
> (1435–36)

My translation here, "salvation," is admittedly slanted: the word means as much "security, safety" in military terms as it does spiritual or existential rescue from evil (as is perhaps implied by "salvation"). But these spiritual associations are certainly present—and Dionysus' question was indeed preceded by a conventional appeal to "Zeus the Savior" (1433), so that we are certainly justified in interpreting this final stage of the contest in terms of "saving" Athens on all fronts: moral and artistic as well as political and military. Indeed, this final scene of the play reasserts powerfully (though still in absurd comic mode) the inseparability of the artistic and the political, the moral and the musical. "The poets make the people in their communities better . . ." (*tous anthrôpous en tais polesin*), it was agreed earlier in the contest (1009–10).

The term used there, "people" (*anthrôpous*), is very inclusive: women and slaves count as *anthrôpoi*, though they would not be included among the "citizens" or even "the Athenians." And this inclusiveness is significant for the ending of the play and for its overall message and appeal. For not only do the responses offered by the two rivals to Dionysus' invitation express the broadest possible conception of what this community/city most needs if it is once again to be secure, strong, unified, and prosperous—i.e., *restored* and (in the terms we discussed in chapter 6) even *reborn*—but the final celebration and procession appear to include the fullest possible range of social types and statuses in the comic celebration of reinvigorated community.

We examined this passage in some detail in chapter 3 (pp. 75–79) and saw that the two poets do not differ radically in their recommendations for changing the city's direction, especially in its choice of whom to trust. But Aeschylus (speaking second, as usual) is given the more extended opportunity to offer specific advice, and shows himself to be a stalwart supporter of Pericles' earlier "war policy": depend on the navy, avoid land-battles, and allow the Peloponnesians to continue invading and occupying Attica, as they have been doing for much of the last twenty-five years.

Both Euripides and Aeschylus have advocated a change of leadership and a renewal of trust in those who are currently out of favor—i.e., Alcibiades on the one hand, and the "distrusted ones" who are "noble and useful" (*chrêstoi*) on the other, a clear enough allusion to those wealthier citizens who were disenfranchised after the events of 411, the ones who "slipped up just once . . ." (689–91, 699). Thus the concerns voiced by the Chorus in the *parabasis* are with us again (see chapter 2, pp. 44–53): for the city to recover its former glories, it needs to revert to the gold and silver standard symbolized by the old coinage (*nomisma*) as well as by the pure blood in the veins of the old aristocracy, rather than following the currently dominant politicians like Cleophon and the rest (1500–14, 1532–33) or hanging out with Socrates (1491–99). This does not mean an outright rejection of all the newly enfranchised citizens (i.e., those ex-slaves who fought at Arginusae), though it may suggest getting rid of several of the currently influential democratic leaders (as does the sneer at "jurymen gobbling up all our resources" in 1466). The mockery and rejection of these unsavable elements in Athenian society resembles the ending of *Clouds* (where Socrates'Think-Shop is burned to the ground with him inside) or of *Acharnians* (where the war-mongering general Lamachus is mocked and humiliated as the hero and his friends feast). Comic resolution and inclusion are rarely total and absolute. Most of "us" (the worthy ones) can feel included, while there must also be others who are not welcome, who do not measure up, who are to be excluded. That is how comedy usually works (see chapter 1, pp. 12–13, chapter 2, pp. 41–43).

On the other hand, it is perhaps noteworthy that in these final scenes Euripides is not mentioned, and his departure (presumably right after 1477) is barely acknowledged: there is no gloating or mockery directed at him at all. It is the politicians and pseudo-intellectuals, rather than Euripides himself (or any other defective playwrights), that are specified as the "outsiders" or enemies to whom comic celebration is not offered.

The Final Celebration: Reconciliation and Community

The procession that begins to make its way out of the orchestra at the end of the play (rather like the procession at the end of Aeschylus' *Oresteia*) contains divinities and humans, men and women, free citizens and (probably) slaves. Although Plouton and Persephone will obviously remain in the Underworld, and so will the cheerfully singing Chorus of Initiates, all of these are part of the send-off celebration for Aeschylus and Dionysus—the final *kômos*—and all of them are focused on Athens, our city, "us," as the beneficiaries of Aeschylus' return "home." Even Plouton speaks now as an Athenian rather than as a universal god of the dead: "Off you go, farewell, Aeschylus, and save our city with your good ideas . . ." (1500–02). Just as in the *parabasis*, where the audience were invited by Aristophanes' Chorus into whole-hearted partnership with all that is best and purest in the city, past and present (chapter 2, pp. 45–48), so here too we are brought to feel that the whole world (and underworld) looks to us and cares about us. This play is saving not just one city, but humankind (all those who care about drama, music, and the arts).

A small but important, even crucial question presents itself at this point for any director—or interpreter—of this play: is Xanthias a part of this final procession? He does not speak (his last words in the play are at 804), and certainly he is not made the focus of attention as he was so frequently at the beginning of the play. But someone has to carry all the paraphernalia of suicide and execution that Plouton points to ("this here . . .!"), requesting that they be conveyed to Cleophon and the others (1504–13), and it would seem inappropriate for Dionysus or Aeschylus to have to carry such objects in their own aristocratic hands. (They are probably carrying torches.) The text gives us no direct clue, and editors and translators of the play differ among themselves in their stage directions as to whether Xanthias is present at all in these later scenes.

It is a significant index of our understanding of the play and of our sense of community, whether we elect to include Xanthias in the final procession and celebrations, or not. It has often been observed that the economy of ancient Greek drama tends to eliminate characters who are not (or are no longer) needed for the action to develop: thus, for example, in Aeschylus' *Oresteia*, Electra is not brought on stage to greet her father in *Agamemnon*, and she likewise departs halfway through *Libation Bearers* and is absent for the revenge and Orestes' final torments. At the end of Sophocles' *Antigone*, no mention is made of the heroine, only of Creon and his immediate family; in Aristophanes' *Birds* Euelpides, the hero's comrade and chief confidant throughout the first half of the play, fades out completely from the second half; and in *Lysistrata* it has been argued by some critics that the heroine herself falls silent or even departs the stage in the closing scene, leaving all the action and words to the Athenian and Spartan men. In most of these examples, it is female or lower-status characters who drop out of view; so it has been argued that the Athenian audience (predominantly male citizens) would prefer to be able to focus on characters most like themselves.

This assumption, or prejudice, may be mistaken. (There are plenty of counter-examples.) Certainly modern audiences expect to see Electra and Lysistrata at these junctures of their respective plays, and directors usually play the scenes accordingly. Likewise, in the modern era we surely expect to see Xanthias taken care of properly, given the play's inclusive message and concern for *all* members of the community, and we may well have some questions in our mind as to exactly how the Chorus' ideas from the *parabasis* (= the poet's, more or less)—and Aeschylus' too, in his responses to Dionysus about saving the city—will be translated into action. What is the attitude to be towards the newly enfranchised (ex-slave) citizens, and how broadly do we expect the benefits of "salvation" to be experienced?

At 530–33, after Dionysus has once again donned his Heracles costume which he had asked Xanthias to wear a moment before, we find him scoffing at the idea that a slave could ever plausibly impersonate Heracles. But Xanthias replies presciently, "You may find yourself needing me again soon, if god so wishes. . . ." And, in the next scene, the two of them again go through a process of exchanging identities and even undergoing identical tests (tortures). So Xanthias indeed provides indispensable service and support, both practical and moral, without which his cowardly and bumbling master would never have succeeded in his quest. It is all the more curious that Dionysus is found singing a little lyric stanza on the topic of the topsy-turviness of a comic world in which a slave might get to lord it over his master:

[Dion.] Wouldn't it be ridiculous, if Xanthias, a slave,
    Were tossing on fancy Milesian quilts
    And kissing a dancing-girl,
    And then asked for a chamber pot—while I
    Was looking at him and wanking my bean;
    And he saw me, and being a fellow-rascal
    Just like me, punched me in the mouth
    And knocked my front teeth out?
                            (541–47)

The humor of this little vignette (crude as it is) seems to depend on the idea that slaves are doomed forever to have to watch their masters having fun and enjoying the delights of life that slaves are denied. To Dionysus, the ultimate "ridiculous" absurdity would be for himself to have to carry a chamber pot, for himself to have to resort to masturbation, while his lowly slave enjoyed fine bedcovers and the favors of a prostitute—with the added indignity and pain that the master is even allowed to hit his slave if he feels annoyed at him, without fear of retaliation or even social disapproval. Yet, as Dionysus tellingly remarks in passing, each of them is really "a rascal" (*panourgos*, 545); each would behave just the same as the other if given the opportunity. And in comedy such opportunities may occur. *Frogs* provides repeated and extensive moments of exchange and usurpation of roles, competition, and complaint, as well as mutual interdependence between these two. So the question, whether anyone remembers Xanthias at the end—especially whether Dionysus in particular has enough fellow-feeling to include his loyal slave in the celebrations (and enough sense of continuity with the past, or common sense, to employ his slave in his customary duties of carrying all the stuff that will be needed on a journey and at its end)—carries considerable symbolic weight.

I should like to think that Xanthias will be part of this final procession, mirroring his role from the opening scene. If not, then we have to reconcile ourselves to the differences between our own modern sensibilities and those of fifth-century Athenians. To them, slavery was natural, normal, indispensable—just as the restriction of citizen rights to men was. Persephone does not speak in our play either; yet her presence and approval of Plouton's decisions are clearly of crucial importance, given the Underworld context and the presence of the Initiate Chorus. Silent characters can still play major roles (think Pylades . . .).

It is noteworthy that in these final scenes the focus has shifted from Dionysus to Aeschylus, and the master of ceremonies is definitely Plouton. Dionysus' last contribution to the dramatic action is his final relegation of the second-place Euripides back to his place among the dead shades. Mockingly misquoting the playwright's own lines in justification of this shameless rejection of him (1471–78), Dionysus makes it clear that the paradoxical ideas and expressions that he had previously found so exciting and "adventurous," now appear merely empty: "Who knows whether life is death, whether breathing is dining and sleeping is a fleece-blanket?" (1477–78). Euripides departs in despair and, from here on, Dionysus has nothing to say. It is the Chorus who speak and sing as representatives of the city at large, in conversation with Aeschylus and Plouton.

Plouton invites Aeschylus and Dionysus inside to be his guests for a feast before "sailing back home" (1479), and the Chorus of Initiates sing a song of blessings (*makarismos*) in honor of Aeschylus and his "extraordinarily acute intelligence . . . and good sense" (1482–85). In returning to his old home above, he will bring benefits to "his citizens . . . and to his own family and friends." Here again, the inclusiveness is significant: women, children, non-Athenians are among the beneficiaries of Aeschylus' return—it is only Socrates and other such pretentious hair-splitters who will fail to appreciate the greatness of "true tragic art" (1491–99). So it is for the celebrants at the Eleusinian Mysteries as well (and other Bacchic rituals, as we saw in chapter 6)—men, women, and children, Athenians, metics and slaves, all can be "saved" through the correct process of presenting themselves to the judgment of Persephone and her husband. Xanthias too? He is after all actually the only human being in this play who has successfully negotiated the passage into the Underworld and back. . . .

Why Aeschylus—What Does This Mean for the Arts in Athens (and Beyond)?

All of this explains well enough why Aristophanes would choose to show Dionysus favoring these various pieces of "good advice" that he receives from the two great tragedians, and how the members of the audience are collectively drawn into acceding to the inclusive message of this ending. But we still have not determined exactly why, in the end, it is Aeschylus whom Dionysus chooses rather than Euripides, or what this entails for the artistic (aesthetic, musical, poetic) "message" of our play. Is Aristophanes, after all, recommending a reversion to older styles of composition and performance, rejecting the latest trends and endorsing the familiar stereotype of Euripides (and the New Music) as being degenerate, effeminate, and vulgar? How are we supposed to interpret Dionysus' decision?

The decision is certainly overdetermined. There are many good reasons why Dionysus should choose Aeschylus. The actual process leading up to the announcement of this decision has been swift and amusingly arbitrary-seeming. Once again it is Plouton who provides the crucial nudge, as he interjects impatiently, "Please, make your decision!" (1467). Immediately Dionysus turns to face the two poets:

> Here is how my decision (*krisis*) will be made about the
>   two of you:
> I will choose the one that my soul (*psychē*) really wants.
> (1467–68)

Then, despite Euripides' frantic reminder that he was the one that Dionysus originally intended to reclaim ("Remember the gods you swore by, to bring me back . . .," 1469–70), Dionysus at last blurts it out: "[That's what] my tongue swore; but it's Aeschylus that I'll choose!" (1471). The witty reminder of Euripides' own notorious line (from *Hippolytus*; see chapter 5, p. 128) just adds zest to this delicious comic moment. The real point was already set up by the mention of Dionysus' "soul" (*psychē*) immediately before. Although many critics have seen this as merely equivalent to a "gut feeling" (i.e., "I'm going with my heart [sc. rather than my intellect and considered judgment]"), similar to his earlier account of how "a sudden yearning grabbed my heart (*kardian*) . . . for a man . . . for Euripides" (53–68), the choice of the term *psychē* at 1468 suggests something different: while "soul" may be a little too spiritual and religious (Platonic, Christian) to be a perfect translation in this context, the word—which has not been used up until this point in the play to refer to Dionysus' feelings or "inner self"—reminds us of the Eleusinian and eschatological dimensions of Dionysus' underworld adventure, and reinforces the notion that this "judgment" of his is going to decide not only the resurrection of one dead poet but also the future (the afterlife) of a whole community, all of us in the audience who have been initiated into the mysteries of Dionysian joy and understanding. In the Underworld, it is your *psychê*, not your *kardia*, that continues to exist (in some capacity) as "you"; and here in the Theater all of us, as quintessential Athenians ("good and useful citizens"), stand to benefit from Dionysus' correct choice.

So Dionysus' soul chooses Aeschylus. The god never explains why. But the reasons are obvious, and numerous: there is no need for explanations. Everyone in the Theater has seen and heard what Aeschylus stands for—the greatness of Athens' past (and especially its military achievements), respect for the traditions of theater, reticence about sexual misbehavior (combined with blatant sexism and snobbery in choice of tragic themes and "heroes"), and an aura of religiosity emanating from his Eleusinian connections as well as his rather conventional and old-fashioned deployment of gods and sacral language in his plays. And they have seen how at every turn Euripides' innovations—the very elements that Dionysus at the beginning of the play claimed were so "adventurous"—have been made to look absurd and pretentious. It is not that Aeschylus' style and themes have emerged as faultless (perfect models for continued imitation)—on the contrary, Euripides' criticisms and mockery have been quite effective in pointing out how far artistic capabilities and audience taste have advanced since Aeschylus' day. But a nostalgia for those great days when Athens' empire was still growing and Aeschylus' plays were new and inspiring haunts the whole contest, even while credit is being assigned to the technical and intellectual innovations that have intervened and that have made a return to Aeschylean dramaturgy by now inconceivable.

Does this mean that the message of *Frogs* is that tragedy, and dramatic art in general, has indeed declined? (If Aeschylus' plays were better than Euripides', and only Aeschylus' miraculous return to life on earth can "save" the city of Athens, then this might seem to imply that in actuality the city is doomed to continued artistic—and moral-political—deterioration.) If the city now lacks "skilled, potent" poets to advise, teach, and inspire it in the way that Aeschylus—or even Sophocles and Euripides—used to do, what can we all look forward to in the years ahead? The final scenes of the play do not in fact seem at all despondent or pessimistic, either in political or in poetical terms. Instead, as we have seen, there seems to be a powerful sense of rejuvenation, of renewed confidence, and even of artistic exuberance, as Plouton and Persephone bless the Dionysian embassy and send it on its way back up—to here, the Theater of Dionysus, where the audience are already sitting and enjoying the show.

Since quite early in the play the audience has already been prepared (maneuvered) to accept this playwright's (and his Chorus') vision of them as intelligent, discriminating, and full of community spirit: we—i.e., all the ones sitting in the theater who properly appreciate Aristophanes' wit and his grasp of what is "fitting" and right, both in the arts and in society at large—"we" are all qualified as true Athenians, and we all can now buy into the recuperation of Aeschylus for the benefit of our whole community. As we observed in chapter 4, the key evaluative terms *sophos* ("clever, expert") and *dexios* ("accomplished, neat") that dominated critical discussion during the early stages of the play have given way later to forms of the word *sunesis* ("understanding, intelligence") and the related adjective *sunetos* ("knowledgeable, wise, discriminating," as at 876, 892, 1483, 1485, 1490). This shift seems to merge the identities and outlooks of judges and audience—and author—closely with one another inasmuch as *sunesis, sunetos* convey a stronger sense of "shared expertise, good sense." (The prefix *sun-* has precisely this sense; and in some Presocratic writers such as Heraclitus the words *xunos/sunos* and *koinos* ("common") were explicitly identified with one another in relation to the "shared" faculty of human reason.) Thus the emphasis shifts from Dionysus' idiosyncratic taste and the individual genius (*sophia, dexiotēs*), towards the audience's collective good sense in judging the wisest poet and the community's best interests as a whole.

In the end it is a combination of practical and moral excellence that is required [*sophia* (a) and (b), from chapter 4], with cleverness, technical skill [*sophia* (c)] apparently taking a back seat. And yet—behind the scenes, as it were, or plotting the whole course of the action (as well as composing all the words, dance steps, and music)—has been a poetic intellect that has shown itself supremely capable of employing *all* the available registers and techniques of the Tragic Art, old and new. For if "blessed man" is a suitable way to invoke Aeschylus and his poetic "intelligence" (1482), it is even more appropriate as a description of our comic playwright himself, the one who has brought about this perfectly happy ending and this occasion of (temporary) salvation for the city.

Although it was Dionysus who began the process (with plenty of help from Xanthias and Heracles), the eventual outcome cannot be credited to him alone: it was not really (or not originally) Dionysus' skill or insight that conjured up the spirit of Aeschylus and restored it to the upper air. (Left to himself, as we've seen, the guy's an idiot!) The miraculous outcome has really been achieved by Aristophanes himself and his "Choruses." Our supreme comic poet, who knows tragedy and all the tragedians of Athens inside out, by this point has established himself (post-Cratinus) as incomparably the supreme dramatist in the city (and he is still alive—the best substitute for any "reborn" or re-imagined Aeschylus . . . or Euripides, for that matter). In earlier years, Aristophanes had sometimes presented himself as a young challenger to the aging, fading Cratinus, and had made fun of the old poet's lack of self-control with wine, with women, and with the art of drama (see chapter 2). Now that Cratinus has passed on, his name is mentioned with reverence (356–67) and Aristophanes is able to position himself as the living heir to the old man's legacy—but without any of the rancor and disruption that we have witnessed in the collision between Aeschylus and Euripides.

Did Aristophanes realize that an era of comedy (as well as tragedy) was coming to an end? Certainly one of the factors that has contributed to the enduring appeal of *Frogs* both to ancient and to modern readers and audiences is the fact that the play so clearly and strikingly constitutes (even if Aristophanes and his audience were not fully aware of this at the time) his last full-blooded engagement with the traditional forms of Old Comedy—including personal abuse, direct address to the audience in a *parabasis*, and extensive choral song and dance. Thus we might think of this play as being almost as much about the past, future, and ideal form of comedy, as it is about old vs. new tragedy and the prospects of continued vitality in tragic drama from the successors of the great three: Aeschylus, Sophocles, and Euripides.

Modern readers and theatergoers tend to see this play as a watershed, a definitive moment in the history of (ancient) theater. Neither tragedy nor comedy was ever quite the same after this—or so the surviving plays indicate: we possess tragedies from none of the successors of Euripides and Sophocles (except perhaps *Rhesus*, whose authorship is uncertain); and while we do have two later plays by Aristophanes, both of them display quite a different character from *Frogs* and his earlier works. We are aware too as we read *Frogs*, not only that total defeat of Athens in the War was to follow within months of the play's production, but that (by an odd historical quirk, i.e., the long-term triumph of Christianity) a whole new "century" was (retrospectively) about to dawn. The conclusion of *Frogs* is thus viewed, however artificially and unjustifiably, as the end of an era. A *fin de siècle* play that contemplates the demise of tragedy yet concludes with an exuberant celebration of past glories and future artistic possibilities leaves many avenues of interpretation open as to who these artists of the future are to be and how seriously they may wish to take the idea of reincorporating the spirit of Aeschylus into their work. The message that pervades the ending of *Frogs* seems really to be not so much "Can we get our poets to write more like Aeschylus?," as "How can we all combine our talents to appreciate and maximize the full potential of the Muse, so that the best of the past and of the present can all be harnessed and appreciated to the full?"

The selection of Aeschylus as the savior of Athens, when all is said and done, involves an endorsement of Tragedy's claim to be serious and "proper," to be legitimate—the "decorum" factor (see chapter 4). Whether we take this in the marital-sexual terms suggested by the contrast between Phrynichus' and Aeschylus' physical figuration of the "Art of Tragedy" (overweight, but monogamous and demure) versus Euripides' (a professional and promiscuous provider of musical pleasures and intellectual provocation), or in the verbal and costuming distinctions between Aeschylus' heroic, grand, larger-than-life representations and Euripides' more domestic and low-life ones (including kings in rags, women in love, and other kinds of sub-heroic "realism"), the issue of decorum—what is "appropriate, required" in the art of tragedy—lies at the heart of the whole contest. Athenian society was (as most societies in the world today continue to be) pervasively androcentric and sexist. The most "potent" poet, the one who has not "lost his little bottle of oil," is likely to prevail in public debate over one who claims to speak for women and the poor, for intellectuals, for musical and theological innovation—and in such respects to be representing social realities truthfully (democratically?), rather than merely nostalgically. Aeschylus stands for an idea (ideal) of the tragic art (and of democracy?) in which certain things are not spoken of or shown, and the audience need not confront the uncomfortable possibilities of female desire, class inequity, or divine ineptitude (or nonexistence), settling instead for an ideal of unity and community in which such divisions have been poetically transcended or obliterated. The superior technical accomplishments of Euripidean rhetorical argumentation or solo singing can be classed as "prostitution" of the art (*porneia*), especially if they required specialized skills from noncitizen performers, while Aeschylus' linguistic enhancements and old-fashioned (epic-citharodic) mannerisms can be viewed as a kind of authenticity, a fidelity to the tragic poet's implied contract. (In much the same way, Cratinus in his late-career *Pytinê* had staged the renunciation of his own wayward past—alcoholism, sluttish music, etc.—and his joyous return to his faithful "wife," the Muse of Comedy, see chapter 1.) In both political and poetical terms, the ending of *Frogs* suggests that its audience and judges should embrace a shared system of values and "intelligence, taste, good sense" (*sunesis*), and should not be so carried away with the latest notions of cleverness and sophistication as to lose touch with the qualities that originally made Athenian tragedy—and the city of Athens—the pride of Greece.

In chapter 6 (pp. 198–99) we observed how the Art of Tragedy herself/itself—and perhaps of Comedy too—seems to be among those who have experienced a "rebirth" or rejuvenation/purification through Dionysus' visit to the Underworld in *Frogs*, and how Aristophanes himself thus emerges as the potential savior of the city, alongside the revivified Aeschylus. We may recall how, when the Chorus of Initiates first arrive, they declare that among those banned from their celebrations are people "who [were] never initiated in the Bacchic rites of bull-eating Cratinus' tongue" (357). As the most famous practitioner (now deceased) of Old Comedy from the previous generation, Cratinus carries many of the same associations as Aeschylus does for tragedy: both of them certainly belong among the old school poets of indisputable vigor and "potency." Perhaps Aristophanes, previously known for his "Euripidizing" tendencies (see chapters 1and 5), as well as for his scathing put-downs of Cratinus, here seeks to reclaim some of the authority of the "Old" while still incorporating the brilliance and panache of the "New," as he restores The Art (The Muse) to her pristine state of purity, health, and proper behavior. Under the trustworthy supervision of the (deceased but rejuvenated and ever- "potent") master poet, Aeschylus, and of Aristophanes himself, still living and in his prime, the spirit of drama cannot go astray.

· 8 ·

Reading and Performing *Frogs* After Aristophanes—Reception

The first production of *Frogs*, at the Lenaea festival of 405 BCE, was a smash hit. Not only did the play win first prize, but the Athenians were impelled to pass a special edict awarding Aristophanes an olive-leaf crown and inviting him to present the play again publicly the next year—a very unusual privilege. We do not know where (or even whether) this second production occurred; and modern scholars disagree as to whether our medieval manuscript texts of the play reproduce the first or second version—or some combination of the two. (In particular, lines 1431–55 seem to contain some duplications and inconsistencies, and many scholars have thought that these must be the result of a splicing together of two different versions, both genuinely Aristophanic.) Such revision for reperformance is common enough, of course, in the world of the theater—most playwrights think of their work as always open to updating, adaptation, and improvement if the prospect of a new production arises. But specific evidence such as this for classical Athens is very rare.

Apart from this alleged second performance, we have no idea whether *Frogs* was ever presented again in a full-scale production with choruses, costumes, original or revised music, etc., in classical or Hellenistic Athens—or if it was, in what venue or context (perhaps in one of the Attic deme theaters? or in South Italy, where

Athenian Comedy seems to have been very popular?) and with what kinds of revisions. A play whose basic premise is that *Euripides has just died* (and Sophocles too) and that Athens therefore needs to retrieve its tragic Grand Master(s) so as not to sink into permanent artistic decline would obviously lose its immediate point very quickly. There were plenty of successful and highly regarded tragedians around in fourth-century Athens—it does not appear that anyone was in fact seriously worrying that tragedy had died or deteriorated. Furthermore, as with all of Aristophanes' plays, most of the topical references would become quite obscure or irrelevant as the decades passed, a problem that did not apply to tragedy. Allegorical or myth-based plays would be more timeless and so fare better with later audiences—and it was indeed the highly allegorical *Wealth* that went on to become by far the most read and best-known of Aristophanes' plays in later centuries.

The first performance of *Frogs*, supervised by Aristophanes himself, took place—presumably—in the Theater of Dionysus. We can say a certain amount about the way it was staged while also leaving open a number of questions that are interesting to think about but impossible to answer. The stage directions that are written in many modern published translations of Aristophanes' plays are entirely the work of the translator: none of this information is supplied in the Greek texts that have come down to us, and translators, editors, and theater historians often have quite widely divergent ideas as to how each play was staged. Nonetheless, archaeology, vase painting, and indications within the plays themselves do allow us to reach agreement on certain points.

The set consisted, as always, of the large wooden stage-building (*skēnē*), representing in this play first Heracles' house and later Plouton's palace. (Did one and the same door work for both, or were there two? Opinions differ. So either we should think of Heracles' house as being at one end of the *skēnē*, Plouton's at the other; or else one large door was used for all entrances and exits, and the sense of space was generally more fluid throughout.) In front of the set was the large earth-floored *orchestra* ("dance-floor"), in which most of the acting and all the dancing took place. Was this *orchestra* circular or rectangular/trapezoidal during this period? The evidence is inconclusive; see Figures 1–1a and b for possible reconstructions, as well as for alternative versions of the one-door or two-door *skênê*. Interactions and transitions between the dance-floor, the acting area in front of the house, and the interior, were quick and easy. (The high, built-up stage that we know from Roman theaters was not introduced until many decades later; possibly there was a low stage, as in Figure 1–1a, but more likely none at all.)

Every comic playwright worked, it appears, with four speaking actors. *Frogs* has thirteen speaking characters in addition to the two choruses; so these four actors had to switch roles repeatedly, sometimes rather quickly (relying heavily on masks and costumes). In addition, there was an indefinite number of nonspeaking actors, some of whom may have doubled as stagehands. How were the actors' roles divided in *Frogs*? One actor obviously played Dionysus throughout. A second perhaps played Xanthias and Plouton; a third Heracles, various servants, and Aeschylus; and the fourth Charon, the Doorkeeper, other servants, and Euripides. Other distributions would be possible; but in any case both the actors playing the two tragedians would need to be skilled singers and convincing parodists of tragic style in general. (The limitation to four actors of course provides one practical reason for the elision of Xanthias from the later parts of the play.) It is possible that an actual (female) "dancing girl" performed the castanet dance while Aeschylus sang Euripidean lyrics (1309–28; cf. Fig. 5–1b); more likely this was a silent male actor/dancer. (Was this "Muse" presented as old and ugly, or young and sexy? See chapter 5.)

The pipe-player (*aulêtês*) who accompanied all the singing probably stood or sat in the center of the orchestra throughout (though he could easily move aside when necessary): he did not count as a character at all (see Fig. 1–1b). The main Chorus (the Initiates) presumably comprised twenty-four members, the usual number for comedies. But it is a notoriously unanswerable problem whether or not the Chorus of Frogs made a visible appearance to sing their interactive-disruptive song while Dionysus was rowing. If they did appear, dancing in full frog-costume (as imagined in Fig. 1–1a), they only had a couple of minutes (50 lines or so) after this scene to change costume and reenter as Mystic Initiates. (Otherwise Aristophanes would have had to employ more than twenty-four chorus members altogether; not impossible.) Some critics have concluded that these frogs must have been invisible (singing through the doorway? or from the sides?). But trying to coordinate scenes between onstage and offstage actors—and especially singers!—is a well-known recipe for chaos in modern theaters, and offstage singers tend to be hard for an audience to hear properly. And if you name your play "The Frogs," your audience probably comes to the theater expecting to see an eye-catching set of animal costumes—as in Aristophanes' *Birds*, *Wasps*; it might be a severe disappointment if they never appeared. Meanwhile, where exactly does Xanthias with all his luggage go (on foot!) while Dionysus is rowing in Charon's boat "across" the Lake? (Round the edge of the orchestra? into the seating area and round the back of the whole theater? off by one side entrance and on again by the other?) Questions about these and other directorial choices often are important for the interpretation and impact of the play; but we cannot answer all of them, and it may well be that different choices were sometimes made even for reperformance in Aristophanes' own day, depending on venue and resources.

Props. Did Xanthias ride a real ass, or just some kind of hobby-horse donkey? Either is perfectly feasible in a large open-air theater, and we really do not know to what extent fifth-century dramatists liked to introduce real/realistic props and effects (chariots, earthquakes, gory corpses, etc.), or whether they preferred more stylized representations. Old Comedy really does seem, however, to seek out extravagant visual effects whenever possible; and an early- or mid-fourth-century painted representation of this scene does include a real donkey (see Fig. 3–1). As for the pile of luggage that Xanthias had been carrying slung from a pole resting on his shoulders in the opening scenes, presumably it is eventually deposited in Plouton's palace and forgotten about. How was Charon's boat represented, and how did it move from one side of the orchestra to the other? If it had wheels, it might remind the audience of the wheeled boat that apparently conveyed a statue of Dionysus during the Anthesteria procession (see chapter 6; also Fig. 1–1a). Chairs were certainly brought on at the beginning of the contest scene for Plouton and Persephone to sit on; presumably these were placed at the back of the orchestra (as in Fig. 1–1b). Was an actual *cithara* used for Euripides' parody at 1285–97? (Maybe; but not necessarily: see chapter 4 p. 143.) But various pieces of machinery and measuring tools—most conspicuously, an enormous pair of scales—were certainly brought in to stand available (at the front of the orchestra? or side? see Fig. 1–1b) until needed: then the coming and going of technicians manipulating these gadgets during the later stages of the contest must have added to the humorous effect.

Costumes and masks. The text makes clear that Dionysus wears both a Heraclean lion-skin and his own traditional saffron robe; and he carries a club too (see Fig. 3–1, though in this painting the saffron robe is missing). Other costumes and masks would be boldly designed so as to be obvious to spectators sitting in the back rows. Most of the masks would have been grotesque and exaggerated, in accordance with standard comic emphasis on the "ugly"; and in addition most of the actors would have padded buttocks and bellies, and wear a dangling or "infibulated" (tied-up) phallus (see Fig. 3–2). They would mostly be dressed in short tunics and full-body tights that covered their legs; and on their feet both actors and chorus members would have worn light slippers/pumps (*kothurnoi*) suitable for dancing and occasional slapstick or acrobatics. The Initiates apparently were costumed in rather cheap-looking, tattered garments (404–14), as Eleusinian worshippers were in real life (chapter 6). The text indicates that some of the Initiates are women, others men (though some scholars have disputed this). Of course all the actual chorus members (choreuts), like the actors, were male.

Performance style. In all of this, the blocking and stage "business"—as well as the vocal and musical execution of Aristophanes' dazzling language and elaborate metrical-choreographical modulations and parodies—must certainly have contributed greatly to the humor and entertainment of the original production. Athenian comic acting, like the costumes, was geared to gross and exaggerated gesture and movement—definitely "over-the-top." But these actors needed also to be able to produce convincing parodies of Aeschylean and Euripidean songs and dances—and parody is most effective when it successfully captures the true idiom of the original (and then proceeds to distort and mangle it). So comic actors needed to understand tragedy well, just as the play's author did.

Given all these demands, it really seems unlikely that any team of actors, designers, director, and pipe-player of the fourth century or later would have been capable of recreating that first performance (or pair of performances) with quite the original flavor and flair, given how much was changing in musical styles and audience tastes. In the future, Aristophanes' *Frogs* would necessarily be—at least partially—someone else's *Frogs*, whether staged, or read. Undoubtedly, however, the play was re-performed in various places, and, as we have seen, a fourth-century vase painting from Apulia (South Italy: the so-called "Berlin Heracles," Fig. 3-1) appears to represent one such performance. Whether or not changes were made in the text for such productions (excisions, rewritings, interpolations; new "business" and fresh topical allusions), they would inevitably look and sound different, and be differently imagined, from that first production.

The Fourth Century—and Beyond

Aristophanes himself remained active for several years after *Frogs* as an author of successful comedies (including *Women in the Assembly* and *Wealth*), and in due course his sons took over the business of producing his and their own plays (see chapter 2). But whereas "old tragedies," especially those of Euripides, were frequently revived in the fourth century in Athens and elsewhere in Greece, and provided excellent opportunities for star actors to show off their talents (like, for example, the plays of Shakespeare, Molière, and Brecht in more recent times), tastes in comedy had changed. There was little or no demand for the old-style comedies of Aristophanes, Cratinus, Eupolis, and the rest. Instead, "New" Comedy, with its tightly plotted "human" dramas of romance, character types, and mistaken identities, had become more appealing than the wild-and-crazy plots, political satire, and hyperbolic fantasies that Aristophanes had offered. Theater was flourishing throughout the Greek world (it was during this period that huge stone theaters came to be built at Epidaurus, Ephesus, Pergamum, and many other cities), but for the most part the comedies presented there were the compositions of Alexis, Eubulus, Menander, Philemon, Diphilus, etc. Old Comedy was old hat—and it is not even clear which type of comedy, Old or New, Aristotle had primarily in mind when he wrote his *Poetics* (probably during the 330s BCE, just as Menander was beginning his career as a playwright): he does mention Aristophanes once as comedy's equivalent to Sophocles in tragedy (*Poetics* 1448a); but there are signs that his ideas of comedy are more decisively shaped by fourth-century styles and priorities. It is possible, however, that the distinction between "Old" and "New" Comedy has been drawn too sharply by many; the overlap and continuities may have been greater than has conventionally been argued. In any case, the loss of the second book of the *Poetics* reduces us to mere speculation; we remain largely in the dark as to what antiquity's greatest drama critic thought about any of Aristophanes' plays.

Although *Frogs* was not being reperformed, it was certainly being read. The Suda (see above, chapter 1 and chapter 2) reports, perhaps fancifully, but tellingly:

> The reputation of the poet even reached the Persians, and the King learned about him from his ambassadors. They say too that Plato, when Dionysius the tyrant of Syracuse asked to learn about the Athenian political system (*politeia*), sent him the compositions of Aristophanes and advised him to study these plays and learn from them about their political system.

Plato himself is said to have kept copies of Aristophanes' plays under his pillow; and the role he gave Aristophanes in his imaginary *Symposium*, in dialogue with Socrates, Alcibiades, and Agathon, measures up brilliantly to the playwright's offbeat and fantastic genius.

No sustained allusions to or imitations of *Frogs* are found in later Greek or Latin authors (though occasional short quotations by admiring or disapproving critics are common). On the other hand, the literary/aesthetic principles that we find articulated in our play, especially the contrast between the old "grand, inflated" style and the new "slender, subtle" one, became central to later Greek and Roman critical theory: among poets, Philetas and Callimachus, Catullus and Propertius follow in these footsteps, while the rhetorical tradition of Theophrastus, Cicero, Dionysius of Halicarnassus, and Quintilian likewise routinely works with a binary in which "grand" and "thin" are always competing options for every aspiring orator (or literary stylist), depending on subject matter and context. The best orator is usually expected to be able to command both, but poetic genres are meant to keep them separate. In none of these discussions does it appear that *Frogs* is being specifically cited, nor any of its particular scenes or tropes deployed: it is rather the case that Aristophanes in *Frogs* (along with, e.g., Cratinus in his *Pytine*) helped to open the gates onto a long and sweeping avenue of subsequent critical debate, which took on its own life and terms of reference. When Old Comedy and Aristophanes were cited in literary critical contexts, it was usually not for their aesthetic discrimination or potential for saving a community through their art, but for their low and unconventional usages of language, uninhibited representations of human ugliness, sexuality, and moral debasement, or outspokenness and fierce mockery of living individuals. And, in those respects, *Frogs* was not the most extreme nor the most typical of Aristophanes' works, hence not the most likely to be quoted or critiqued: it is usually the more overtly "political" plays that crop up in these discussions—along with the notorious depiction of Socrates in *Clouds*, of course.

By the early third century BCE, as "Hellenism" had spread to all corners of the Mediterranean and western Asia, and the Attic Greek dialect was becoming established as the "common" (*koinē*) language for the educated classes in all those regions, the cachet of classical (fifth-fourth century) Athenian literature continued to grow. Scholars at Alexandria, Pergamum, and elsewhere collected the best of the "classic" texts, and schoolteachers everywhere were consolidating the canon of appropriate authors to teach to young potential orators and bureaucrats. Standardized, "correct" spelling, grammar, vocabulary, and idiom were expected among the educated class all over the Hellenized world, and this standard was the Attic Greek of Lysias and Demosthenes, Xenophon and Plato. Homer of course continued to be central to every Greek's education, but not as a model of style. Along with the orators and philosophical texts, Attic drama was a vital component of the school curriculum. Euripides and Menander were especially prominent since their Greek was relatively easy to read and they provided many good examples of moralizing and argumentative speech-composition. But the plays of Aristophanes, Eupolis, and Cratinus were also admired as examples of authentic Athenian discourse from the great days of Pericles. Their plays were valued by professional scholars too—a significant new breed—both for the wealth of historical and biographical information (or comically inflected misinformation) that they contained, and for the rare or specialized words that cropped up in certain comic contexts (e.g., involving food, furniture, crafts, or religion). So scholars such as Eratosthenes (chief librarian at Alexandria, second century BCE) wrote full-scale monographs on the history of Old Comedy, and an ever-growing body of "glosses" (*glôssai*) and "notes" (*hypomnêmata*) on matters of diction, spelling, grammar, meter, prosopography, and history began to accrue around the plays—the core of the extensive scholia that eventually came to be written all over the margins of our medieval manuscripts (see Fig. 8–1).

But the status of Aristophanes' plays as models of Greek style for students was always somewhat uncertain throughout later antiquity and the Middle Ages. Whereas nobody could deny the authentically Attic quality of Aristophanic Greek, nor the boldness and outspokenness of his plays' denunciations of disreputable individuals and their immoral behavior (vivid examples of Athens' famed "freedom of expression," *parrhêsia*), it was also all too obvious to any reader that the plays were full of obscenities and indecencies, that Aristophanes' language was often grotesque and full of extravagant puns and wordplays, and that many of the leading characters (including even divinities) were speaking and behaving in shameless and socially unacceptable ways. What kind of model could these plays be for youngsters in school? Here again, Euripides and Menander were generally regarded as offering more morally acceptable and decorous objects of study and more consistently correct and normal language—as well as being still highly performable in the theater. So it is likely that Aristophanes' plays were read in excerpted or bowdlerized versions (at least, in the schools); and probably little effort was made to preserve or restore (let alone teach) the music or choreography that had been such vital components of the original productions.

We possess one (garbled and truncated, but clearly recognizable) example of such critical/moralistic views, recorded in a work attributed to Plutarch, *A Comparison of Aristophanes and Menander*.

> In Aristophanes we find coarseness and vulgarity of language; not in Menander. Uneducated, ordinary people enjoy antitheses, rhymes, and word-plays, and Aristophanes employs these all over the place, but Menander only rarely, as educated people prefer. . . . [So whereas Menander's work] is full of charm and merry wit, satisfying and acceptable in all contexts—theaters, discussions, banquets, schools, and dramatic competitions—Aristophanes' poetry is like a whore . . . full of licentiousness and malice. . . . His wit is bitter and rough, biting and wounding . . . and he seems to have written only for the envious and malicious. . . .

A much more enthusiastic assessment of Aristophanes is offered by the Roman educator Quintilian (*Inst. Orat.* 10. 1. 65, ca. 90 CE):

> Old Comedy is almost unique in preserving intact that pure grace of the Attic dialect, together with the eloquent expression of freedom. . . . It is mighty, elegant, and charming . . . and apart from Homer there is no other kind of poetry better suited to the training of orators. There are quite a few authors, but the best are Aristophanes, Eupolis, and Cratinus.

Clearly at this period the plays of Cratinus and Eupolis were still available, as well as Aristophanes'; and this is confirmed by a famous assertion by Horace in his *Satires*, which also demonstrates well the symbolic position that Old Comedy had by now attained in elite Greek and Roman circles:

> Eupolis, Cratinus and Aristophanes, and the other poets
> Of Old Comedy . . . used to mark out and expose
> With great freedom anyone who was bad—thief, adulterer
>   etc . . . .
> . . . That's where Lucilius' [sc. and hence my own] satires
>   come from . . .
>   (*Sermones* 1. 4. 1–6)

Horace is citing these three Old Attic Comedians as precedents for the social practice of criticizing by name individual contemporaries who are behaving badly, as a way of exposing their vices and thereby improving the morals of the whole community. Although Horace's own practice and style as a satirist does not in fact much resemble Aristophanes' (his language and meter are generally much tamer and more regular, his obscenities and scatology fewer and more restrained, his fantasies infinitely less bold), the citation of Old Comedy as the beacon of frank, outspoken criticism and fearless exposure of vice persisted throughout the classical and late antique periods, and into the Renaissance as well. Thus the verse satirists who followed in Horace's footsteps (Martial and Juvenal at imperial Rome; Ben Jonson in Renaissance England; Jonathan Swift and Alexander Pope in Enlightenment England, etc.) adopt almost none of Aristophanes' stylistic or formal elements, but nonetheless often present themselves (sometimes explicitly—especially in the case of Jonson) as his successors in the social project of cleansing and improving their community through personal invective.

So Aristophanes' plays (and those of other masters of Old Comedy) continued to be read and admired by educated Romans and Greeks. But they were not performed, nor were they directly imitated or adapted, the way Menander's and his rivals' had been (most notably, for the future of European stage comedy, by Plautus and Terence). For the most part it was the "spirit" of Aristophanic comedy that functioned as a catalyst for subsequent writers—right into the twentieth century—more than any particular play or scene. And the author who most whole-heartedly imbibed this spirit was the brilliant prose satirist-dialogist-fantasist Lucian of Samosata (Syria), in the second century CE, who clearly knew Aristophanes' plays well and makes clear allusions here and there to *Frogs* (especially in his *Dialogues of the Dead*) and to other plays as well. But even Lucian never directly imitated any of the plays in a sustained way, and his own prose medium was far removed from the verbal, metrical, and musical extravagances of Old Comedy. (In those respects the Roman comic playwright Plautus was closer, but his plots were derived largely from the New Comic tradition and from indigenous Italian theater forms.) So in the end Lucian was probably the author who most effectively kept the Aristophanic spirit alive—to inspire later comedians and satirists.

By the end of the second century CE the range of Old Comic texts covered in the schools and circulated among the educated public began to shrink. The *Onomasticum* of Julius Pollux and the *Deipnosophists* of Athenaeus both contain hundreds of quotations from all three comic poets, but, from this point on, texts of Cratinus and Eupolis seem to fade from the scene, with Aristophanes emerging as sole survivor. And even with Aristophanes, as with the three great tragedians, a smallish selection of his comedies, eleven out of the original forty or so, ended up being consolidated as the canon for school reading: *Frogs* was included, presumably because of its literary/aesthetic focus, relative lack of obscenity, and famous passages of moralizing and exhortation, and the play thus went on to become part of the canon of Western dramatic literarure. The title of our play, *Frogs* (*Batrachoi* in Greek; *Ranae* in Latin), seems to have remained consistent.

As the centuries passed, and more and more of "classical" Greek literature was lost (largely through neglect rather than active deletion or censorship), three plays in particular, *Wealth*, *Clouds*, and *Frogs*, established themselves as by far the most commonly copied and read. This "triad" is found in over two hundred extant Byzantine and early Renaissance manuscripts, of which the oldest surviving one was written in the early tenth century and now resides in Ravenna. (It is actually the only manuscript to contain all eleven plays, including *Thesmophoriazusae*, which apparently was less popular for didactic purposes than the other plays because of its racy subject matter.) The Ravenna's beautifully written text of *Frogs* has quite full marginal notes (scholia) to assist the reader in making sense of Aristophanes' text (see Fig. 8–1); and other manuscripts, also containing our play, most of them copied during the period 1000–1200 CE (usually in Byzantium-Constantinople or Thessaloniki), likewise offer extensive scholia. Indeed, the scholia of Aristophanes are the most copious of any ancient Greek author except Homer. There was so much to comment on—problems of language and dialect, issues of prosopography and history, explaining convoluted jokes. . . . And indeed there are many places where these scholiasts' comments enable modern scholars to arrive at a much surer understanding of the context and meaning of particular phrases and lines than would otherwise have been possible.

Byzantine clerics, from St. John Chrysostom to Photius to Thomas Magister, liked to borrow accusatory or self-justificatory passages from Aristophanes' plays and work them into their own homilies and critical discussions; and during periods of literary and scholarly "Renaissance" at Constantinople further scholarly aids were compiled, such as the Suda (see chapter 2), with all its valuable information about Aristophanes and his plays. On the other hand, Greek Orthodox interpretation of scripture (unlike that of the Roman Catholicism of the Latin West) did not approve of drama: painted icons and beautiful rhetorical narratives were good, but not three-dimensional, in-the-flesh impersonations. Accordingly it does not appear that classical drama, as such, was performed at all, even though it was quite intensively read. And since Menander was by now lost completely—for reasons that are hard to account for—it was the Aristophanic triad that was copied, studied, and excerpted for examples of the best of ancient comedy.

Figure 8–1. The page of the parchment manuscript R (Ravennas 429: tenth century CE) that contains the opening lines of *Frogs*. Note the heading *ARISTOFANOUS BATRA* (with abbreviation for *XOI* written above = "ARISTOPHANES' FROGS"), marginal commentary (scholia) written all around the main columns of lines, and abbreviations for speakers' names (*Xan/th* or *X/th*, and *Di/o*) to the left of the lines where relevant.

The original MS is in the Biblioteca Classense, Ravenna. This photo is from the facsimile edition, *Aristophanis comoediae undecim cum scholiis: Codex ravennas 137, 4, A*, ed. J. van Leeuwen (Leiden 1904).

1498 to the Present

As the project of preserving and studying the classical Greek legacy shifted from Constantinople (after the Ottoman conquest in 1453) to Italy and Western Europe, manuscripts were collected, copied, and studied there anew, and scholars in the rest of Europe learned how to read Greek, a language they had ignored for centuries. Aristophanes was clearly a high priority for them: the first printed edition of Aristophanes (Venice 1498, the "Aldine" edition) preceded the first complete edition of Euripides by five years, the first Sophocles edition by four years, and the first Aeschylus edition by fifty-nine years. In due course further editions of Aristophanes' Greek text appeared in Basel (1524, 1532) and elsewhere. During the fifteenth and early sixteenth centuries, *Wealth* attracted by far the most scholarly attention, and this was the first Aristophanes play to be translated (into Latin prose: 1440 in Florence; into Latin verse: 1501 in Parma; into German: 1531); also the first to be performed in the modern era (in Latin, by students in Zwickau, 1521; in Greek at Cambridge, in 1536). By contrast, *Frogs* did not begin to enjoy this kind of attention until well into the eighteenth century.

During the sixteenth century, the favorite mode of appreciating—and teaching—Aristophanes seems still to have been by means of excerpts of short passages, often termed "florilegia." Most significantly, and influentially, Erasmus included hundreds of Aristophanic passages in his *Adagia* (1500), a kind of dictionary of Greek and Latin quotations of a proverbial or witty character: only Cicero, Homer, and Plutarch were better represented in his collection than Aristophanes, with Horace, Plato, Lucian, and the rest trailing well behind. Erasmus also (in his *De Ratione Studii*, 1511) made a point of recommending the reading of Aristophanes as a high priority for the teaching of classical Greek prose style:

> I would assign first place to Lucian, second to Demosthenes, and third to Herodotus; again, among the poets, first place to Aristophanes, second to Homer, third to Euripides. For Menander, to whom I would have given even the first place, is not extant.

Perhaps the most important stages in the opening up of Aristophanes to a wider reading public came with the translation of all of the plays, first into Latin (by Andreas Divus, Venice 1538) and then into Italian (by the brothers Rositini, Venice 1545), soon followed by the French version of Pierre de Ronsard (Paris 1549). (N. Frischlin's Latin version, Paris 1589, was also quite widely known and read.) But English translations were much slower to appear (first *Wealth* in 1651); and *Frogs* apparently had to wait until 1785, when Charles Dunster's version was published in Oxford (though Pierre Brumoy's *Dissertation on Ancient Comedy* had been translated into English by 1759 and contained a version of *Frogs*). Throughout this period (indeed, right up into the twentieth century), the pattern continued whereby Aristophanes' name and reputation were widely known—often provoking intense admiration or disapproval—while relatively little attempt was made to stage or directly adapt his work (in sharp contrast, e.g., to the plays of the three great Greek tragedians, or the Roman comedians). Thus we find eloquent expressions of praise for Aristophanes and his comic-satiric ideals from Ben Jonson, John Dryden, Samuel Coleridge, and Percy B. Shelley, and we encounter the phenomenon of the eighteenth-century dramatist and actor Samuel Foote, renowned as "the English Aristophanes" for his mimes and satirical stand-up-comic routines. Only rarely, however, did a poet or playwright (usually a highly educated one) work directly with one of Aristophanes' actual plays: Jean Racine (seventeenth century) adapted *Wasps*; Goethe adapted *Birds* (1780, 1789), and his brother-in-law, J. G. Schlosser, produced the first German translation of *Frogs* (1783, Basel); Robert Browning wrote a well-informed and interesting drama, *The Apology of Aristophanes*, based in part on *Thesmophoriazusae* and *Frogs* (1875); but none of these made much impact on the reading or theatergoing public. Other comic dramatists such as Molière and the masters of Italian Commedia show no sign of being aware of Aristophanes at all, any more than Shakespeare had been. (The contrast between this and the status of the tragedies of Euripides and Seneca in Elizabethan England or Louis XIV's France is stark.) Meanwhile, moralistic and/or philosophical critics from time to time would continue to express disdain for Aristophanes' crudity and alleged anti-intellectualism (especially because of *Clouds* and its contribution to the prosecution and death of Socrates): so, for example, Boileau ("poisonous tongues and shameless buffoonery") and Voltaire in France.

It was not until the late nineteenth century that more widespread familiarity with the plays began to produce significant growth in their popularity and influence outside the walls of academia. The writings of Friedrich Nietzsche and Heinrich Heine in Germany, and James Frazer and Jane Harrison in Britain, brought a new excitement about the ritual origins, Dionysian effects, and musical dimensions of drama, while the steady decline of state-sponsored Christian belief and its sexual repressiveness, along with "modernist" assaults on many of the conventional aesthetic forms of previous centuries, all opened up Western audiences' eyes and ears to more extravagant, earthy, and multi-hued entertainments. The possibilities offered by Aristophanic adaptations for contemporary political satire and commentary were also obvious and irresistible—a "classic" and highly respectable precedent for subversive or revolutionary drama. The plays of Aristophanes were ready and waiting: as Max Beerbohm exclaimed in wonder, "Who is more modern than he?" (Many of Brecht's prescriptions for "epic theater," for example, are already found fully fledged in the works of Old Comedy.) In previous centuries, most of the authors who cited or borrowed from Aristophanes for his social commentary or personal invective had done so from quite conservative and reactionary positions of their own (and Aristophanes does indeed often ridicule "new" ideas and progressive artistic endeavors—including Socrates and Euripides!); but henceforth his style of comedy—and often his actual plays—tended more often to be adopted for progressive causes and/or as a means of antigovernment critique. And while *Frogs* has not been the most-performed (productions of *Birds*, *Lysistrata*, *Peace*, and *Clouds* have been more numerous), our play has remained prominent on course reading lists, and has not been neglected by college—and occasionally professional—performers throughout the twentieth century and into the twenty-first.

Overall we may trace four main forms of "reception" of *Frogs*, though sometimes these overlap with one another: (i) reading the Greek text, usually at school; (ii) reading/sampling the play in English (or other languages), especially by other writers as a jumping-off point for their own critical theorizing and/or adaptation (often involving some contemporary Battle of Ancients vs. Moderns); (iii) the growing industry (since ca. 1955) of idiomatic, up-to-date translations geared to students in universities and to theater-makers and readers of all kinds who need have no particular knowledge of ancient Greek culture or language; and, (iv) actual performances of *Frogs* (in Greek or other languages). Let us look at these in turn—though we will find some of the categories at times collapsing into one another.

(i) Unlike the best-known Latin classics (e.g., the *Aeneid* and *Metamorphoses*, or the comedies of Plautus and Terence), or even such Greek classics as Homer, Plato, and Euripides, the plays of Aristophanes have always been too difficult for more than a relatively small number of advanced students and professional classicists to read accurately in the original language. The fact that these works also contain so much crude language and amusingly immoral/indecent behavior further reduced the likelihood until recently that young students would be introduced to these plays in their entirety, though this has been less of an issue with *Frogs* than with some other plays that contain more extensive sexual content (especially *Lysistrata, Thesmophoriazusae*). Briefly, we may say that the reading of Aristophanes in the original Greek over the centuries has only occurred within communities of scholars (e.g., monasteries, or prep/public schools and universities), that is to say, a very small population, mostly elite and well-educated. During the nineteenth century, the most widely used edition of the Greek text in British schools was that of T. Mitchell, with English notes (1839). A vast improvement has been seen on this front since the mid-twentieth century, and students nowadays are fortunate that several first-rate editions and commentaries have been published for *Frogs* that make understanding and appreciation of the play in its original Greek much more achievable: in particular, the editions of W. B. Stanford (1963), K. J. Dover (1993; abridged ed. 1997), and A. H. Sommerstein (1996) are all excellent, and the bilingual Loeb edition by J. W. Henderson (vol. IV, 2002) presents another source of reliable help.

(ii) It is a very different story when we turn to Aristophanes' impact via modern translations or at secondhand, especially since the late nineteenth century. As we have seen, it was generally the "spirit" of Aristophanic humor that loomed (in the background, mostly) among creative artists and critics up into the nineteenth century, while firsthand knowledge of his plays tended to be small. Thus, several of the most brilliant figures of European satire and grotesque-fantastic comedy certainly belong in the Aristophanic tradition, but they usually seem to be more directly influenced by the comments of Horace, Quintilian, and Plutarch, and by reading Lucian's works (which were sometimes transmitted in the same manuscript tradition as Aristophanes' plays, and are far easier reading in their witty Attic prose) than by any particular Aristophanic play. Rabelais, for example, is known to have owned a text of Aristophanes, yet nowhere does his writing directly allude to or adapt anything specific from the plays.

One particularly lively and witty exchange of barbs, accompanied by unusually close engagement with Aristophanes' actual works (including *Frogs*), was generated by Ben Jonson in his *Every Man Out of his Humour* (1602), a play whose main characters are rival writers, arguing about the value of literature and the best style of poetry. In the course of the play, various arguments are presented to defend "comicall satyre" (by which Jonson apparently means a blend of Old Comedy and Horatian satire) both from the assaults of previous antitheatrical critics and from recent legislation introduced by the Archbishop of Canterbury to prohibit direct personal mockery of individuals by name. Cordatus, a member of Jonson's Grex (chorus) in the play, provides a brief (and not very accurate) history of *Vetus Comoedia* in justification of the idea that innovation is always appropriate; and Jonson's friend Jasper Mayne wrote a poem to him the next year congratulating him for his effective use of "th'old Comicke freedome."

Henry Fielding was another witty and enthusiastic Aristophanean. In his youth he composed a translation of *Wealth*, and he also incorporated several elements of *Frogs* into *The Author's Farce* (1730). Among his twenty-six comedies performed at the Haymarket, London, were several tragic spoofs, including *Tom Thumb*; and in his novel *Tom Jones* the introductory Chapter of Book 13 invokes Genius: "Come thou, that hast inspired thy Aristophanes, thy Lucian, thy Cervantes, thy Rabelais, thy Molière, thy Shakespear, thy Swift, thy Marivaux, fill my pages with Humour—till Mankind learn the Good Nature to laugh only at the Follies of others and the Humility to grieve at their own." But there are surprisingly few successors to Fielding in the next 150 years who show any real knowledge of Aristophanes' plays, and only since the late 1800s—and especially the 1950s—have quite broad segments of the population, including writers, visual artists, and theater-makers, become as familiar with the full range of Aristophanes' comedies as they have been for centuries with the works of Sophocles and Euripides. For this we obviously have to thank the boom in translations.

(iii) Translations (especially English): for those not trained as Classicists who have actually wanted to read *Frogs* for themselves, the possibilities have varied greatly depending on which country they have lived in. British and American readers had to wait until the nineteenth century to sample any of Aristophanes' plays other than *Wealth*, *Birds*, or *Clouds*. The vital—"breakthrough"—volume of translations was coordinated by J. H. Frere between 1817 and 1820 (but not satisfactorily published until 1837); for this he contributed his own verse translation of *Frogs*, along with a long and lively introduction and several chunks of commentary sandwiched between scenes of the play.

In his introduction Frere included a thoughtful and perceptive discussion of the different goals and approaches of the "faithful" vs. the "spirited" translator, and his own translation of *Frogs* is remarkably lively and accessible, even almost 200 years later. It is not surprising that it held the field for almost a century:

[Eur.] I mean it; I shall now proceed to expose him
as a bad composer, awkward, uninventive,
repeating the same strain perpetually.
[Chorus] I stand in wonder and perplext
    to think of what will follow next.
    Will he dare to criticise
    the noble bard, that did devise
    our oldest, boldest harmonies,
    whose mighty music we revere?
    Much I marvel, much I fear.

(1249–60)

Frere's versions eventually became the Everyman Library edition of Aristophanes, which was the version read by most English readers between 1837 and the e.arly twentieth century.

Gilbert Murray's 1902 version of the play, done mainly in rhyming couplets, was genteel and mild; clever in places but decidedly tame. The argumentative, intellectualizing Euripides in this version is clearly recognizable as George Bernard Shaw, a common identification in later decades too, as we shall see. Despite Murray's progressive views and lively writing style (and brilliant command of Greek), he was conspicuously prudish and not very musical. So we find, for example, Xanthias and Dionysus avoiding any reference to shitting or farting: "Don't shift your luggage pole across and say, "I want to blow my nose!" . . . "I have to sneeze" (7–10); and the frog chorus sings cheerful rhyming and not very disruptive limericks. Like the rest of Murray's translations of tragedy and comedy, this one sold well, was often reprinted, and remained the best-known version of the play up until the 1950s. The virtues and limitations can be seen in the following sample (939–44):

    [Eur.] I had the Drama straight from you, all bloated and
        uncertain,
    weighed down with rich and heavy words, puffed out past
        comprehension.
    I took the case in hand; applied treatment for such distension,

Beetroot, light phrases, little walks, hot book-juice, and
   cold reasoning;
then fed her up on solos . . .
[Dion., aside] With Cephisophon for seasoning!

The next translation of significance to appear—done rather in the manner of Gilbert and Sullivan—was part of the complete edition of the plays by Benjamin Bickley Rogers (1902; Loeb Library edition 1924). The rhythms and patter already sounded rather old-fashioned at the time they appeared (including plentiful sprinklings of "thou" and "ye"), but in places achieved an attractive flow and neatness. (Rogers was only slightly bolder than Murray, however, in his treatment of scatology and obscenity: so "belly-ache" and "ease myself" in 7–10; and in some plays whole passages are omitted.) Rogers' editions contained much useful scholarship, and the skillful and witty Englishness of the translations (as well as the pervasive presence of Loeb editions throughout the English-speaking world) kept them in the public domain long after other Victorian-style translations of the classics had been consigned to oblivion. But they seem rarely to have been used for performances.

Up until the mid-twentieth century and the era of paperbacks, the standard versions of *Frogs* available to readers in English were thus those of Frere, Murray, and Rogers. But since the 1950s the range of Aristophanic options for readers and performers has been enormously expanded. For the first time, translators began to attempt honestly to convey a fuller range of the linguistic registers presented by the original, and the hip, up-to-date qualities of Aristophanic language at last became recognizable on the English page, with all the alternations/combinations of high poetry and low colloquialism, serious moralizing and gross obscenity, smart-ass repartee and lyric fantasy—all those qualities that make his Greek so uniquely exciting and resonant and his dramaturgy so extraordinarily inclusive of different and contrasting social levels and comic registers. It is regrettable that William Arrowsmith, perhaps the most gifted of all translators of Aristophanes (and Euripides too) into English, never tackled *Frogs*. (His *Clouds* and *Birds* are superb.)

But in his edition of *Aristophanes: Four Comedies* (first published in 1962) he had the wisdom to include Richmond Lattimore's new version of *Frogs*. As always, Lattimore (in the view of many, the finest twentieth-century translator of Homer, and also an excellent translator of tragedy) succeeds in being both accurate and stylish, poetic yet quick-moving and performable. This translation won the Bollingen Poetry Translation Prize. A couple of samples:

> [Chorus] All now must observe the sacred silence: we ban
>   from our choruses any
> whose brain cannot fathom the gist of our wit; whose
>   hearts and feelings are dirty;
> who never has witnessed and never partaken in genuine
>   cult of the Muses . . .
> who gets up to speak in the public assembly and nibbles at
>   the fees of the poets
> just because they once made a fool of him in the plays that
>   our fathers established.
> Such men I forbid, and again I forbid, and again I forbid
>   them a third time . . .
>
> (354–56, 367–69)

> [Eur.] When I took over our craft from you, I instantly
>   became aware
> that she was gassy from being stuffed with heavy text and
>   noisy air,
> so I eased her aches and reduced the swelling and took
>   away the weights and heats
> with neat conceits and tripping feets, with parsnips,
>   radishes and beets.
> I gave her mashed and predigested baby-food strained from
>   my books,
>   then fed her on solo-arias . . .
>
> (939–44)

Dudley Fitts' 1959 version was much freer; pleasantly breezy, accessible, but less gutsy than Lattimore's. It was often used for stage productions during the 1960s–90s. Two specimens:

[Dion.] Say something, Aischylos. You heard the man.
[Eur.] He's going into one of his Portentous Silences.
It's a favourite trick of his to impress the audience.
[Dion.] Euripides, please don't talk so much!

(832–36)

[Eur.] And this I teach the crowd to say:
    "From day to day
    in every way,
    I'm clearly growing better."
My verses bring them new insight:
    night after night
    they think aright
    on things that really matter.

(971–78)

Other up-to-date translations, mainly intended for use in college courses (in some cases, with quite copious explanatory notes as well as stage directions) followed, most of them sticking close to the original Greek, some even choosing prose rather than verse in their determination to make the play easier to read and understand (and teach) at a basic level.

R. H. Webb's version in rhyming four-stressed couplets (1962), subsequently included in the widely-used college edition of all Aristophanes' plays edited by Moses Hadas, was not one of the most successful of these, frequently turning trite and sing-songy:

[Aesch.] Of what ills is Euripides not the cause?
Pimps he brings on in defiance of laws,
a woman in a temple becoming a mother,
a woman lying with her own brother,
"no life equals life" asserting,
our whole city thus subverting . . .

(1077–82)

The contrast between this and Lattimore's snappier and much less artificial sounding version of this passage, which still manages to include rhyme and rhythmic punch, is telling:

> [Aesch.] That's what he's begun. What hasn't he done?
> His nurses go propositioning others.
> His heroines have their babies in church
> or sleep with their brothers,
> or go around murmuring: "*Is* life life?"
> So our city is rife
> with the clerk and the jerk . . . etc.
>
> (Lattimore, 1077–82)

The lively Penguin version of David Barrett (1964), despite its hyper-Englishness in places, has vigor and pace, while staying quite close to the original Greek. The frog-limericks are bouncier and less verbally stilted than Murray's:

> [Dion.] I don't want to row any more. [Frogs] Brekekex.
> [Dion.] For my bottom is getting so sore. [Frogs] Brekekex.
> [Dion] And what do you care?
>   You are nothing but air
>   and I find you a bit of a bore.
> [Frogs] Brekekekex koax koax.
> Your remarks are offensive in tone
> and we'd like to make some of our own:
>   our plantation of reeds
>   for all musical needs
> in the very best circles is known . . .
>
> (221–35)

Numerous translations have appeared since the 1960s, some seeking performability (e.g., Kenneth McLeish, Paul Roche), others focused mainly on enabling a reader to grasp as much as possible of Aristophanes' original meaning, with copious notes and stage directions explaining and supplementing the translation, while less effort is devoted to replicating the rhythms, energy, or poetry of the original.

Outstanding among these latter is Alan Sommerstein's version in the Aris & Phillips series (1996; subsequently adopted by Penguin), while Jeffrey Henderson's Loeb, Stephen Halliwell's Oxford version (1994), and Michael Ewans' "translation with theatrical commentary" (2011) are all helpful and reliable, giving the reader a good sense of what is happening on stage and how the lines would have been understood, in literal terms, by the original audience.

One additional version deserves special mention for its remarkable inventiveness and pizzazz: Douglas Young's *The Puddocks* (1958, two editions), a Scots version composed for performances at St. Andrews University. Although on the printed page the dialect initially looks quite forbidding (and Young accordingly provides a glossary at the back), when pronounced out loud and performed, it quickly becomes more accessible, as audience reactions and critical reviews confirm. The translation is also accurate and close to the Greek. Overall, it deserves to rank almost on a level with Gavin Douglas' Middle Scots *Eneados* (1513; arguably the finest of all "British" translations of Vergil's epic) as an example of what nonstandard English can achieve by way of verbal music, colorful vocabulary, and wit in translating "the classics." A couple of specimens may speak for themselves:

> [Aesch.] What crimes is he no guilty o?
> Shawed procuresses on the stage,—
> bairnbirths in chaipels, did he no?
> sisters wi brithers beddit tae,—
> weemen that say "Life's nae real life!"
> And wi aa this oor country nou
> is stappit fou o bureaucrats
> and sleekit puggy-demagogues
> aye swickan the democracy . . .
>
> (1079–86)

> [Chorus] Richt it is this haly chorus suld exhort the public
>   weel
> wi oor lengthened sage advices. First of aa, then, we appeal,
> citizens suld aa be equals, nane of us sul live in fear.

Gin a body slipt a wee, whan Phrynichos made aa thon steer,
nou, we say, maun aa thae fautours hae the chance tae clear
 their faut;
aince acquit, byganes be byganes: ilka backspang be forgot.

(686–91)

In general, translations aimed specifically at stage performance are likely to be freer than those intended primarily for reading; and this is especially true for Aristophanes. Indeed, it may be said that for his plays adaptation usually works better than attempts at close translation, though of course much depends on the style and goals of each production.

(iv) Actual Productions . . .

Performances of *Frogs* since the classical period, whether in translation or in the original Greek, have mostly taken place—or originated—at universities and schools. Students have always enjoyed performing comedy if given the opportunity; and the cachet of a distinguished classical (even "Attic") pedigree, along with the eagerness of professors and institutions of learning to demonstrate the relevance of the Greek past to the educational and artistic programs of the present, has been remarkably successful in keeping Aristophanes alive, on stage. By contrast, until quite recently professional theater companies were far less willing to produce Old Comedy than Greek tragedy, partly because of the problems of indecency and obscenity (which of course are part of the appeal for students), and partly because so much in the comedies is tied closely to the original context of fifth-century Athens and is therefore less easily reoriented than the tragedies to the horizons of modern audiences.

The staging of Aristophanes in Greek or Latin began at European universities in the 1500s. Already in 1536 England witnessed a production of *Wealth* at St. John's College, Cambridge, partly motivated by the director/teacher's desire to show off his theories of correct pronunciation. Many of these college productions doubtless never made it into the history books. (Research is ongoing.) *Wealth*, *Birds*, and *Clouds* were by far the most frequently performed, and several other plays languished untried. The earliest record (rather vague) of a production of *Frogs* comes from Berlin in 1843–44, while the first known performances of the play in Britain took place in the 1870s at a small private theater in Edinburgh, produced by H. F. Jenkin, using Frere's translation. From that point, the habit of staging Aristophanic comedies as well as tragedies, whether in Greek or in English, caught on as an annual or biennial event at Cambridge and Oxford, soon followed by Harvard, Berkeley, King's College London, and many other campuses in Britain and the United States. *Frogs*, as one of the least politically subversive or sexually explicit, as well as one of the most musically and culturally engaging, was quite frequently chosen (while never rivaling *Clouds* or *Birds* in popularity). Several of these college productions included specially commissioned music (Hubert Parry's score for the 1892 Oxford *Frogs* was especially successful, employing extensive pastiche from earlier and contemporary operas), and they often drew considerable attention from both local and national reviewers (*The Times*, *The Athenaeum*, *The Oxford Magazine*, *The Temple Bar*, etc.). The unmanly qualities and unusual saffron dress of Dionysus gave opportunities for actors to "mince" provocatively and behave in various "effeminate" or queer ways that appealed greatly to many late nineteenth-century male Oxbridge theatergoers (while also offending others, of course); and at least one Oxford production also made the most of the Charon scene by adapting it to parody a rowing lesson being administered to a novice undergraduate crew-member (see Fig. 8–2).

As Edith Hall, Fiona Macintosh, and others have shown, Aristophanes continued to be regarded as a highly entertaining but safely conservative comic voice throughout the Early Modern period and well into the nineteenth century. But by the later nineteenth century the potentially revolutionary and/or politically progressive elements in his plays were increasingly recognized—and highlighted

in productions. So at last *Lysistrata*, long neglected in colleges and hardly ever performed, became a popular stage vehicle for the suffragette movement; *Peace* and other comedies were adapted as antiwar plays. The satirical and disruptive qualities of Aristophanic comedy were now coming more into their own. At the same time, both *Clouds* and *Frogs* (and perhaps *Thesmophoriazusae* too, though this play was still too troublesome for most performers or audiences, even at colleges, to approach, right up until the 1970s) appear to present rather a conservative intellectual and artistic agenda, so these plays tended to inspire productions that were geared more to highlighting the fantastic and witty than the politically or socially innovative. Like Aristophanes' own audience in *Frogs* ("every one has his little book and learns all the clever stuff . . ."), campus audiences would be expected to recognize the Aeschylean and Euripidean allusions, and even perhaps catch some of the Greek puns and jokes—a valid source of comic satisfaction, indeed, but not a recipe for large-scale box office success. Few professional theater companies were interested.

One important development was the founding of the National Theater in Greece. After a fitful beginning (1880–1932), this became established as an important promoter of ancient Greek tragedy and comedy in performance, and by the 1940s the institution of annual festivals at the outdoor theaters in Epidaurus and Athens (Herodes Atticus Theater) brought growing national and international recognition. In the first half of the twentieth century, tragedies tended to dominate their repertoire, and the few comedies that were presented, including several productions of *Frogs*, were done in rather a conservative and unadventurous style. Bolder new approaches (in

◀

Figure 8-2. Program cover (designed by Charles Wellington Furse) for the 1892 production of *Frogs* by the Oxford University Dramatic Society at the New Theatre, Oxford.
(John Johnson Collection, OUDS Box 2, Bodleian Library, Oxford). Photo courtesy of the Bodleian Libraries, The University of Oxford.

Modern Greek, as was usual for this festival) were pioneered by the Art Theatre of Karolos Koun during the 1940s–70s, including more ritualistic choral movement, eclectic, often eastern-influenced music, and adaptation of traditional shadow-puppet elements. In his *Frogs*, Koun cannily incorporated music that recalled that of his own previous production of Aeschylus' *Persians*, thus bringing about a very appropriate dialogue between the comic and tragic idioms. Meanwhile the GNT itself tended to maintain a more mainstream approach, especially in the elegant and splashy productions of Alexis Solomos, which generally stayed closer to Western European and American models of musical theater and drew large and enthusiastic audiences over two decades. Overall, these Modern Greek performances of Aristophanes seem to have been more successful in combining words and music, choral and solo performance, and bold visual and design elements in a big outdoor theater space—and thus to have reached larger audiences—than other productions around the world. Since the 1960s, the opportunity for explicit or covert political commentary offered by Aristophanes' plays has often given a sharper edge to Greek productions; but *Frogs* does not lend itself to such treatment as easily as some other comedies do. On the other hand, for Greek performers and audiences (unlike the rest of Europe), the sense of continuity, real or imagined, in "national" democratic traditions and indigenous musical and art forms has always been an important issue in restaging these dramas—and *Frogs* provides particularly rich opportunities for such cultural self-analysis and comparison.

Elsewhere in Europe, *Frogs* has generally been a popular and relatively uncontroversial choice for production. Whereas some Aristophanic plays have inspired radical adaptation in order to provide a platform for modern social and political agendas, *Frogs* usually is presented fairly "straight"—though the choice always has to be made for each production, between a more "scholarly" restaging of the text that retains all the original references, personal names, etc., and a more contemporary rewriting that might streamline and update such references, and even perhaps cut out certain segments that might not work so well for a modern audience.

Many different approaches are taken. The music of the choruses, and of the old and new tragedian, may be based on the idiom(s) of a certain period or may be contemporary; the language may be rhythmical poetry or slangy prose, and may be fairly uniform or vary wildly in level and tone (as Aristophanes' does); costumes may be "authentic" (Dionysus in his saffron robe, Heracles' lion-skin; etc.) or modernized (Euripides as a beatnik, or rock star); obviously Christian symbols and language may be adopted for their associations with "salvation" and "rebirth"—or may be carefully avoided so as not to cause offense; etc. One element is never missing, however: the frog chorus must always sing or chant *BREKEKEKEX KOAX KOAX*. This scene, and this sound, has become one of the most famous in all drama, and no audience would tolerate its excision.

In recent decades, some of the more memorable productions include the following:

The (professional, but University College London–derived) London Small Theatre put together a long-running (and touring: 1991–1995) production that subsequently evolved into an Aquila Co. production: the witty adaptation (in English) was by Fiona Laird, and the quick-moving and stylish production was co-directed by Peter Meineck (founder of Aquila). "Authentic" and modernized elements were seamlessly combined, and the tiny cast (all excellent singers) succeeded in creating many effective and funny musical and poetic contrasts (e.g., Aeschylus singing over a barber-shop quartet, Euripides rapping to hand percussion), with plenty of zany stage business to keep everything moving.

A King's College, London production (performed in ancient Greek) in 1988 toured the UK and college campuses in the USA, with the lyrics adapted to fit musical theater songs of the 1920s–30s: a curiously tame and stilted effect though ingenious in its planning.

An Italian production at the Syracuse festival of 2002 had large back-panels decorated with pictures resembling prominent politicians, which were taken down at the last minute and not used, apparently as a result of government pressure.

By far the "biggest" productions of *Frogs* in the USA, in terms of artistic ambition and public recognition, have been the collaborations between Burt Shevelove and Stephen Sondheim. Shevelove's original adaptation, performed at Yale in 1941 (i.e., another college-initiated production), made prominent use of the gymnasium's swimming pool for the Charon scene, with the Yale swim team in the pool as the (synchronized) frog chorus. In 1974, Shevelove resuscitated this production in the same venue, but with newly commissioned lyrics and music by Stephen Sondheim—with whom he had already collaborated on *A Funny Thing Happened on the Way to the Forum*, a masterful and widely acclaimed adaptation of three plays by Plautus. (Sondheim had also been the lyricist for Leonard Bernstein's *West Side Story*, and was fast establishing himself as America's most original and accomplished composer for the musical stage.) After a long hiatus, another—much revised—version of their *Frogs* was staged on Broadway in 2004, with many new songs by Sondheim (see cover illustration).

The basic premise of Shevelove's adaptation is that Aeschylus is Shakespeare and Euripides is G. B. Shaw. It is an intelligent idea, though disappointing insofar as the two playwrights merely quote their own lines verbatim rather than parodying each other's in exaggerated form as they do in Aristophanes. (Obviously, too, the cultural resonance for Americans in 1974 or 2004 of Shaw and Shakespeare is far smaller than that of Aeschylus and Euripides for the Athenians of 405 BCE.) But the most extraordinary aspect of both the 1974 and 2004 productions is Sondheim's inventiveness in combining music and words, which in its own way may be called a match for Aristophanes' verbal and rhythmic wit. For example:

DIONYSOS:

> I, Dionysos, god of drama, am going to travel
> to the Underworld and bring back a great writer who can
>   speak
> to the problems of our society and give us comfort, wit
>   and wisdom.
> And also challenge our complacencies.

XANTHIAS:

Who are you gonna bring back?

DIONYSOS:

Shaw.

XANTHIAS:

Oh . . . who?

<A little later . . .>

DIONYSOS:

George—Bernard—Shaw.
I knew if I stuck to it,
I'd somehow get through it.
At times I thought, "Oh, screw it!"
But proceed I did,
And oh, you kid—!

I just met Shaw!
I got to meet Shaw!
There isn't any doubt
The man's without
A single flaw!

I talked to Shaw,
I said to him, "Shaw,
The world is in a crisis."
He said, "Listen, Dionysos,
What you need is Shaw.
I'll go with you," says Shaw.
"I happen to be free,

And who could be
A bigger draw?"

That instant generosity,
That's Shaw!
The verbal virtuosity,
That's Shaw!
The fearless animosity,
That mind with such velocity—
All right, there's the pomposity,
But that's just Shaw.
[*Reluctantly*]
And maybe some verbosity,
But still you'll be
In awe.

This is obviously adaptation, not "translation"—but both the spirit and the technical genius of Aristophanes are evident. So is the element of collaboration: it is quite clear that no single artistic vision created these productions—they were the result of the collective input of playwright, composer, director(s), and lead actor (in 2004, Nathan Lane as Dionysus). The story line as well as several of the musical numbers was much altered from one production to the other (in particular, a love interest was added by Shevelove in 2004, with Dionysus acknowledging during the course of the play that part of his reason for descending to the Underworld is to retrieve his long-lost love, Ariadne). So it was doubtless for Aristophanes too and his fellow artists: one idea suggests another, each performer adds his own voice, and the production continues to evolve.

To conclude: there are many potentially viable ways to perform Aristophanes' *Frogs* and to bring its author's amazing vision of the world and of the possibilities of Dionysian art to modern audiences. Writers, musicians, designers, and actors will doubtless continue to explore several of these ways in the years ahead. Studious reconstructions and bold reimaginings all have their place: stage plays, musical extravaganzas, movies, digital animations . . . anything can work. (Perhaps the most successful of all recreations/adaptations of 'Aristophanes' in the modern world so far has been the animated sequence from John Cameron Mitchell's *Hedwig and the Angry Inch* (2001), in which "The Origin of Love" as narrated by 'Aristophanes' in Plato's *Symposium* is brought fantastically to animated life—viewable on YouTube.) With models of comic creativity before our eyes such as the Marx Brothers, Mel Brooks, Monty Python, or South Park, and texts of Aristophanes too in our hands, carefully annotated but also imaginatively supplemented by translations and adaptations of all kinds, in various languages and media, we look to the students, theater companies, directors, and composers of the future to take fuller advantage of these unparalleled resources. To be sure, the creative linguistic and musical genius, humanistic vision, and social-political edge of Aristophanes are hard to convey all at once and in a unified combination: any modern recreation of *Frogs* is bound to have to make choices as to which aspects of the original it will go for, which it will forego. But Aristophanes—and *Frogs* in particular—is very much of our time. We need to be saved; and this Dionysus is on the right track towards saving us all with his Art.

Suggestions for Further Reading

On the staging of *Frogs* (and of Old Comedy in general), the commentaries of Stanford (1963), Dover (1993), and Sommerstein (1996) are all helpful, though not always in agreement with one another; also the translation "with theatrical commentary" by Ewans (2011). See too Slater (2002), Revermann (2006). For the resources and conventions of ancient Greek theatrical performance, see Csapo and Slater (1995); on acting, Easterling and Hall (2002).

On the reception of Aristophanes from the fourth century to the present, valuable in general are Solomos (1960/1974), and Hall and Wrigley (2007): Hall's introductory chapter, "Aristophanic laughter across the centuries," is particularly good. For the history and transmission of Aristophanes' Greek text, see Reynolds and Wilson (1991) index s.v. "Aristophanes," Dover (1993) 76–103, and Sommerstein (2010). A complete list of all known translations of Aristophanes' plays published up to 1920 (in any language) is provided by Giannopoulou (2007). For more recent years, a full list of published English translations of Aristophanes is provided in the Appendix (pp. 253–67) of Walton (2006). Invaluable for researchers in all languages, but especially English, is the Archive of Performance of Greek and Roman Drama (APGRD) at the University of Oxford, available online at http://www.apgrd.ox.ac.uk/.

For discussion of the place of Aristophanes and—especially—attitudes to "Old Comic" license in Renaissance and Early Modern criticism, as well as the degree of firsthand knowledge of his plays shown by European writers in general during this period, see especially Solomos (1960/1974) 252–76, and Steggle (2007), Hall (2007).

Van Steen (2000) provides a fascinating discussion of the history of productions of Aristophanes' plays in Greece, especially since World War II, focusing mainly on political issues and notions of cultural heritage, but also on approaches to translation, design, tone, and performance style. On English-language performance of *Frogs*, recommended are Wrigley (2007), and especially Gamel (2007), a discussion that ranges more widely than just the Shevelove and Sondheim collaborations on *Frogs*. Also in the same Wrigley and Hall volume are essays by M. Silk on the King's College, London, productions of *Frogs* in ancient Greek ("Translating/Transposing Aristophanes") and by F. Schironi on the 2002 Syracuse festival production of *Frogs* (in Italian) that apparently drew government intervention. In general, Walton (1987) is a good guide to modern performances of Greek tragedy and comedy, in all countries up to that date.

Among translators themselves, helpful and interesting essays about their goals and methods are to be found in the introductions to Frere (1837) and Lattimore (1962). Robson (2009) 188–218 has a good discussion of the general issues facing translators and adaptors of Aristophanes, and well-chosen examples (but it is not focused on *Frogs*). See too Sommerstein (2006), Silk (2007), and, on general principles, Hardwick (2000).

There is, as far as I am aware, just one video recording of a *Frogs* production that has ever been released: the London Small Theatre's excellent touring version from 1991, on VHS: no longer available. CDs of the music from Sondheim's *Frogs* (both the 1974 and the 2004 versions) are available, but no DVDs of the stage productions.

Glossary of Personal and Geographical Names

Names in CAPITALS (Upper Case) = historical persons and places. Names in lower case = mythical or imaginary persons and places.

(Only the names of ancient persons and places are included in this Glossary. For modern (post-medieval) names discussed in the text, see General Index.)

Acheron: river or lake in the Underworld across which the dead are ferried 162

Achilles: Greek hero of Homer's *Iliad*; leader of the Myrmidons, from Phthia 89, 104, 123, 134, 193

Aeacus: one of three mythical judges of the dead in the Underworld (with Minos and Rhadamanthus) 68, 162, 167, 171

AEGEAN SEA: the body of water that separates mainland Greece from the mainland of Anatolia (modern-day Turkey) 38–39, 78

AEGINA: an island in the center of the Saronic Gulf, 17 miles from Athens 24, 37

Aegisthus: adulterous partner of Clytaemestra; the two of them murdered Agamemnon and were later killed by Orestes (the subject of Aeschylus' *Oresteia*) 205

Aeneas: Trojan prince, eventual founder of Rome; hero of Vergil's *Aeneid*   16, 193

AESCHYLUS: Athenian tragic poet (lived ca. 525–455)   passim.

AESOP: semi-legendary slave-sage of the sixth century, reputed author of animal fables and lead character in many low-life anecdotes   26

Agamemnon: son of Atreus, brother of Menelaus; king of Mycenae/Argos; leader of Greek forces at Troy; on returning home, he was killed by his wife Clytaemestra   104, 163, 209. *See also* General Index, "*Oresteia.*"

AGATHON: successful Athenian tragic poet of the late-fifth century; renowned for his musical innovations, and also for his own good looks and gay lifestyle   100–101, 119, 141–43, 226

ALCAEUS: famous sixth-century lyric poet from Mytilene (Lesbos)   89, 149

ALCIBIADES: aristocratic Athenian statesman and military commander (lived ca. 450–404); adopted by Pericles and continued his pro-democratic policies. His checkered career included periods of exile spent helping the Spartans   19, 22, 49–52, 76, 78, 114, 177–78, 203–207, 226

ALCMAN: seventh-century choral lyric poet at Sparta   135–36

ALCMEONIDS: an aristocratic Athenian family claiming descent from the hero Alcmaeon; prominent members included Pericles and Alcibiades   48

ALEXIS: fourth-century playwright of Athenian "Middle" and "New" Comedy   226

AMEIPSIAS: Athenian comic poet, rival of Aristophanes   20, 107

AMPHIDAMAS: eighth-century king of Chalcis (Euboea); his funeral celebrations were said to have included a poetic competition at which Hesiod won the prize   84

ANACREON: lyric poet (lived ca. 570–500), renowned for his elegant style and popularity with symposiasts   26, 89, 118

ANAXAGORAS: early scientist-philosopher (lived ca. 500–428); his works do not survive, but one of his controversial theories was that the heavenly bodies were not divine but large lumps of red-hot rock. He is said to have been prosecuted at Athens for impiety   26, 153

Andromeda: daughter of the Ethiopian king Cepheus, rescued by Perseus from a sea-monster. A much-admired tragedy by Euripides (now lost) was based on this story   **116, 127**

Antigone: daughter of Oedipus; main character of Sophocles' play   **117, 126, 193, 209**

ANTIPHON: Athenian politician and orator (lived ca. 480–411); one of the leaders of the oligarchic coup of 411, for which he was subsequently tried and executed   **49**

APELLES: famous fourth-century Greek painter   **83**

Aphrodite: goddess of love and sex   **55, 83, 97, 105, 113, 154, 185, 188**

Apollo: god of music (esp. lyre, *cithara*), medicine, prophecy, and (male) adolescence   **67, 84, 93, 126, 152, 154, 179, 185**

Arachne: Lydian princess skilled at weaving; foolishly challenged Athena to a contest   **83**

ARARUS: son of Aristophanes (lived ca. 420–350?); produced two of his father's latest plays, and himself went on to compose successful comedies (starting 375 BCE)   **25, 30**

ARCHEDEMUS: Athenian pro-democratic politician of late-fifth century   **7**

ARCHILOCHUS: famous iambic-invective poet (seventh century)   **6, 26, 82, 85, 163, 165**

ARGINUSAE: three small islands between Lesbos and the west coast of Anatolia (modern-day Turkey), where the Athenians won a naval victory over the Spartans in 406 BCE   **24, 39, 45, 50, 52, 67, 190, 207**

ARGOS: a city located in the southern region of the Argive plain in the Peloponnesus, about sixty miles west of Athens   **62**

ARION: semi-legendary singer and musician from Lesbos (seventh century); spent much of his career at Corinth; credited by some with "inventing" dithyramb and even tragedy   **186**

ARISTIDES: esteemed Athenian politician and commander during the Persian Wars   **19, 166**

ARISTOPHANES: Athenian comic poet (fifth century)   passim.

ARISTOTLE: philosopher-scientist (lived 384–322) from Macedonia; after 367, mostly resided in Athens   5, 8, 14, 35, 95–97, 119, 123, 131, 226

Artemis: goddess of hunting and animals, virginity, and (female) adolescence   154

Asclepius: hero or god (son of Apollo), founder/patron of the art of medicine   163–64

ASTYDAMAS: Athenian tragic poet (fourth century), son of Morsimus and great-grand-nephew of Aeschylus; his son (also named Astydamas) was likewise a successful tragedian   117

Athena: goddess of wisdom, war, and the arts; patron divinity of Athens   12, 46, 83, 152–53, 181

ATHENAEUS: eclectic second- to third-century CE Greek author, whose fifteen-book *Deipnosophistai* ("Dinner-experts") contains innumerable anecdotes and explanations (of varying degrees of reliability) about food, fashions, music, sexual behaviors, and other aspects of classical Greek culture.

ATHENS, ATHENIANS: main city in the plain of Attica. "Athenians" can refer to all the citizens residing in Attica   passim.

ATTICA: a large region in southeast Greece dominated and ruled by Athens   10, 12, 32–33, 35, 39, 46, 78, 157, 159, 174–75, 177, 185, 190, 207

Attis: youthful Anatolian consort of the goddess Cybele   174

Bellerophon: Corinthian hero who rode the winged horse Pegasus and killed the Chimaera; his attempt to fly up to heaven and subsequent punishment were staged in a (lost) tragedy by Euripides   106, 126

Bendis: Thracian goddess whose cult became popular in late-fifth-century Athens   174

BUPALUS: sculptor from Chios (sixth century); victim of Hipponax's invective poems   6

BYZANTIUM: a Greek city situated just to the west of the Black Sea, on the eastern end of the Sea of Marmara; later named Constantinople, and now Istanbul. From the 4th to the 15th century it was the capital of the Eastern Roman or Byzantine Empire. The culture's interest in their Greek heritage and language ensured the preservation and study of much classical Greek literature.   19, 23, 232

Calchas: chief seer (*mantis*) for the Greeks at Troy; mentioned in Aeschylus' *Agamemnon*   83

CALLIAS: wealthy Athenian politician (lived ca. 450–370); sponsor of artists and intellectuals   20, 37

CALLIMACHUS: influential Hellenistic poet (lived ca. 305–240), based in Alexandria   95, 123, 227

CALLISTRATUS: producer of Aristophanes' earliest comedies (420s)   23, 29

CARCINUS: Athenian tragic poet of mid-fifth century   117–118

CARIA: a region of southwestern Anatolia (modern-day Turkey)   137, 143, 145, 184

CATULLUS: Roman poet of the late Republic (lived ca. 87–54)   145, 227

CEPHISOPHON: collaborator with Euripides, esp. on musical aspects   29, 74, 129, 140, 146, 241

Cerberus: three-headed dog who guarded the entrance (and exit) to the Underworld   63, 155, 164, 171

Charon: ferryman of dead souls across Acheron/Styx to the Underworld; see Fig. 6–1   x, 53, 66–67, 161–62, 166, 169, 222–23, 247, 252

CHOERILUS: early Athenian tragic poet, predecessor and rival of Aeschylus   119–120

CICERO: Roman orator, politician, and intellectual of late Republic (lived 106–43)   95, 123, 227, 234

CINESIAS: Athenian dithyrambic poet of later fifth century   141–42, 147

CLEIGENES: Athenian bathhouse owner (?) and politician in later fifth century   37

CLEISTHENES (i): founder of the original Athenian democracy in 510–508   38

CLEISTHENES (ii): Athenian politician of the late-fifth century, ridiculed by comedians for his effeminate appearance and habits   37, 116

CLEON: most influential pro-democratic politician in Athens between 427 and 422; mocked by Aristophanes in several plays   23, 25, 29, 31, 36–37, 49, 56, 204–205

CLEOPHON: most influential pro-democratic politician in Athens between 410 and 404; staunch supporter of the anti-Spartan war effort; executed in 404   19, 37, 43, 48, 50, 52, 146, 200, 204, 207, 209

CLITOPHON: well-known Athenian intellectual of late-fifth century; friend of Euripides   37

Clytaemestra: wife (and killer) of Agamemnon and lover of Aegisthus; appears in several Greek tragedies. (Sometimes spelled Clytemnestra.)   125–26, 205

CORINTH: large city on the isthmus connecting the Peloponnesus to central Greece   51, 186

CRATES: pioneer of "Old" Comedy in Athens (lived ca. 490–430)   5, 8, 17

CRATINUS: Aristophanes' most famous rival (and predecessor) as a comic playwright in Athens (lived ca. 470–420)   9, 14, 16–19, 23, 49, 85, 119, 123, 146, 165, 188–89, 198, 216, 218–219, 225, 227–31

Creon: king of Thebes after Oedipus' fall from power; appears in several Greek tragedies   209

CRETE: large island to the southeast of mainland Greece; its biggest city was Knossos, one of whose legendary kings was Minos   138, 178, 185, 198

CRITIAS: pro-Spartan Athenian aristocrat (lived ca. 460–403); leader of the oligarchic junta ("Thirty Tyrants") at the end of the Peloponnesian War in 404   51

Cybele: Near Eastern goddess (also known as "Great Mother"), closely associated by the Greeks with Dionysus; worshipped in Athens at least since the early-fifth century   143, 174, 184

Cycnus: son of Ares, killed by Heracles   124

CYPSELUS: brilliant but ruthless monarch ("tyrant") of Corinth in seventh century   205

CYRENE: famous dancer/courtesan in late-fifth-century Athens. (Also the name of a major Greek city in Libya, North Africa.)   146–47

DAMON: musical theorist of the mid-fifth century   **94**

Danaus: father whose fifty daughters killed their new husbands, the fifty sons of Aegyptus (their cousins) on their wedding night. This story was the subject of Aeschylus' *Suppliant Maidens*   **126**

DARIUS: king of Persia who attempted to subjugate Greece (ruled 521–486). His ghost appears in Aeschylus' tragedy *The Persians* (472)   **105, 164, 166**

DECELEA: a village in northern Attica, occupied by the Spartans (following Alcibiades' advice) as a military post during the later stages of the Peloponnesian War, in order to disrupt agriculture and impede the transportation of goods by land into Athens   **39, 46, 50, 78, 177**

DELOS: island in the center of the ring of islands known as the Cyclades in the Aegean Sea to the east of mainland Greece; sacred to Apollo and Artemis   **84**

DELPHI: town on the southwestern slope of Mount Parnassus in Phocis; the site of the Delphic oracle, sacred to Pythian Apollo   **81, 84, 176**

Demeter: goddess of agriculture; sister of Zeus and mother of Korê (Persephone). She and Korê were worshipped in the Eleusinian Mysteries   **7, 72, 161, 175–77, 181–82**

DEMOCRITUS: influential Greek philosopher-scientist from Abdera in Thrace (lived ca. 460–400)   **95–96, 156**

DEMOSTHENES: Athenian orator and pro-democratic statesman (lived 384–322)   **228, 234**

DIAGORAS: lyric poet and renowned atheist of the late-fifth century; prosecuted in Athens for desecrating the Eleusinian Mysteries   **180**

Dicaeopolis: protagonist of Aristophanes' play *Acharnians* who declares a private peace treaty with Sparta   **57, 183, 194.** *See also* General Index, "*Acharnians.*"

Dictynna: Cretan goddess, frequently identified with the Greek Artemis   **148**

DIONYSIUS OF HALICARNASSUS: Greek historian, literary critic, and teacher of rhetoric in Rome during the first century BCE   **123, 227**

Dionysus: Greek god of music, wine, transformation, and drama; son of Zeus and Semele; also known as Bacchus, Iacchus, Bromius; one of his epithets is *eleutherios* ("liberator"): see ELEUTHERAE passim. *See also* General Index, *"Bacchae."*

DIPHILUS: playwright of the "New" Comedy, active in Athens in the late-fourth century   226

Electra: daughter of Agamemnon and Clytaemestra, sister of Orestes; in several tragedies the two of them successfully plot revenge on their mother and Aegisthus for Agamemnon's murder   109, 126, 130, 147, 209–210

ELEUSIS: a town about twelve miles northwest of Athens, famous for its annual festival of the Mysteries (see Demeter)   10, 175–77, 179–82, 206. *See also* General Index, "Mystery cult."

ELEUTHERAE: a small town in the northern part of Attica, on the border with Boeotia. The City Dionysia festival was supposedly transferred to Athens from here. The name means "Free, Liberated."   189

Empousa: an Underworld creature who changes her shape and devours the unwary   170

EPICHARMUS: renowned comic playwright from Sicily (early-fifth century), little of whose work has survived   9, 15

EPIDAURUS: a small town near Argos in the Peloponnesus. A majestic theater was constructed there in the fourth century BCE, with a seating capacity of approximately 15,000 people and exceptional acoustics. It is still used for modern outdoor performances of ancient Greek tragedy and comedy   10, 226, 249

ERASINIDES: Athenian politician and general, prosecuted and executed for his conduct at the naval battle of Arginusae in 406   40

ERATOSTHENES: Hellenistic scholar and chief librarian at Alexandria (lived ca. 285–184 BCE)   228

Erinys: also known as "Fury," a chthonian power of retribution for blood-guilt, particularly within the family   154

Eris: Greek goddess and personification of Strife   81

Eteocles: son of Oedipus. He and his brother Polynices killed each other while fighting for control of Thebes. This story is the subject of Aeschylus' *Seven against Thebes*   104

EUBULUS: Athenian comic poet of the late-fourth century 226

EUPHORION: tragedian in mid-fifth-century Athens; son of Aeschylus 117

EUPOLIS: Athenian comic playwright of the late-fifth century, contemporary of Aristophanes 14, 16–17, 19, 23, 28, 29, 49, 166, 225, 228–31

EURIPIDES: Athenian tragic poet (lived ca. 480–407/6) passim.

Eurydice: wife of Orpheus; after she died, he visited the Underworld and tried through his powers of music and song to bring her back with him to the world of the living 63

FOUR HUNDRED: oligarchic council in Athens led by Antiphon, Pisander, and Phrynichus that in 411 overthrew the democratic constitution in a peaceful coup 49–52

Gilgamesh: semi-legendary king of Uruk (in Sumeria) and hero of the Akkadian/Hittite *Epic of Gilgamesh* 169, 193

GORGIAS: influential sophist and rhetorician from Leontini (Sicily) who spent time in Athens during the late-fifth century 95–96, 114, 128

Hades: Greek god, brother of Zeus and king of the Underworld; also known as Plouton (Pluto) 19, 63, 66, 71, 79, 84, 101, 115, 159–61, 169, 171, 175, 181, 190, 194–95, 211. *See also* General Index, "Underworld."

Hecate: a Greco-Roman goddess associated with magic, crossroads, and the Underworld 148

Hector: the greatest Trojan warrior in Homer's *Iliad* 104, 121

Helen: famously beautiful daughter of Zeus and Leda, and wife of Menelaus. Her abduction by Paris/Alexandros led to the Trojan War 13, 125, 188–89

HELLESPONT: a narrow strait in northwestern Anatolia (modern-day Turkey) that links the Aegean Sea to the Sea of Marmara and thus separates Europe from the Asian mainland (like the Bosporus) 39

Hera: Greek goddess, wife of Zeus 83

Heracles: great Greek hero, son of Zeus and Alcmene. His twelve labors for King Eurystheus included the capture of Cerberus from the Underworld 8, 13, 20, 53, 61–71, 87, 100–101, 104, 126, 152, 155, 164, 169–72, 174, 176, 180, 191, 193–94, 197–98, 210, 216, 221–22, 225, 251

HERACLITUS: Pre-Socratic philosopher from Ephesus (wrote ca. 500) whose enigmatic writings emphasized the paradoxical unity of opposites   **93, 179, 215**

Hermes: Greek messenger god, son of Zeus and Maia. One of his roles is to guide souls on their journey to the Underworld (*psychopompos*); see Fig. 6–1   **13, 158, 160–61**

HERODOTUS: Greek historian from Halicarnassus who wrote about the Persian Wars (lived ca. 484–425)   **89, 93, 234**

HESIOD: early Greek poet, author of the hexameter poems *Theogony* and *Works and Days* (probably eighth century)   **26, 81, 84–85, 89–93, 103, 113, 135, 153, 163, 165, 184**

Hippolytus: son of Theseus and stepson of Phaedra; following Phaedra's suicide and false accusation of rape, he was banished and cursed by Theseus and died in a chariot crash. This story is the subject of Euripides' *Hippolytus*   **124–25, 128, 193, 213**

HIPPONAX: foul-mouthed Greek iambic poet from Ephesus (mid-sixth century)   **6, 82**

HOMER: early Greek poet to whom are attributed the epic hexameter poems the *Iliad* and *Odyssey* (probably eighth century)   **v, 26, 82, 84–85, 90–94, 103–104, 108, 110, 113, 121–22, 135, 153, 155, 160, 162, 165, 175, 184, 228–29, 232, 234, 237, 242**

HORACE: Roman lyric and satiric poet of late Republic and Augustan period (lived 65–8 BCE), particularly influenced by Greek poets such as Alcaeus, Sappho, Archilochus, and Anacreon   **145, 230, 234, 238**

HYPERBOLUS: leading Athenian pro-democratic politician, much satirized in comedy (d. 411)   **37**

Hypermestra: the only one of Danaus' fifty daughters who refused his orders to kill her husband (Lynceus) on their wedding night. Her love for Lynceus is the subject of Aeschylus' *Danaids* (now lost)   **125**

Iacchus: another name or aspect of Dionysus, particularly associated with the Eleusinian Mysteries   **58, 68, 152, 180–81, 183**

Icarius: mythical Attic farmer who entertained Dionysus and received from him the gift of wine   **185–86, 190**

INITIATES (chorus of): one of two choruses in *Frogs*, consisting of celebrants in the Eleusinian Mysteries   7, 43, 58, 66, 68, 70, 152, 167, 169, 170–75, 177–78, 180–81, 183, 195, 197–98, 200, 208, 212, 219, 222–24. See also *General Index*, "Mystery cult."

ION: professional Homeric reciter (*rhapsode*) who is Socrates' interlocutor in Plato's dialogue *Ion*   82, 104

IOPHON: Athenian tragic poet of the late-fifth century; son of Sophocles   30, 100–101, 117

Iphigenia: daughter of Agamemnon and Clytaemestra who was sacrificed by her father so that the Greek army could sail to Troy from Aulis   193

JUVENAL: Roman satiric poet of the late-first and early-second century CE   230

LAMACHUS: Athenian general of the later fifth century, ridiculed in Aristophanes' *Acharnians* (424)   73, 208

LESBOS: an island in the northeast Aegean Sea, close to the coast of Anatolia (modern-day Turkey)   39, 138, 144–45

LUCIAN: Greek prose satirist-dialogist-comic fantasist of the second century CE (originally from Samosata in Syria)   231, 234, 239

LUCILIUS: early Roman satiric poet (lived ca. 180–102/1 BCE)   230

LYCAMBES: a (possibly fictitious) nobleman from the island of Paros who was the target (along with the rest of his family) of many of Archilochus' most savage invective poems, and allegedly was driven to suicide as a result   6

LYCIS: Athenian comic playwright, contemporary with Aristophanes   20, 107

Lycurgus: legendary Thessalian king who persecuted Dionysus and was horribly punished   184

Lynceus: husband of Hypermestra and the only one of Aegyptus' sons to be spared by his bride on his wedding night. He then became king of Argos   125

LYSANDER: Spartan general who obtained Athens' surrender in 404 and helped to install the Thirty Tyrants there (d. 395)   51

LYSIAS: renowned orator from Syracuse who settled in Athens (lived ca. 458–380) **228**

Lysistrata: chief character of Aristophanes' comedy of this title (411); she organizes a sex-strike by all the women of Greece to make the men call a truce to the Peloponnesian War   **40, 56 (pl), 57, 151, 209–210**. *See also* General Index, "*Lysistrata*."

MACEDONIA: the region of Greece north of Thessaly and west of Thrace; the main city was Pella, where in the late-fifth century King Archelaus ruled.

MAGNES: pioneer of early Athenian comedy (early- to mid-fifth century)   **8, 20**

MARATHON: a small town in Attica, a little more than 20 miles northeast of Athens. In the Battle of Marathon (490 BCE) the Athenian infantry, aided by the Plataeans, defeated the much larger Persian army. Aeschylus was said to have fought in that battle   **22, 38, 41, 53, 113, 129, 147, 154**

Marsyas: a satyr or silenus from Phrygia or Lydia, virtuoso of the *aulos*; rashly challenged Apollo to a musical contest   **84**

MARTIAL: Roman epigrammatist and satiric poet of the late first century CE   **230**

MELANIPPIDES: dithyrambic poet from Melos; pioneer of the "New Music" who was said to have replaced sung stanzas with purely instrumental interludes (mid-fifth century)   **141**

MENANDER: preeminent Athenian playwright of "New" Comedy (lived ca. 342–292)   **13–14, 23, 34, 127, 226, 228–29, 232, 234**

MILTIADES: Athenian aristocrat and general of the late-sixth and early-fifth century; commander-in-chief at the Battle of Marathon   **19, 166**

Minos: mythical king of Crete who became a judge of the dead in the Underworld along with his brother Rhadamanthus and Aeacus   **162, 167**

Mopsus: seer who (in one story) brought about the death of Calchas by defeating him in a contest of divination after the Trojan War   **83**

MORSIMUS: grandnephew of Aeschylus and tragic poet in Athens (late-fifth century)   **117**

Musaeus: legendary Greek poet, said to have been Orpheus' pupil; various hymns and mystic and oracular verses were attributed to him   26, 103

Muses: daughters of Zeus and Mnêmosynê (Memory); goddesses of literature, music, and dance to whom Greek poets and singers often appealed for inspiration; sometimes said to be nine in number   18–19, 25, 67, 84, 90–91, 107, 119, 122–23, 154, 242

MYTILENE: the biggest city on the island of Lesbos, distinguished for its cultural and musical heritage, including the famous sixth-century poet-singers Sappho and Alcaeus.

NICOCHARES: comic poet of early-fourth century; son of Philonides, Aristophanes' contemporary and collaborator   29

NICOMACHUS: probably the overseer of the public inscription of the Athenian laws (late-fifth and early-fourth century)   52

Nikê: Greek goddess of victory   47, 154

OLBIA: a Greek town on the distant north coast of the Black Sea (in modern-day Ukraine)   179

OLYMPUS (i): mountain on which the gods were imagined to make their home, located in Pieria in northern Greece   155

OLYMPUS (ii): Phrygian musician active in Greece in the seventh century, particularly associated with the double-pipes (*auloi*); semi-legendary (said to be son or pupil of Marsyas), but regarded by Plato, Aristotle, and others as having composed the best of the traditional Greek *aulos* melodies   133

Orpheus: mythical singer, son of Apollo and a Muse, who tried to lead his dead wife back from the Underworld through his powers of music and song; also credited with poems ("Orphic Hymns") narrating the origins of the world and also providing instructions for a pure life that would lead to salvation for the soul after death   26, 63, 103, 164, 174, 176, 179. See also *General Index*, "Orphic texts."

Pan: Greek god of shepherds and flocks, associated with the *syrinx* (pan-pipe); father of the satyrs   67, 74, 100, 154

Paris/Alexandros: Trojan prince (son of Priam) whose abduction of Helen led to the Trojan War   13, 18, 83, 125, 188–89

Patroclus: Greek warrior, intimate friend of Achilles in the *Iliad* 122

Pentheus: king of Thebes who was driven mad by Dionysus for refusing to recognize his divinity and worship, and was finally torn to pieces by his mother Agave and her fellow maenads. This story is the subject of Euripides' *Bacchae* 184, 187, 189–90, 193

PERICLES: preeminent Athenian statesman during the mid-fifth century (lived ca. 495–429) 18–19, 22, 31, 38, 48–50, 52, 78, 166, 189, 205, 207, 228

Persephone (Pherephatta): daughter of Demeter, wife of Plouton/Pluto (Hades), and queen of the Underworld; also called Korê. She and Demeter were worshipped in the Eleusinian Mysteries 7, 58, 63, 68–69, 71–72, 76, 78, 154, 161, 170, 174–75, 178, 181, 184, 191, 193–94, 202, 208, 211–212, 215, 224

Phaedra: daughter of Minos; wife of Theseus; committed suicide after Aphrodite made her fall in love with her stepson Hippolytus. This story is the subject of Euripides' *Hippolytus* 105–106, 113, 124–25

Phales: god/personification of the phallus in procession and the *phallikon* song at festivals of Dionysus 5

PHERECRATES: Athenian comic playwright of the mid- to late-fifth century 14, 17, 85, 95, 147

PHILEMON: renowned poet of "New" Comedy (lived ca. 360–268) 23, 226

PHILETAS: Hellenistic poet in Alexandria, particularly famed for his elegies (mid-fourth to early-third century) 227

PHILIPPUS (i): father of Aristophanes 23–24

PHILIPPUS (ii): comic poet in late-fifth century Athens, son of Aristophanes 25

Philocleon: protagonist of Aristophanes' play *Wasps* who is consumed by a desire to serve on juries (out of his devotion to Cleon) 25

PHILOCLES: Athenian tragic playwright of the mid-fifth century; nephew of Aeschylus 117

PHILONIDES: Athenian comic poet; also credited with being the producer (*chorêgos*) of *Frogs* (late-fifth century)   **23, 28–29**

PHILOXENUS: dithyrambic poet from Cythera, active in Athens and then Syracuse; particularly known for varying the modes and rhythms of his songs (lived ca. 435–380)   **141**

PHRYNICHUS (i): early Athenian tragic playwright of the late-sixth and early-fifth century   **17, 19–20, 85–86, 107**

PHRYNICHUS (ii): Athenian politician and a ringleader of the oligarchic coup in 411 (the Four Hundred)   **49–50, 52**

PHRYNICHUS (iii): Athenian comic poet of the fifth century, contemporary and rival of Aristophanes   **118–119, 132–33, 136, 143, 149, 217**

PHRYNIS: citharode and composer of *nomoi* from Mytilene, active in Athens in the mid-fifth century. He was credited with increasing the number of *cithara* strings and introducing greater harmonic modulation and rhythmic variety   **141**

PINDAR: renowned Greek choral lyric poet from Boeotia (lived 518–438)   **89, 163**

PIRAEUS: the main harbor for Athens; itself a large city, connected to Athens by the "Long Walls"   **39, 51**

PISANDER: Athenian politician and a ringleader of the Four Hundred in 411   **49–50**

Pisetaerus: main character in Aristophanes' play *The Birds*, who collaborates with all kinds of birds in establishing a city in the sky   **57, 183, 194**. *See also* General Index, "*Birds.*"

PLATAEA: a town in southern Boeotia; the Greek (Spartan-led) infantry victory in the Battle of Plataea (479 BCE) effectively ended the Persian invasion of mainland Greece   **154**

Plathanē: the innkeeper in Aristophanes' *Frogs*   **171**

PLATO: Athenian philosopher who mostly wrote in the form of Socratic dialogues (lived 429–347)   **vi, 17, 22, 27–28, 40, 85, 93–94, 104, 142, 156, 162–63, 204, 226, 228, 234, 237**

PLAUTUS: Roman comic playwright (lived ca. 254–184 BCE) **28, 34, 55, 231, 237, 252**

Plouton/Pluto: Greek god, brother of Zeus and king of the Underworld, also known as Hades; husband of Persephone **8, 51, 58–59, 63, 69, 71–72, 75–76, 78, 83, 102, 161, 165, 171–72, 191, 194–95, 202, 208–209, 211–213, 215, 222, 224**

PLUTARCH: Greek biographer, historian, and moral philosopher (lived ca. 46–120 CE) **96, 132, 205, 229, 234, 238**

POLLUX, Julius: Greek second century CE author of a lexicon/thesaurus (*Onomasticon*) of which portions are preserved, providing definitions of many rare technical terms some of which pertain to the theater, music, and rhetoric **231**

Poseidon: god of the sea and earthquakes; brother of Zeus **126**

PRATINAS: renowned author of satyr-plays (as well as tragedies); from Phlius in the Argolid, but active in Athens in the early-fifth century **118**

PRODICUS: Greek intellectual (sophist) from Ceos, active in Athens in the late-fifth century; expounded theories on ethics, linguistics, religion, and anthropology **94, 153**

Prometheus: son of Iapetus, associated with the origin of fire and human culture, and with the creation of human beings **13**. See also General Index, "*Prometheus Bound.*"

PRONOMOS: star *aulos* player from Thebes, active in late-fifth century Athenian theater performances **139**

PROPERTIUS: Roman elegiac poet of the later-first century BCE who claimed to be a "Roman Callimachus." **227**

PROTAGORAS: renowned intellectual and teacher of rhetoric (sophist) from Abdera (lived ca. 490–420); famous for his relativist and phenomenal theories **82, 93–94, 128**

Pylades: companion of Orestes and son of Strophius, king of Phocis. He assists Orestes in killing Clytaemestra and Aegisthus, and later marries Electra **211**

PYLOS: a town on the southwestern tip of the Peloponnesus **185**

PYTHANGELUS: lesser-known Athenian tragic poet of the late-fifth century   101

QUINTILIAN: Roman rhetorician and educator of the late-first century CE   95, 227, 229, 238

Rhadamanthus: one of three mythical judges in the Underworld (with Minos and Aeacus)   162, 167

Sabazius: a Thracian-Phrygian god associated by the Greeks with Dionysus, and worshipped as such in Athens during the later-fifth century   174

SALAMIS: a small island in the Saronic Gulf about 10 miles west of Athens. At the Battle of Salamis (480 BCE) a Greek navy led by the Athenian Themistocles defeated the Persian invading forces   22, 38, 41, 78, 129, 154

SAPPHO: renowned female lyric poet from Lesbos (sixth century)   26, 89, 144

Semele: daughter of Cadmus, king of Thebes; mother of Dionysus, by Zeus   63, 183

SIMONIDES: famous and versatile fifth-century Greek poet (lived ca. 556–468)   26, 82, 93

SOCRATES: Athenian intellectual (lived 469–399)   13, 17, 22, 26–28, 51, 82, 93, 103, 115, 129, 153, 156, 204, 207–208, 212, 226–27, 236. *See also* General Index, "*Clouds*."

SOLON: Athenian statesman, lawgiver, and poet of the sixth century   19, 92, 166

SOPHOCLES: Athenian tragic poet (lived ca. 495–406)   22, 30, 66, 71, 86, 100–101, 116–20, 129, 134, 140–41, 163, 195, 209, 215, 217, 221, 226, 234, 239

STESICHORUS: Greek choral lyric poet of the sixth century from South Italy   89, 135–36

Strepsiades: main character of Aristophanes' play *The Clouds*, who at first seeks to learn rhetoric from Socrates but ends up turning against him and burning down his school   194. *See also* General Index, "*Clouds*."

Stheneboea: wife of Proetus, king of Tiryns; she tried to seduce the hero Bellerophon, and when he rejected her she accused him of sexual assault; eventually, after her deceit was discovered, she attempted to escape on the winged horse Pegasus but fell off and drowned. The story was the subject of a celebrated play by Euripides (now lost)   **105, 113, 125**

SUDA: the Suda or Souda (sometimes referred to as "Suidas", as if this were an individual author) is a huge tenth century CE (Byzantine) Greek encyclopedia, with over 30,000 entries, many drawing from ancient sources that have since been lost. It contains many important but otherwise unknown items of literary history, though it is often impossible to tell whether these are based on ancient or Christian-era sources and how reliable or fantastic their testimony is   **19, 23, 37, 55, 226, 232**

SYRACUSE: the largest and most powerful Greek city in Sicily; home to a strong theatrical tradition independent from that of Athens   **9–10, 226, 251, 256**

Tantalus: father of Pelops and grandfather of Atreus and Thyestes; he served the gods a feast of human flesh (his own son's) and was punished with eternal torments in the Underworld   **161**

Tartarus: deepest and darkest part of the Underworld, where the worst sinners were punished   **161–62**. *See also* General Index, "Underworld."

TERENCE: Roman comic poet (lived ca. 190–159) whose plays adhere closely to the tradition of Menander's New Comedy   **13, 55, 231, 237**

TERPANDER: early (seventh-century, semi-legendary) Greek virtuoso musician and poet, known as an innovator on the lyre and *cithara*; originally came from Antissa (Lesbos) but also was said to have been active in Sparta   **119, 133, 135**

Teucer: half-brother of Ajax; a Greek hero at Troy, who appeared as a character in several Greek tragedies, including at least one by Aeschylus (now lost)   **122, 135**

Thamyris: mythical singer and *cithara*-player from Thrace who challenged the Muses to a competition, and was consequently blinded by them   **84**

Thanatos: personification of Death   **63, 155, 179**

THEBES: a large city in Boeotia, about fifty miles northwest of Athens; mythical home of both Dionysus and Heracles. During the classical period Thebes and Athens were usually at loggerheads, and often at war   **184–85, 189**

THEOPHRASTUS: a pupil of Aristotle (fourth century); author of an influential book (now lost) on rhetoric   **123, 227**

THERAMENES: Athenian politician of late-fifth century, remarkable for his shifting allegiances and continuing success under different regimes between 411 and 404   **19, 37, 40, 49–50**

Theseus: son of Aegeus (or Poseidon); mythical king of Athens, and the Athenians' most popular hero; often regarded as their founding father, and credited with exploits designed to some degree to rival the labors of (Dorian) Heracles   **63, 126, 176**

THESPIS: semi-legendary (sixth century) Athenian dramatist, said to have been the inventor of tragedy. None of his writings survive   **119**

THESSALONIKI (SALONICA): a city in Macedonia (northeast Greece) founded in the late-fourth century BCE. During the Middle Ages it was the second largest city in the Byzantine Empire and its scholars played an important role in the preservation of classical Greek culture   **232**

Thetis: sea-nymph, wife of Peleus and mother of Achilles (e.g., in the *Iliad*)   **184**

THIRTY TYRANTS: junta of pro-Spartan Athenian oligarchs, led by Critias, who collaborated with Lysander to bring about the surrender of Athens to Sparta at the end of the Peloponnesian War (404); they subsequently massacred hundreds of their pro-democratic opponents before being deposed in 403   **51**

THRACE, THRACIAN: an extensive region to the north (and its non-Greek speaking inhabitants), covering what is today northeastern Greece, southeastern Bulgaria, and northwest Turkey   **33, 48, 137, 164, 174**

THRASYBULUS: Athenian politician of late-fifth and early-fourth century, a stalwart supporter of the people against oligarchic opposition   **40, 50**

THUCYDIDES: Athenian historian of the Peloponnesian War (lived ca. 460–400)   **22, 93, 128, 204**

TIMOTHEUS: innovative poet and musician from Miletus (lived ca. 450–360); fragments of his poetry survive **141, 147**

Teiresias: blind seer of Thebes; a prominent character in several Greek tragedies **160, 187**

Titans: an old generation of gods, sons of Ouranus, led by Cronus and Iapetus; overthrown by Zeus and the Olympian gods **18, 184**

Tityus: a son of Earth, he attempted to violate the goddess Leto and was punished with eternal torments in Tartarus **161**

Trygaeus: main character in Aristophanes' play *Peace* who succeeds in finding the missing goddess Peace and organizing a rescue mission to bring her back **57, 183**. *See also* General Index, "*Peace.*"

VERGIL: Rome's most famous poet (lived 70–19 BCE); author of the *Aeneid* **162, 245**

Xanthias: name of Dionysus' (human) slave in *Frogs*. The name means "red-headed, sandy-haired." **33–34, 40, 53, 57, 59, 61, 66–71, 79, 101, 107–108, 152, 155, 166, 169–72, 180, 190–91, 197–98, 209–212, 216, 222–23, 240, 253**; see Fig. 3–1.

XENOCLES: son of Carcinus; successful late-fifth century tragic poet in Athens **100–101, 117**

XENOPHANES: boldly original Ionian philosopher-scientist (sixth century) **93, 153**

XENOPHON: distinguished Athenian soldier and author (lived ca. 428–354) **22, 228**

Zeus: king of the Olympian gods, and "father" of their divine household **63, 100, 105–106, 122, 126, 152, 155–59, 161, 183–85, 206**

ZEUXIS: famous (semi-legendary) Greek painter of late-fifth and early-fourth century **83**

Bibliography

Anderson, W. B. 1966. *Ethos and Education in Greek Music.* Cambridge, Mass.
Apte, M. L. 1985. *Humor and Laughter: an Anthropological Approach.* Ithaca.
Arrowsmith, W. (ed.) 1969. *Aristophanes. Four Comedies.* Ann Arbor.
Bakola, E. 2010. *Cratinus and the Art of Comedy.* Oxford.
Barker, A. 1984. *Greek Musical Writings.* Vol. 1. Cambridge.
———. 1989. *Greek Musical Writings.* Vol. 2. Cambridge.
Battezzato, L. 2009. "Metre and Music," in F. Budelmann (ed.), *Cambridge Companion to Greek Lyric.* Cambridge, 130–46.
Bierl, A. 2001/2009. *Ritual and Performativity: the Chorus of Old Comedy.* Trans. A. Hollmann, Washington, DC.
Biles, Z. 2011. *Aristophanes and the Poetics of Competition.* Cambridge.
Bowie, A. 1993. *Aristophanes: Myth, Ritual, and Comedy.* Cambridge.
Burkert, W. 1977/1985. *Greek Religion.* Trans. J. Raffan, Cambridge, Mass.
———. 1987. *Ancient Mystery Cults.* Cambridge, Mass.
Calame, C. 1998. *Choruses of Young Women in Ancient Greece.* 2nd ed. Trans. D. Collins, Lanham.
Carpenter, T. H. and C. A. Faraone (eds.) 1993. *Masks of Dionysus.* Ithaca.
Cartledge, P. 1990. *Aristophanes and his Theatre of the Absurd.* Bristol.
Clinton, K. 1992. *Myth and Cult: The Iconography of the Eleusinian Mysteries.* Stockholm.
Cole, S. G. 2007. "Finding Dionysus," in D. Ogden (ed.), *A [Blackwell] Companion to Greek Religion,* Oxford, 327–41.

Comotti, G. 1989. *Music in Greek and Roman Society*. Trans. R. Munson, Baltimore.
Csapo, E. 2000a. "From Aristophanes to Menander?," in M. Depew and D. Obbink (eds.), *Matrices of Genre*, Cambridge, Mass., 115–33.
———. 2000b. "Euripidean New Music," *Illinois Classical Studies* 24–25: 399–426.
———. 2003. "The Dolphins of Dionysus," in E. Csapo and M. Miller (eds.), *Poetry, Theory, Praxis*, Oxford, 69–98.
———. 2004. "The Politics of the New Music," in P. Murray and P. Wilson (eds.), *Music and the Muses*, Oxford, 207–48.
Csapo, E. and M. Miller (eds.) 2007. *The Origins of Theater in Ancient Greece and Beyond*. Cambridge.
Csapo, E. and W. J. Slater. 1995. *The Context of Ancient Theater*. Ann Arbor.
Denniston, J. D. 1927. "Technical Terms in Aristophanes," *Classical Quarterly* 21: 117–19.
De Ste Croix, G. E. M. 1972. *The Origins of the Peloponnesian War*. London.
Detienne, M. 1996. *The Masters of Truth in Ancient Greece*. Trans. J. Lloyd, 2nd ed., Cambridge, Mass.
Dodd, D. B. and C. A. Faraone (eds.) 2003. *Initiation in Greek Rituals and Narratives*. New York.
Dover, K. J. (ed.) 1993. *Aristophanes. Frogs*. Oxford.
———. 1972. *Aristophanic Comedy*. Berkeley.
Easterling, P. E. and E. Hall (eds.) 2002. *Greek and Roman Actors*. Cambridge.
Edmonds, R. G. III. 2004. *Myths of the Underworld Journey: Plato, Aristophanes, and the 'Orphic' Gold Tablets*. Cambridge.
Ehrenberg, V. 1962. *The People of Aristophanes*. 3rd ed, New York.
Ewans, M. (ed. & trans.) 2011. *Aristophanes. Lysistrata, The Women's Festival, and Frogs*. Norman, Okla.
Feeney, D. 1991. *The Gods in Epic*. Oxford.
Ferrari, G. R. F. 1989. "Plato and Poetry," in G. Kennedy (ed.), *Cambridge History of Literary Criticism*, 92–148.
Foley, H. P. 1980. "The Masque of Dionysus," *Transactions of the American Philological Association* 110: 107–33.
———. (ed.) 1994. *The Homeric Hymn to Demeter*. Princeton.
Ford, A. 2002. *The Origins of Criticism*. Princeton.
Frere, J. H. (trans.) [1837] 1939. *Aristophanes. The Frogs: a Verse Translation*. London.
Frye, N. 1957. *Anatomy of Criticism*. Princeton.

Gamel, M.-K. 2007. "Sondheim Floats," in Hall and Wrigley 2007, 209–30.
Giannopoulou, V. 2007. "Aristophanes in Translation Before 1920," in Hall and Wrigley 2007, 309–42.
Goldhill, S. 1991. *The Poet's Voice*. Cambridge.
Graf, F. and S. I. Johnston. 2007. *Ritual Texts for the Afterlife*. New York.
Griffith, M. 1990. "Contest and Contradiction in Early Greek Poetry," in M. Griffith and D. J. Mastronarde (eds.), *Cabinet of the Muses*, Atlanta, 185–207.
Hall, E. 2007. "The English-speaking Aristophanes, 1650–1914," in Hall and Wrigley 2007, 65–88.
Hall, E. and A. Wrigley (eds.) 2007. *Aristophanes in Performance, 421 BC–AD 2007*, London.
Halliwell, S. 1991. "Comic Satire and Freedom of Speech in Classical Athens," *Journal of Hellenic Studies* 111: 48–70.
———. 2008. *Greek Laughter*. Cambridge.
Hardwick, L. P. 2000. *Translating Words, Translating Cultures*. London.
Harvey, D. and J. Wilkins (eds.). 2000. *The Rivals of Aristophanes*. London.
Henderson, J. 1990. "The Demos and the Comic Competition," in Winkler, J. J. and F. Zeitlin (eds.). *Nothing to Do with Dionysos?* Princeton, 271–313.
——— (ed.). 2002. *Aristophanes. Frogs, Assemblywomen, Wealth*. Cambridge, Mass.
Henrichs, A. 1982. "Changing Dionysian Identities," in B. Meyer and E. P. Sanders (eds.), *Jewish and Christian Self-Definition*. Vol. 3, Philadelphia. 137–60.
Herington, C. J. 1985. *Poetry into Drama*. Berkeley.
Hubbard, T. K. 1991. *The Mask of Comedy. Aristophanes and the Intertextual Parabasis*. Ithaca.
Hunter, R. 2009. *Critical Moments in Classical Literature*, Cambridge.
Jens, W. (ed.). 1971. *Die Bauformen der griechischen Tragödie*. Munich.
Johnston, S. I. 1999. *The Restless Dead: Encounters between the Living and the Dead in Ancient Greece*. Berkeley.
Kerferd, G. 1981. *The Sophistic Movement*. Cambridge.
Lada-Richards, I. 1999. *Initiating Dionysus. Ritual and Theatre in Aristophanes' Frogs*. Oxford.
Laird, F. (adapter/director) 1991. *Frogs: a Comedy* (London Small Theatre), Aquila Productions, VHS video-recording.
Lattimore, R. (trans.) 1962. *Aristophanes. Frogs*. New York.

Lloyd, M. 1992. *The Agon in Euripides.* Oxford.
Lowe, N. J. 1993. "Aristophanes' Books," *Annals of Scholarship* 10: 63–83.
MacDowell, D. M. (ed.) 1971. *Aristophanes. Wasps.* Oxford.
———. 1995. *Aristophanes and Athens.* Oxford.
Marrou, H. 1956. *History of Education in Antiquity.* Trans. G. Lamb, Madison.
McGlew, J. F. 2002. *Citizens on Stage: Comedy and Political Culture in the Athenian Democracy.* Ann Arbor.
Ogden, D. 2001. *Greek and Roman Necromancy.* Princeton.
Olson, S. D. (ed.) 2004. *Aristophanes. Acharnians.* Oxford.
O'Sullivan, N. 1992. *Alcidamas, Aristophanes and the Beginnings of Greek Stylistic Theory.* Stuttgart (Hermes Einzelschr. 60).
Padilla, M. 1992. "The Heraclean Dionysus: Theatrical and Social Renewal in Aristophanes' *Frogs*," *Arethusa* 25: 359–84.
Parker, L. 1997. *The Songs of Aristophanes.* Oxford.
Parker, R. 1996. *Athenian Religion: A History.* Oxford.
———. 2005. *Polytheism and Society at Athens.* Oxford.
Power, T. 2010. *The Culture of Kitharôidia.* Washington, DC.
Reckford, K. J. 1987. *Aristophanes' Old-and-New Comedy.* Chapel Hill.
Revermann, M. 2006. "The Competence of Theatre Audiences in Fifth- and Fourth Century Athens," *Journal of Hellenic Studies* 126: 99–124.
———. 2006. *Comic Business.* Oxford.
———. 2013. (ed.) *The Cambridge Companion to Greek Comedy.* Cambridge.
Reynolds, L. D. and N. G. Wilson. 1991. *Scribes and Scholars.* 3rd ed., Oxford.
Richardson, N. J. 1975. "Homeric Professors in the Age of the Sophists," *Proceedings of the Cambridge Philological Society* 21: 65–81.
Robson, J. 2009. *Aristophanes: An Introduction.* London.
Roselli, D. K. 2011. *Theater of the People.* Austin.
Rosen, R. M. 1988. *Old Comedy and the Iambographic Tradition.* Atlanta.
———. 2000. "Cratinus' *Pytinê* and the Construction of the Comic Self," in Harvey and Wilkins, 23–39.
———. 2004. "Aristophanes' *Frogs* and the *Contest of Homer and Hesiod*," *Transactions of the Proceedings of the American Philological Association* 134: 295–322.
Rosen, R. M. and I. Sluiter (eds.) 2004. *Free Speech in Classical Athens.* Leiden.
Rosenmeyer, T. G. 1955. "Aeschylus, Gorgias, and *apatê*." *Americal Journal of Philology* 76: 225–60.
Rothwell, Jr, K. S. 2007. *Nature, Culture, and the Origins of Greek Comedy. A Study of Animal Choruses.* Cambridge.

Ruffell, I. A. 2002. "A Total Write-off: Aristophanes, Cratinus, and the Rhetoric of Comic Competition," *Classical Quarterly* n.s. 52: 138–62.
Russell, D. A. 1981. *Criticism in Antiquity*. London.
Rusten, J. S. (ed.) 2011. *The Birth of Comedy. Texts, Documents and Art from Athenian Competitions, 486–280*. Baltimore.
Scott, W. C. 1984. *Musical Design in Aeschylean Theater*. Hanover.
Schironi, F. 2007. "A Poet without 'Gravity': Aristophanes on the Italian Stage," in Hall and Wrigley 2007, 267–75.
Seaford, R. 1981. "Dionysiac Drama and the Dionysian Mysteries," *Classical Quarterly* n.s. 31: 252–71.
———. 2006. *Dionysos*. London.
Segal, C. P. 1961. "The Character and Cults of Dionysus and the Unity of the *Frogs*," *Harvard Studies in Classical Philology* 65: 207–42.
———. 1962. "Gorgias and the Psychology of the *logos*," *Harvard Studies in Classical Philology* 66: 99–155.
———. 1997. *Dionysian Poetics and Euripides' Bacchae*. 2nd ed., Princeton.
Sifakis, G. M. 1992. "The Structure of Aristophanic Comedy," in *Journal of Hellenic Studies* 112: 123–42.
Silk, M. S. 2000. *Aristophanes and the Definition of Comedy*. Oxford.
———. 2007. "Translating/Transposing Aristophanes," in Hall and Wrigley 2007, 287–308.
Slater, N. W. 2002. *Spectator Politics: Metatheatre and Performance in Aristophanes*. Philadelphia.
Solomos, A. 1960/1974. *The Living Aristophanes*. Trans. A. Solomos and M. Felheim, Ann Arbor.
Sommerstein, A. H. (ed.) 1996. *Aristophanes. Frogs*. Warminster.
———. 2006. "How Aristophanes Got his A&P," in L. A. Kozak and J. W. Rich (eds) *Playing Around Aristophanes: Essays in Honor of Alan Sommerstein*. Oxford, 126–39.
———. 2010. "The history of the text of Aristophanes," in G. W. Dobrov (ed.) *Brill's Companion to the Study of Greek Comedy*. Leiden, 399–422
Stanford, W. B. 1942. *Aeschylus in his Style*. Dublin.
———. (ed.) 1963. *Aristophanes. Frogs*. London.
Steggle, M. 2007. "Aristophanes in Early Modern England," in Hall and Wrigley 2007, 52–65.
Storey, E. 2003. *Eupolis Poet of Old Comedy*. Oxford.
Tell, H. 2011. *Plato's Counterfeit Sophists*, Cambridge, Mass. (Hellenic Studies Series 44).
Van Steen, G. 2000. *Venom in Verse: Aristophanes in Modern Greece*. Princeton.

Vermeule, E. T. 1979. *Aspects of Death*. Berkeley.
Versnel, H. 1990. *Inconsistencies in Greek Religion*. Vol. 1, Leiden.
———. 1993. *Inconsistencies in Greek Religion*. Vol. 2, Leiden.
Walsh, G. 1984. *The Varieties of Enchantment*. Chapel Hill.
Walton, J. M. 1987. *Living Greek Theatre*. New York.
———. 2006. *Found in Translation: Greek Drama in English*. Cambridge.
Wehrli, F. 1946. "Der erhabene und der schlichte Stil in der poetisch-rhetorischen Theorie der Antike," in O. Gigon (ed.) *Phyllobolia für Peter von der Mühll*, Basel. 9–34.
West, M. L. 1992. *Ancient Greek Music*. Oxford.
Whitman, C. H. 1964. *Aristophanes and the Comic Hero*. Cambridge, Mass.
Willi, A. 2002. *The Languages of Aristophanes*. Oxford.
Wilson, P. 2000. *The Athenian Institution of the Khorêgia*. Cambridge.
———. (ed.) 2007. *The Greek Theater and Festivals: Documentary Studies*. Oxford.
Woodbury, L. 1976. "Aristophanes' *Frogs* and Athenian Literacy," *Transactions of the American Philological Association* 106: 349–57.
Wright, M. 2009. "Literary Prizes and Literary Criticism in Antiquity," *Classical Antiquity* 28: 138–77.
Wrigley, A. 2007. "Aristophanes Revitalized! Music and Spectacle on the Academic Stage," in Hall and Wrigley, 136–54.
Young, D. (trans.) 1958. *The Puddocks: a Verse Play in Scots, from the Greek of Aristophanes*. 2nd ed., Makarsbield.

General Index

Acharnians, The (of Aristophanes), 5, 10, 13, 16, 24, 30, 36, 56–57, 73, 183, 194, 204, 208
Acting and actors, 8, 28, 117, 132, 136, 139–40, 222, 224–25, 254. *See also* Staging, Reperformance
Adaptation, 10, 116, 235, 237, 246–56
Aesthetics, ancient Greek criteria for, 71, 86–114, 213
  influence of *Frogs* on later theories of, 89, 97–98, 114, 123, 227
Afterlife, 63, 150–52, 160–99; *see also* Religion, Soul
agōn: *see* Competition
Aldine edition of Aristophanes, 234
Anthesteria festival, 67, 157–58, 198, 224
Apology of Socrates (by Plato), 26, 27, 28, 40, 92–93, 235
Aquila Theatre Company, *see* Meineck, Peter
Arrowsmith, William, 241–42
Assemblywomen, The (of Aristophanes), 16, 56, 151, 225

Atheism, 129, 180
Audience, ancient Athenian, 31–35, 52–54, 99, 115–16, 154–57, 159, 162, 165, 171, 174–75, 185, 209, 215
  different levels of sophistication of, 31–35, 53–54, 102–103, 108, 154–55, 192, 196
  as community, 34–35, 52, 70, 99, 182, 197–99, 200, 209–12, 215–216, 218
  as addressees within the play, 44–45, 69–70, 99, 171, 197, 208, 217
auloi (double-pipes), *aulētēs* (piper), 9, 32, 30, 81, 89, 116, 136, 131–32, 138–45, 176, 180, 184, 222 (and Figs. 1–1a and 1b, 5–1b)
Austen, Jane, 8

Bacchae, The (of Euripides), 12, 128, 180–82, 184–85, 187, 190, 192
Babylonians, The (of Aristophanes), 16, 29, 36, 49
Banqueters, The (of Aristophanes), 16, 29, 94

barbitos (type of lyre), 144, 187 (and Fig. 5–1a)
Battle of Frogs and Mice, The (burlesque epic poem), 82
Barrett, David, 244
Beerbohm, Max, 236
Birds, The (of Aristophanes), 13, 16, 56–57, 118, 155, 183, 194, 209, 223, 236, 246–47
Boileau-Despréaux, Nicolas, 236
Brecht, Bertolt, 225, 236
Brooks, Mel, 255
Browning, Robert, 235
Brumoy, Pierre, 235
Burial customs, Greek, 66, 162–66, 172–80

chorêgos (chorus-director and/or theater producer), 10, 23, 28–30, 81, 99, 181, 203
Chorus, in general, 4–5, 10, 25–26, 34, 81, 99, 115–116, 124, 138, 158–59, 203
  in Old Comedy, 8–9, 159, 196
  of frogs, 67, 157–59, 197–98, 222–23, 251 (and Figs. 1–1a, 8–2)
  of Initiates, 68, 176, 180–83, 197, 208, 212, 222 (and Fig. 1–1b)
  choreography, 30, 34, 72, 89, 95, 98, 105, 116, 132–33, 137–38, 142, 147, 216, 224, 229
  See also Dance, Phallus
cithara (concert lyre), 81, 89, 119, 133, 135–36, 139–41, 143, 224
City Dionysia at Athens, 4–5, 9, 10, 16, 25, 83–84, 115, 116, 132, 138, 139, 157, 195
Clouds, The (of Aristophanes), 13, 16, 19, 25, 27, 28, 56, 97, 108–109, 115, 194, 204, 208, 227, 231, 236, 241, 246–47, 249
Coinage, Athenian (gold, silver, bronze), 40–41, 45–48, 110, 207
  as metaphor for human character, 41, 47, 207
Comedy, comic drama
  origins of in Greece, 4–12, 14–16, 21, 89, 173, 185, 196. *See also* Chorus, Phallus
  "Old/Middle/New" distinctions, 14–15, 55–56, 127, 165, 216–17, 221, 225–26, 229–31
  in relation to other Greek types of literature and drama, 30, 120–21, 238
  conventions and formal structure of Aristophanic, 8–9, 12–16, 59–60, 79, 165
  predecessors and rivals to Aristophanes in, 8–9, 14, 16–21, 23–24, 49, 85–86, 123, 165–66, 188–89, 216, 219, 228–31
  typical themes in, 6–9, 12–21, 56–57, 79, 155, 165–66, 196, 203. *See also* Humor
Competition (*agôn*), in Greek society, 80–88
  in Greek music and performance, 3, 25, 34, 74, 81
  in tragedy and comedy, 3, 10–12, 16, 28, 54, 70, 80–114, 194–95, 201–219
Contest between Homer and Hesiod, 84, 113
Costumes, 20, 61, 68–69, 71, 73, 109, 112, 118, 131, 176, 222, 224, 251 (and Figs. 3–1, 3–2a and 2b)
Criticism
  of art and literature, 20, 34, 54, 71, 91–114. *See also* Aesthetics, Judgment
  ad hominem, of politicians in comedy, 9, 19, 29, 31, 35–37, 188, 205–206, 227, 230, 236
  See also Invective
Cult, *see* Burial customs, Festivals, Heroes, Religion

Dance, 4–5, 15, 18, 25, 52, 68, 76, 83, 89, 92, 95–96, 98, 109, 115, 116, 118, 137, 143, 146, 147, 181, 183, 186–88, 197, 199, 216–217, 221–22, 225 (and Figs. 5–1a and 1b). *See also* Chorus

Dante Alighieri, 8, 162

Demes (of Attica), 10, 23, 24, 32, 35, 39, 174, 185–86

   deme theaters and performances, 10, 116, 220

Democracy (Athenian), ideology of, 31–32, 37–43, 49–50, 87–88, 111, 114, 127–28, 218

   and slaves, 32–24, 124. *See also* Slaves

   and women, 31, 35, 40–41, 124, 151

   and aristocrats, 24, 30–31, 48–51, 87, 209

   leadership of, 44, 48–51, 114, 203–208. *See also* Glossary, "Alcibiades," "Four Hundred," "Thirty tyrants"

Dionysia (festivals at Athens) *See* Anthesteria, City Dionysia, Lenaea, Rural Dionysia

Dithyramb, 29, 82–83, 119, 133, 138, 141–42, 148, 203

Donkey (ridden by Xanthias), 61, 170, 223 (and Fig. 3–1). *See also* Props

Dryden, John, 235

Editions and translations of *Frogs*, 220–58 (and Fig. 8–1)

Education, ancient Athenian in music and poetry, 25–27, 34, 54, 82, 92–93, 95–97, 102, 228. *See also* Chorus, *Clouds*, Literacy

Erasmus, 234

Everyman (as comic hero), 57, 79, 192

Festivals, *see* Anthesteria, City Dionysia, Lenaea, Rural Dionysia

Fielding, Henry, 239

Fitts, Dudley, 242–43

Foote, Samuel, 235

Frazer, James, 236

Frere, J. H., 239–40, 241, 247

Frogs (species *Pelophylax Ridibundus*), 20, 158–59, 183, 198

Gender, 35, 85, 111, 125–26, 187, 207, 209–10, 218, 247

   of musical/poetic performers, 73, 95, 100, 142–46, 190, 218–19, 222 (and Fig. 5–1b)

   and sexual humor, 5–6, 13, 15, 85, 105–106, 109–13, 125–26, 143–46, 227, 237, 247

Gerytades (of Aristophanes), 85

Gods, *see* Religion. (*See also* Glossary, under individual gods' and goddesses' names.)

Goethe, Johann Wolfgang von, 163, 235

Great Idea (in comedy), 56–59, 66, 75, 79

Hero

   in comedy, 56–57, 155, 183, 192, and passim

   hero cults in Athens, 153, 163–65, 194

   Dionysus as, 183–89, 193–94, 196–99, and passim

   Heracles as, 104, 126, 152, 155, 164–65, 169–72, 174, 176, 190–91, 193–94

   Aeschylus as, 163–65, 191, 194–95, 197

Homeric Hymn

   to *Demeter*, 7, 175

   to *Dionysus*, 186

Hoplite, 24, 190. *See also* Marines

Humor, 3, 5–9, 69, 73, 169, 171, 209–12, 232, 249, and passim. *See also* Comedy

iambos, iambic poetry, 5–7, 9, 14, 21, 25, 36, 82. *See also* Invective
Impiety, 52, 128–29. *See also* Atheism, *and* Glossary, "Eleusinian Mysteries"
Initiation, *see* Mystery cult
Innovation in music, poetry and drama, 18–19, 98–103, 107–110, 113, 115–49, 214, 218, 238–39
Inspiration, 18, 90–91, 122–23, 154, 187
Instruments, musical, *see auloi, barbitos, cithara, krotala,* lyre
Invective, 5–7, 9, 17, 19, 25, 35, 37, 51, 82, 230, 236. *See also iambos*
Ion (of Plato), 82, 104

Jonson, Ben, 28, 230, 235, 238–39
Judgment (*krisis*) in artistic contests, 71, 84, 86–114, 200–19
of Paris, 83, 188
See also Competition

katabasis ("descent" into the Underworld), 174–77, 191–98. *See also* Underworld
Knights, The (of Aristophanes), 16, 19, 29, 36, 49, 56, 204, 205
kômôidia, see Comedy
kômos, 4–5, 15, 60, 78, 89, 155, 158, 196, 200, 208
Koun, Karolos, 250
krisis, see Judgment
krotala (castanets), 142, 145–146, 187, 222 (and Figs. 5–1a and 1b)

Laird, Fiona, 251, 257
Lane, Nathan, 254
Language and poetic style, 6, 8, 34, 73, 110–13, 120–21, 132–33, 147–48, 194, 224, 227, 227–32, 239–46. *See also* Obscenity
Lattimore, Richmond, 242

lazzi (comic routines), 107
lekythion (oil-bottle), 113, 129–31
Lenaea festival at Athens, 9, 83–84, 85, 157, 220
Liberation, 183, 186, 189, 198. *See also* Salvation, *and* Glossary, "Dionysus," "Eleutherae"
Life of Aristophanes, The (in Suda), 23–34
Literacy in Athens, 26–27, 34, 54, 114, 116–117. *See also* Audience, Education
London Small Theatre, *see* Laird, Meineck
Lyre (*lura*), 67, 140, 143, 187. *See also barbitos, cithara*
Lyric (poetry), *see* Chorus, Monody, Music
Lysistrata (of Aristophanes), 13, 16, 30, 40–41, 56–57, 151, 204, 209, 236, 237, 241, 249

Marines (on Athenian triremes), 24, 190
Marshes, 58, 67, 157, 158, 159, 198. *See also* Anthesteria, frogs
Marx Brothers, 34, 255
Masks, 5, 8, 62, 140, 187, 188, 192, 196, 222, 224, 255 (and Figs. 3–2a and 2b)
Meineck, Peter, 251, 257
Metatheater (dramatic self-reflexivity), 1, 109, 152, 159, 197, and passim
Meters, 27, 59–60, 74, 78, 86, 97, 112–113, 125, 131, 133–37, 140, 142–44, 147–48, 224, 230–31
Metics (*metoikoi* = resident aliens), 10, 32–33, 39, 157, 174, 190, 212
Milton, John, 120, 121
Mitchell, John Cameron, 255
Mockery, 4, 6–8, 36–37, 82, 176, 181–82, 208, 214, 227, 238. *See also* Invective

Molière, 55, 225, 235
Monody, 16, 89, 113, 138–48
Monty Python, 255
Murray, Gilbert, 240–41
Muse, Muses. *See* Glossary
Music, in Greek drama, 27, 74, 85, 94, 97, 105, 113, 118, 131–49, 229, 247, 249–51
   personified as Muse and/or "Art of Tragedy", 73, 95, 100, 111, 142–43, 198, 217–219, 222
   and Athenian education, 25–27, 96–97
Mystery cult, 18, 151, 172–83, 199. *See also* Chorus of Initiates, Orphic texts; *and* Glossary, "Eleusis," "Initiates."
   Frogs as suggesting mystery cult initiation, 53, 172–99

National Theater of Greece, 249–50
Necromancy, 118, 161–62, 164, 166
Nietzsche, Friedrich, 236
nomos, nomisma ("law" and "coinage"), 45–48, 207

Obscenity and scatology, 6–8, 176, 228–29, 231, 240–41, 246
Odyssey, The (of Homer), 8, 18, 121, 160–61
Oil-bottle, *see lekythion*
Oligarchic revolution (in Athens), 22–23, 48–51, 203–204. *See also* Glossary, "Four Hundred" and "Thirty Tyrants."
Oresteia, The (of Aeschylus), 85, 109, 124–26, 130, 134–36, 163, 205, 208, 209
Orphic texts and doctrines, 26, 151, 172–73, 178–83, 184, 186–88, 199

Panathenaic competitions, 12, 81, 135
Parabasis, 9–10, 15, 18, 20, 24, 29, 40, 42–48, 60, 69–70, 108, 114, 207–208, 210, 217

Parody, 16–18, 20, 82, 117–118, 159, 180–82, 224–25, 247, 252, and passim
Parry, Hubert, 247
Peace (of Aristophanes), 16, 30, 56–57, 183, 204, 205, 236, 249
Phaedo (of Plato), 26, 162, 163
Phallus, as part of comic costume, 4, 71, 109, 112, 131, 196, 224 (and Figs. 3–2a and 2b)
   phallic songs as part of Dionysian/Bacchic ritual, 4, 14, 173, 196
Philosophy and beliefs, 26, 27–28, 35–36, 93–94, 150–99
Politics, *see* Democracy, Oligarchic revolution, War
Pope, Alexander, 230
Prizes, *see* Competition, Judgment
Producer, *see choregos*
Production, nature of the original, 9–11, 61–79, 221–25, 255. *See also choregos*, Realism, Staging
Prometheus Bound (of Aeschylus), 123–24, 133–34
Propriety, artistic and moral (*decorum*), 35, 98–113, 115, 121–22, 127, 214, 217–218, 228–29
Props, 61, 72, 74, 110, 223–24
Puddocks, The, 245–46
Purity, 40, 46–48, 53, 141, 176–83, 219

Rabelais, Francois, 238
Racine, Jean, 28, 235
Ravenna manuscript, 232 (and Fig. 8–1)
Realism, lack of in Old Comedy, 13, 55–56, 62, 66, 155, 162, 166, 169–70, 241
Reception of *Frogs, see* Adaptation, Editions and translations, Reperformance
Rejuvenation, 173, 181, 191, 196, 207, 215

Religion (Greek), 11–12, 128, 150–66, and passim
  role of belief in, 129, 153–57, 160–65, 174, 196
  Dionysus' place in, 11–12, 157–99
  See also Afterlife, Festivals, Mystery cult, Orphic texts, Ritual
Reperformance (of *Frogs* and other plays), 10, 116, 120, 204, 220, 222–23, 234, 236, 246–56
Republic, The (of Plato), 103, 104, 162
Rhetoric, 26, 93, 128. *See also* Sophists
Rites of passage, 172–73, 192–97, 199
Ritual, *see* Burial customs, Chorus, Festivals, Mystery cult, Rites of passage
Rogers, Benjamin Bickley, 241
Rural Dionysia (*Dionysia kat' agrous*), 10, 116, 157

Salvation, 20, 58–59, 75–76, 78–79, 150–99, 206, 251. *See also* Afterlife
Satire, 9, 14, 18, 226, 230, 236, 238
Satyrs and satyr-drama, 16, 30, 61–62, 84, 116, 127, 141, 155, 184, 187–88, 190, 203 (and Fig. 5–1a)
Scatology, *see* Obscenity
Schlosser, J. G., 235
Scholarship on *Frogs*
  modern, 237–38, 244–45
  scholia as representative of ancient, 36, 37, 134, 228, 232 (and Fig. 8–1)
scholia, see Scholarship
Sex
  Athenian sexual behaviors and attitudes, 4–5, 13, 15, 126–27, 142, 188, 190, 217–218
  sexual jokes, 85, 109, 142–47, 222, 227, 237, 247
  (*See also* Gender, Humor, Obscenity)
Shakespeare, William, 28, 34, 55, 117, 120, 163, 225, 235, 252–54

Shaw, G. B., 240, 252–54
Shevelove, Burt, 252–54. *See also* Sondheim, Stephen
Slaves
  position of in Athens, 32–34, 62, 69, 170–72, 174, 198, 207–10
  relationship to their masters, 33–34, 62, 107, 209–12
  becoming citizens, 33, 39–40, 45, 50, 67, 198, 207, 212
Solomos, Alexis, *see* National Theater of Greece
Sondheim, Stephen, 252–54, 257. *See also* front cover illustration
sophia (wisdom, skill, poetic genius), 43, 75, 80–114, 201, 215–16. *See also* Wisdom
Sophists, 26, 82, 93–96, 128, 153. *See also* Glossary, "Gorgias," "Prodicus," "Protagoras."
Soul (*psychê*), 20, 53, 58, 66, 151–52, 160–83, 213–14 (and Fig. 6–1). *See also* Afterlife, Salvation
South Park, 255
Staging, 61–79, 221–25, 245, 255. *See also* Reperformance
Stranger, Dionysus as, 184, 189–90
Style, old vs new, inflated vs. thin, 18–19, 27, 73–75, 94–95, 111, 115–49, 200, 213–214, 227; *see also* Decorum
Swift, Jonathan, 230
Symposium, 4, 81–82, 118, 140, 190, 226 (*see also* Fig. 5–1b)
Symposium, The (of Plato), 17, 28, 31, 82, 226, 255

Teacher, poet as, 28–30, 35, 44, 52–53, 73–74, 76, 82, 92–93, 99–100, 102–14, 215, 228, 234, 243. *See also chorêgos*
technê (art, skill), 25, 73, 83, 92–96, 98, 101, 102, 111, 119, 124, 198

Theater of Dionysus (at Athens),
　　topography and design of, 9–11,
　　21, 221–25 (and Figs. 1–1a and 1b)
Thesmophoriazusae, The (of
　　Aristophanes), 16, 56, 126–27, 131,
　　142, 143, 151, 232, 237, 249
Torture, 47–48, 69, 172, 194, 198, 210
Tragedy (Greek)
　　history of, 8, 89–90, 119, 133, 184–85
　　old and new style(s) of, 8, 27, 52,
　　　73–74, 95, 115–49, 214–19, 221,
　　　252–54
Translation of *Frogs*, 235, 237, 239–46,
　　256–57
Transmission of the text of
　　Aristophanes' plays, 3, 16, 77,
　　225–38. *See also* Editions, Ravenna
　　manuscript (and Fig. 8–1)
Triad, Byzantine, of Aristophanes' plays,
　　232
Trireme (warship), 24, 66–67, 166, 194
　　(and Fig. 6–2)

Underworld, topography of, 66–68,
　　160–62, 166–72, 178–82, 197–99.
　　See also Glossary, "Acheron,"
　　"Charon."
　　heroic/poetic quest to, 8, 19, 53, 63,
　　　150–51, 155, 160–61, 164–65, 169,
　　　172–74, 190–91
　　monsters in, 63, 67–68, 170, 173

Van Gennep, Arnold, 172–73. *See also*
　　Rites of passage

Vase-paintings, 4, 61, 66, 84, 118, 126,
　　159, 160, 185, 188, 221, 225. *See also*
　　Figs. 3–1, 5–1a and 1b, 6–1
Virility or "potency" (of poets), 18, 66,
　　100, 113, 115, 129–31, 215, 218–19.
　　See also lekythion, Phallus
Voltaire, 236

War, as suitable subject for epics and
　　tragedies, 73, 91, 103–105, 110,
　　121–22, 214
　　Peloponnesian War (between Athens
　　　and Sparta), 12, 22–23, 38, 48–51,
　　　78, 177–78, 200, 203–204, 217
　　Aristophanes' views about, 30–31.
　　　*See also Acharnians, Lysistrata,
　　　Peace*
Wasps, The (of Aristophanes), 16, 25,
　　29, 36, 49, 117–18, 204, 205, 223,
　　235
Wealth (of Aristophanes), 16, 30, 51, 57,
　　151, 155, 221, 225, 231, 234–36, 239,
　　246–47
Webb, R. H., 243
Wilde, Oscar, 13, 55
Wine (and Wine-jug), 4, 18, 62, 123,
　　154, 158, 163, 171, 183, 185–88, 190,
　　197, 216
Wisdom, poetry's claim to, 34–35,
　　90–94, 114, 203, 206, 215–16, 218.
　　See also sophia, Teacher
Women, *see* Gender

Young, Douglas, *see Puddocks*

Made in the USA
Monee, IL
22 April 2022